Guide
to Choral
Masterpieces

MELVIN BERGER

Guide to Choral Masterpieces

A Listener's Guide

ANCHOR BOOKS
DOUBLEDAY
New York London Toronto Sydney Auckland

An Anchor Book
PUBLISHED BY DOUBLEDAY
a division of Bantam Doubleday Dell Publishing Group, Inc.
1540 Broadway, New York, New York 10036

Anchor Books, Doubleday, and the portrayal of an anchor
are trademarks of Doubleday, a division of Bantam Doubleday Dell
Publishing Group, Inc.

The author acknowledges with sincere thanks the following individuals and companies for permission to reprint the texts and translations of the following works:

BEETHOVEN: *Fantasia for Piano, Chorus, and Orchestra*, Op. 80. Symphony No. 9, Op. 125, "Choral Symphony." Bernard Lozea, BMG Classics, Inc. (Successor-in-interest to RCA Records). Used with permission.

BLOCH: Sacred Service (Avodath hakodesh). M. R. Roberts. Broude Brothers Ltd. English text by David Stevens, copyright by Broude Brothers. Used by permission.

BRAHMS: *Ein deutsches Requiem*, Op. 45. Alto Rhapsody, Op. 53. Evelyn K. Lorek. Telarc International Corporation. Translation by Steve Ledbetter, courtesy of Telarc International Corporation.

MENDELSSOHN: The First Walpurgis Night, Op. 60. Bernard Lozea. BMG Classics, Inc. (Successor-in-interest to RCA Records). Used with permission.

THOMPSON: Americana (composer's program notes). The Peaceable Kingdom. The Testament of Freedom. Robert Schuneman. E. C. Schirmer Music Company. Used with permission.

WALTON: Belshazzar's Feast. Susan Brailove. Oxford University Press. Text selection and arrangement by Osbert Sitwell, copyright 1931. Reproduced by permission of Oxford University Press.

Library of Congress Cataloging-in-Publication Data

Berger, Melvin.
Guide to choral masterpieces: a listener's guide/Melvin Berger.
1st Anchor Books ed.
p.   cm.
Discography: p.
Includes bibliographical references.
1. Choral music.   I. Title.
ML1500.B47   1993
782.5—dc20   93-18714
CIP   MN

ISBN 0-385-42248-2
Copyright © 1993 by Melvin Berger
All Rights Reserved
Printed in the United States of America
First Anchor Books Edition: September 1993

1   3   5   7   9   10   8   6   4   2

It is not enough that the artist should be well prepared for the public. The public must be well prepared for what it is going to hear.

—Hector Berlioz

Contents

Preface

Guide to Choral Masterpieces discusses approximately one hundred of the best-known and most popular major choral works by nearly forty outstanding composers, arranged alphabetically by composer. For each composer there is a brief biography, followed by discussions of the individual works considered in chronological order. In general, background information on when, why, and where the particular piece was written is presented first, followed by a discussion of the music itself. Among the special features are the inclusion of selected texts, a section of standard texts (Mass, Requiem Mass, Te Deum, Stabat Mater, Magnificat), and the approximate timing of each composition. The Glossary at the end of the book defines any unfamiliar words, and the Discography is included to help anyone building a collection of recorded choral music.

In writing this book, I had in mind all those who enjoy choral music:

- Listeners, for whom this book presents information calculated to enhance and deepen their appreciation
- Those who sing in a choir or study choral music, for whom this book offers an opportunity to become familiar with the most significant choral works, making such people better performers and increasing their grasp of the repertoire
- Choral directors and teachers, for whom this book compiles in one volume both background and musical information on a large number of important choral works by composers ranging from Josquin to Orff, Britten, and Walton

In making the selection of compositions, I drew on my many years of experience writing books on musical subjects, program notes, liner notes, choral texts, and choral arrangements. To introduce some degree of objectivity into the selection process, I also studied record company and music publisher catalogs and lists of choir and orchestra performances, and I discussed my choices with many choral directors.

My greatest hope is that this book may play some small part in encouraging more people to enjoy the pleasures of singing in a choral group or listening to the enduring masterpieces of the choral repertoire.

Guide
to Choral
Masterpieces

JOHANN SEBASTIAN BACH

Born March 21, 1685, in Eisenach, Germany
Died July 28, 1750, in Leipzig

"The glory of God and the recreation of the mind." Thus did Johann Sebastian Bach define the aim and the purpose of his music. On the top of the first page of each of his sacred compositions he wrote JJ *(Jesu Juva,* "Jesus, help") and at the end he inscribed SDG *(Soli Deo Gloria,* "To God alone the glory").

In his vocal music Bach was able to realize most perfectly and clearly his vision of music as worship. If he had written only the most familiar of his choral masterpieces—the *Passion According to St. Matthew* and the Mass in B minor—his position as a leading composer of sacred choral music would be assured. Add to that, however, the seven other major works discussed here, plus the hundreds of other outstanding vocal works he composed, and you come to appreciate the towering achievements of this most remarkable man.

Bach was born into a family of musicians that stretched back several generations. Although his father taught him violin and an older brother taught him to play keyboard instruments, Bach largely taught himself by studying the music of others. In his early years he served his apprenticeship as a violinist and organist in various minor German court positions. His first significant appointment was to the court at Weimar (1708–17), where he developed a reputation as an organist and as a composer for that instrument. His next position took him to Anhalt-Cöthen (1717–23), where he was mostly concerned with the creation of instrumental and chamber music compositions.

It was in his final, crowning position, as cantor of St. Thomas and the other churches in Leipzig, that he turned to the production of his most important sacred choral works—the two Passions, the *Mass in B minor,* the *Magnificat,* and the *Christmas Oratorio.*

Regrettably, the music of Johann Sebastian Bach—some of the most glorious music ever composed—did not fare well during his lifetime or through almost a century following his death. He was a bit cantankerous and complained bitterly of the poor quality of the performers he had to work with in the various court and church positions he held during his lifetime. (According to one famous story, Bach remarked that a bassoonist in his orchestra sounded like a nanny goat *(Zippelfaggotist),* and he later went after the unfortunate player with his dagger!) Although Bach was very well regarded in the cities in which he lived, it was largely a local reputation, as his compositions were rarely heard in other cities.

It took nearly a century after his death for Bach's music to be rediscovered, after which it was usually performed in the distorted, highly romantic style of the nineteenth century. By the mid-twentieth century these excesses in performance style were corrected as performers sought, on the basis of advances in musical scholarship, to go for "authentic" presentations of his music. Now, at the end of the twentieth century, as in any good debate some feel that those espousing "authentic" Bach have robbed his music of much of its fire and passion. Many performers today are seeking a way to juxtapose modern sensibilities and tastes with the most informed understanding of how Bach himself presented his music.

In their search for authenticity, choral directors have long sought evidence of the performance practices favored by Bach. One valuable source is the memorandum that the composer submitted to the Leipzig city council in 1730 suggesting the numbers of performers necessary for the proper presentation of music in Leipzig's churches. In this memorandum Bach recommended assigning three or four singers to each part, including one to sing the solos, making for a choir of between sixteen and twenty vocalists. For the orchestra he suggested two or three first violins and a like number of second violins, four violas, two cellos, one bass, two or three oboes, one or two bassoons, three trumpets, timpani, and a continuo of cello and harpsichord or organ. For the *Mass in B minor,* though, he added two transverse flutes, two oboe d'amores, and a corno di caccia (hunting horn).

The Bach choral works discussed here are ordered by BWV number; BWV stands for *Bach Werke Verzeichnis,* Wolfgang Schmieder's 1950 thematic catalog of Bach's music.

CANTATA NO. 4: CHRIST LAG IN TODESBANDEN, BWV 4
(Christ Lay in the Bonds of Death)

30 minutes

Bach had the task of composing cantatas for the Sunday services and feast days in the various churches in which he worked. It is estimated that he wrote about three hundred cantatas, roughly five complete annual cycles of Christian observance. Of these, approximately two hundred have been preserved, including about fifteen secular cantatas.

It was probably for performance on Easter Day 1708 that Bach composed *Christ Lag;* he wrote it for four-part choir and string orchestra (violins I and II, violas I and II, and continuo of cellos, basses, and organ). Later, when preparing the cantata for performance in Leipzig, he doubled some of the voice parts and instrumental parts with a cornetto and three trombones.

Bach structured the cantata as a set of variations on an eponymous 1524 Easter chorale with words by Martin Luther. The seven vocal movements of the cantata use, unchanged, the seven verses of Luther's text.

The cantata opens with an instrumental *Sinfonia* in which the first violins, after several repetitions of a descending half step (a frequent symbol of pain and despair in Bach's music), start the chorale melody—which itself begins with a descending half step.

The following seven vocal movements, each one a variation of the chorale melody, are symmetrically arranged. Verses one and seven are for choir and orchestra. In verse one, a chorale fantasia, Bach treats the chorale melody as a cantus firmus—the chorale melody appears in held notes sung by the sopranos—to which the other voices add contrapuntal lines. Verse seven is a simple, four-part harmonization of the chorale, with the instruments doubling the voice parts.

Verses two and six are duets—the former for soprano and alto, the latter for soprano and tenor. The two-note descending figure is heard prominently in verse two, both at the start—as the two voices solemnly intone, *"Den Tod"* ("The death")—and in the continuo throughout. In both verses the two voices follow each other in close imitation.

The next pair, verses three and five, are basically arias for tenor and bass respectively (although verse three is traditionally sung by the entire tenor section of the choir). The fiery character of verse three is established by the violins playing their forceful, aggressive line. Verse five, with its introduction of the Paschal Lamb, projects a quiet and reverential tone.

Verse four for choir and continuo stands alone. The chorale melody is heard in the alto, with the other voices weaving their vigorous polyphonic lines around it.

SINFONIA

VERSUS I (Chor)

Christ lag in Todesbanden

Für unsre Sünd gegeben,
Er ist wieder erstanden
Und hat uns bracht das Leben;
Des wir sollen fröhlich sein,
Gott loben und ihm dankbar
    sein
Und singen Halleluja,
Halleluja!

SINFONIA

VERSE I (Chorus)

Christ lay in the bonds of
    death,
sent to us for our sins,
He has risen again
and brought us new life.
For this we should rejoice,
praise the Lord and give thanks

and sing Hallelujah,
Hallelujah!

VERSUS II (Chor-Sopran, Chor-Alt)

Den Tod niemand zwingen
  kunnt
Bei allen Menschenkindern,
Das macht' alles unsre Sünd,
Kein Unschuld war zu finden.
Davon kam der Tod so bald
Und nahm über uns Gewalt,
Hielt uns in seinem Reich
  gefangen.
Halleluja!

VERSE II (Sopranos and Altos)

Death none could command

amongst all mankind,
this came from our sin,
no innocence could be found.
Hence death came so soon
and took power over us,
held us captives in his realm.

Hallelujah!

VERSUS III (Chor-Tenor)

Jesus Christus, Gottes Sohn,
An unser Statt ist kommen
Und hat die Sünde weggetan,
Damit dem Tod genommen
All sein Recht und sein Gewalt,
Da bleibet nichts denn Tods
  Gestalt,
Den Stachl hat er verloren.
Halleluja!

VERSE III (Tenors)

Jesus Christ, Son of God,
in our place has come
and has removed our sin,
thus taking from death
all its right and strength,
till nought was left but death's
  skeleton,
he has lost his sting.
Hallelujah!

VERSUS IV (Chor)

Es war ein wunderlicher Krieg,
Da Tod und Leben rungen,
Das Leben da behielt den Sieg,
Es hat den Tod verschlungen.
Die Schrift hat verkündigt das,
Wie ein Tod den andern fraß,
Ein Spott aus dem Tod ist
  worden.
Halleluja!

VERSE IV (Chorus)

It was a strange war,
when death and life fought,
life carried the victory,
it swallowed death.
The Scriptures had forecast this,
as one death ate the other,
a farce has become of death.

Hallelujah!

VERSUS V (Baß)

Hier ist das rechte Osterlamm,
Davon Gott hat geboten.

VERSE V (Bass)

Here is the proper Easter Lamb,
of which the Lord commanded.

Das ist hoch an des Kreuzes
    Stamm
In heißer Lieb gebraten,
Das Blut zeichnet unsre Tür,
Das hält der Glaub dem Tode
    für,
Der Würger kann uns nicht
    mehr schaden.
Halleluja!

That was high on the cross's
    beam
burning in fervent love.
The blood marks our door,
this our creed holds death to be,
the killer can no longer harm
    us!
Hallelujah!

*VERSUS VI (Chor-Sopran,
    Chor-Tenor)*

*VERSE VI (Sopranos and
    Tenors)*

So feiern wir das hohe Fest

Thus we celebrate the High
    Feast,

Mit Herzensfreud und Wonne,
Das uns der Herre scheinen
    läßt,
Er ist selber die Sonne,
Der durch seiner Gnade Glanz
Erleuchtet unsre Herzen ganz,
Der Sünden Nacht ist
    verschwunden.
Halleluja!

with joy of heart and bliss
that our Lord lets shine for us
Himself the sun withall,
who with His mercy bright
illumines all our hearts.
The night of sin has
    disappeared.
Hallelujah!

VERSUS VII (Choral)

VERSE VII (Chorale)

Wir essen und wir leben wohl
Im rechten Osterfladen,
Der alte Sauerteig nicht soll
Sein bei dem Wort der Gnaden,
Christus will die Koste sein
Und speisen die Seel allein,
Der Glaub will keins andern
    leben.
Halleluja!

We eat and we live very well
of proper Easter Cake,
the old-worn leaven shall not be
with the word of Mercy—
Christ shall our food now be,
He alone feed our soul,
our creed will not live by any
    other.
Hallelujah!

CANTATA NO. 80: EIN FESTE BURG IST UNSER GOTT, BWV 80
(A Mighty Fortress Is Our God)

32 minutes

Around the year 1529, Martin Luther translated the Latin of Psalm 46, *"Deus noster refugium,"* into German as *"Ein feste Burg ist unser Gott"* (which is, in English, "A Mighty Fortress is Our God") and created a setting of the psalm, probably by playing the tune on his flute for composer Johann Walter to notate and harmonize. Since then a number of composers, including Mendelssohn, Wagner, and Meyerbeer, have used Luther's psalm melody in their original works. But there is little question that Bach's cantata based on that melody makes the most magnificent use of the stirring tune.

Bach composed the cantata in Leipzig for the Feast of the Reformation on October 31, 1724, by reworking his cantata of 1715, *Alles, was von Gott geboren,* BWV 80a. He may have made further revisions for the two hundredth anniversary of the Augsburg Confession in 1730. Modern editions usually call for four soloists, four-part choir, and large orchestra.

The cantata opens with a massive movement for choir and orchestra that is lent a special sheen by the high-pitched trumpets. The next three movements—a duet for soprano and bass (with the soprano singing the melody while the bass adds energetic decorations), a bass recitative, and an affecting soprano aria—lead to a choral movement in which the unison choir forcefully limns out the Luther melody against especially busy and dense writing for the orchestra. (One of the instruments in this movement is a *taille,* which is taken to be a tenor oboe or oboe da caccia; in modern performances the part is usually played by English horn.) Bach follows with two smaller movements—a tenor recitative and an imitative duet for alto and tenor with obbligato oboe da caccia (English horn) and solo violin. The cantata ends with everyone joining in the final presentation of the chorale.

NR. 1 CHOR

Ein feste Burg ist unser Gott,
Ein gute Wehr und Waffen;
Er hilft uns frei aus aller Not,
Die uns jetzt hat betroffen.
Der alte böse Feind,
Mit Ernst er's jetzt meint,
Groß Macht und viel List
Sein grausam Rüstung ist,
Auf Erd ist nicht seinsgleichen.

NR. 2 ARIE (Baß) MIT CHORAL (Chor-Sopran)

ARIE

Alles, was von Gott geboren,
Ist zum Siegen auserkoren.
Wer bei Christi Blutpanier

In der Taufe Treu geschworen,
Siegt im Geiste für und für.

CHORAL

Mit unsrer Macht ist nichts getan,
Wir sind gar bald verloren.
Es streit' vor uns der rechte Mann,
Den Gott selbst hat erkoren.

Fragst du, wer er ist?
Er heißt Jesus Christ,
Der Herre Zebaoth,

NO. 1 CHORUS

A mighty fortress is our God,
a trusty shield and sword.
He sets us free from every ill
that ever did beset us.
The ancient evil fiend
doth compass us around;
with might and craft
in grimmest armour clad
on earth he has no equal.

NO. 2 ARIA (Bass) WITH CHORALE (Sopranos)

ARIA

Every creature born of God
has victorious destiny.
Who to Christ's blood
allegiance swore
when baptized by His blood
His spirit conquers evermore.

CHORALE

Of our own power can we do
naught—
we soon are lost forever.
The righteous man doth strive
for us,
whom God Himself hath
chosen.
Dost question who He is?
He is called Jesus Christ,
the Lord of Sabaoth;

Und ist kein andrer Gott,	there is no other God
Das Feld muß er behalten.	and He must hold the field.

NR. 3 REZITATIV (Baß)

Erwäge doch, Kind Gottes, die
   so große Liebe,
Da Jesus sich
Mit seinem Blute dir
   verschriebe,
Womit er dich
Zum Kriege wider Satans Heer
   und wider Welt und Sünde
Geworben hat!
Gib nicht in deiner Seele
Dem Satan und den Lastern
   statt!
Laß nicht dein Herz,
Den Himmel Gottes auf der
   Erden,
Zur Wüste werden!
Bereue deine Schuld mit
   Schmerz,
Daß Christi Geist mit dir sich
   fest verbinde!

NO. 3 RECITATIVE (Bass)

Consider, Child of God, that
   love so great
how Jesus did
with His own blood cancel thy
   sin,
with which for thee
victorious against Satan's host,
   against the world and sin
did ever strive!
Let not within thy soul
the devil's blasphemy to enter!

Let not thy heart,
which is God's kingdom upon
   earth
become a desert!
Bemoan thy guilt in bitter grief,

so that with Christ's spirit thou
   mayst fast be bound!

NR. 4 ARIE (Sopran)

Komm in mein Herzenshaus,
Herr Jesu, mein Verlangen!
   Treib Welt und Satan aus

   Und laß dein Bild in mir
      erneuert prangen!
   Weg, schnöder Sündengraus!

NO. 4 ARIA (Soprano)

Enter now into my heart
Lord Jesus, my heart's longing!
   Drive the world and Satan
      out
   and let Thine image glow in
      me afresh!
   Hence, hateful dread of sin!

NR. 5 CHORAL

Und wenn die Welt voll Teufel
   wär
Und wollten uns verschlingen,

NO. 5 CHORALE

And if the world were full of
   devils
wholly to engulf us,

So fürchten wir uns nicht so
sehr,
Es soll uns doch gelingen.
Der Fürst dieser Welt,
Wie saur er sich stellt,
Tut er uns doch nicht,
Das macht, er ist gericht',
Ein Wörtlein kann ihn fällen.

then we'd not be at all afraid,

in spite of all we'd conquer.
The Prince of this great world,
however grim he be
can naught avail,
he'll surely stand his trial,
the smallest word his downfall
brings.

NR. 6 REZITATIV (Tenor)

So stehe denn bei Christi
blutgefärbter Fahne,
O Seele, fest
Und glaube, daß dein Haupt
dich nicht verläßt,
Ja, daß sein Sieg
Auch dir den Weg zu deiner
Krone bahne!
Tritt freudig an den Krieg!
Wirst du nur Gottes Wort
So hören und bewahren,
So wird der Feind gezwungen
auszufahren,
Dein Heiland bleibt dein Hort!

NO. 6 RECITATIVE (Tenor)

The stand beside the
bloodstained flag of Christ,
O soul, stand fast
and believe that this thy head
shall not desert thee;
ay, that His victory
shall lead thee also to a glorious
crown!
Step joyful into war!
Wilt thou the Word of God
not only hear, but keep,
then shall the enemy retreat in
shame,
thy Saviour be thy shield!

NR. 7 DUETT (Alt und Tenor)

Wie selig sind doch die, die
Gott im Munde tragen,
Doch selger ist das Herz, das
ihn im Glauben trägt!
Es bleibet unbesiegt und kann
die Feinde schlagen
Und wird zuletzt gekrönt, wenn
es den Tod erlegt.

NO. 7 DUET (Alto and Tenor)

Blessed are they, with God's
Word on their lips;
more blessed is the heart, that
bears Him strong in faith!
Unconquered He remains, His
enemies shall fall,
and at the time of death shall
win a glorious crown.

NR. 8 CHORAL	*NO. 8 CHORALE*
Das Wort sie sollen lassen stahn	They shall cling to the Word of God,
Und kein' Dank dazu haben.	and then receive no thanks,
Er ist bei uns wohl auf dem Plan	sure He is with us through life's span
Mit seinem Geist und Gaben.	with all His gifts and comfort.
Nehmen sie uns den Leib,	If they our body take,
Gut, Ehr, Kind und Weib,	our goods, our honour, children, wives,
Laß fahren dahin,	let them all go;
Sie habens kein' Gewinn;	for them it profits none;
Das Reich muß uns doch bleiben.	the kingdom yet doth ours remain.

CANTATA NO. 106: GOTTES ZEIT IST DIE ALLERBESTE ZEIT, BWV 106, "ACTUS TRAGICUS"
(God's Time Is the Best Time)

25 minutes

Bach probably composed his funeral cantata, *Gottes Zeit,* in 1707, on the occasion of the death of his uncle, Tobias Lämmerhirt (1639–1707). Although Bach was very clear about the makeup of the extremely distinctive orchestra—two recorders, two violas da gamba, and continuo—there is some ambiguity about whether or not he wanted a soprano soloist to go with the alto, tenor, and bass soloists and mixed choir. The uncertainty appears in the central choral movement, *"Es ist der alte Bund,"* which various conductors have sung by the entire choir, by a soprano soloist with the altos, tenors, and basses of the choir, or by four soloists.

The cantata starts with an instrumental sinfonia (which Bach calls "sonatina"); it establishes the basic tone of the entire work

—tragic, but with an air of acceptance and resignation. Two special features are the long/short/short rhythmic pattern that runs through this and several subsequent movements, and the musical sighing of the two recorders.

After announcing, *"Gottes Zeit ist die allerbeste Zeit,"* the choir immediately launches into a vigorous fugue, whose forward motion Bach interrupts only once when he, in a bit of word painting, has the sopranos sustain a note for ten beats on the word *"lange"* ("long"). Two solos follow—the tenor asking help for humankind in numbering its days, and the bass calling for people to put their affairs in order, since the coming of death is inevitable.

The chorus that is the central focus—musically, structurally, and liturgically—of the cantata comes next: musically because of the dramatic and emotional power of every note in the score; structurally because it is the climax, the apex, of the overall arch shape of the cantata; and liturgically because it juxtaposes the two central Christian beliefs about death—that everyone must die (sung by the lower three voices) and that death represents the opportunity to become one with the Lord Jesus (sung by the soprano or sopranos). In the deeply moving conclusion to this section, the rest of the voices and then the orchestra fade away, leaving the soprano to end alone.

Balancing the two solos that precede the pivotal chorus are two solos that follow, for alto and bass. The former, probably meant to be sung by a boy alto, flows without pause into the bass solo, to which the alto then adds a slow-moving melody, *"Mit Fried und Freud."* The counterpart to the opening choral fugue is a magnificent chorale, which brings the entire cantata to a glorious conclusion.

NR. 1 SONATINA

NO. 1 SONATINA

NR. 2 CHOR UND SOLI
CHOR

NO. 2 CHORUS AND SOLOS
CHORUS

Gottes Zeit ist die allerbeste
Zeit.
In ihm leben, weben und sind
wir, solange er will.
Apg. 17, 28
In ihm sterben wir zur rechten
Zeit, wenn er will.

God's time is the best time.

In Him we live and move and
have our being, for as long as
He wills it.
In Him we die at the time
appointed, whenever He wills
it.

ARIOSO (Tenor)

ARIOSO (Tenor)

Ach, Herr, lehre uns bedenken,
daß wir sterben müssen, auf
daß wir klug werden. *Psalm 90,
12*

O Lord, teach us to reflect that
we must die,
when we are most cunning!

ARIE (Baß)

ARIA (Bass)

Bestelle dein Haus; denn du
wirst sterben und nicht lebendig bleiben! *Jesaja 38, 1*

Set thine house in order! For
thou shalt die, and not live.

CHOR

CHORUS

Es ist der alte Bund: Mensch,
du mußt sterben!
Sirach 14, 18
Ja, komm, Herr Jesu!
Offenb. Joh. 22, 20

It is the old oath—Man, thou
art to die!

Even so, come, Lord Jesus!

NR. 3 SOLI UND CHOR

NO. 3 SOLOS AND CHORUS

ARIE (Alt)

ARIA (Alto)

In deine Hände befehl ich
meinen Geist; du hast mich
erlöset, Herr, du getreuer
Gott. *Psalm 31, 6*

Into Thy hands I commend my
spirit; for Thou hast delivered me, Lord, mine own true
God.

ARIOSO (Baß)

Heute wirst du mit mir im
   Paradies sein.   *Lukas 23, 43*

CHORAL (Chor-Alt)

Mit Fried und Freud ich fahr
   dahin
In Gottes Willen,
Getrost ist mir mein Herz und
   Sinn,
Sanft und stille.
Wie Gott mir verheißen hat:

Der Tod ist mein Schlaf
   worden.   *Martin Luther*

ARIOSO (Bass)

Today shalt thou be with Me in
   Paradise.

CHORALE (Altos)

In peace and joy I journey
   hence
And do God's will.
My heart and mind do comfort
   find
Gentle and still.
As God's word has been my
   command,
In sleep of death I slumber find.

NR. 4 CHOR

Glorie, Lob, Ehr und
   Herrlichkeit
Sei dir, Gott Vater und Sohn
   bereit',
Dem Heilgen Geist mit Namen!
Die göttlich Kraft
Mach uns sieghaft
Durch Jesum Christum,
   Amen.   *Adam Reusner*

NO. 4 CHORUS

Praise and glory, blessing,
   honour
To Thee, O Lord, both Father,
   Son
And the Name of Holy Spirit!
The divine power
Us victory gives
Through Jesus Christ our Lord,
   Amen.

JESU, MEINE FREUDE, BWV 227
(Jesus, My Joy)

21 minutes

In the late 1720s, during Bach's tenure as cantor of the St.
Thomas Church in Leipzig, it was the custom, on the death of a
prominent church member, to replace Vespers with a funeral
service. Almost surely, Bach composed his motet, *Jesu, meine*

Freude, for such an event, although neither the exact date nor the name of the person being thus honored has come down to us. (The motet originated in the thirteenth century as a narrowly defined type of sacred vocal composition. By Bach's time, though, the term referred to a variety of different kinds of sacred choral works.)

Bach composed *Jesu, meine Freude* for five-part choir (two sopranos, alto, tenor, bass) without continuo or any indication of instrumental parts. Some evidence exists, though, that performances of that time supported the vocal parts with organ or other instruments. In our own day many choir directors find that they can get better performances with the help of some instrumental background.

Although the eleven movements of *Jesu, meine Freude* appear to be highly integrated, Bach based them on two separate sources. The odd-numbered movements are the six verses of a chorale composed by Johann Crüger in Berlin in 1653, with a text by Johann Franck. Bach composed completely original music—much freer in style—for the even-numbered movements. He drew the text from St. Paul's Epistle to the Romans, chapter 8, verses 1, 2, 3, 9, 10, and 11, which compare the limited span of human life with the eternity of heavenly existence.

Despite the disparate derivations, the eleven movements follow one another perfectly naturally and comfortably. Further, Bach has structured them into a perfect arch shape around a central five-part fugue, giving the entire composition a symmetrical organization that some call a musical palindrome. Movements one and eleven are literally—and musically—identical. Movements two and ten start the same way and are both chordal, even though number ten is only half as long as number two. Movements three and nine present variations on the chorale; the latter, a long movement, uses the chorale melody as a cantus firmus. Movements four and eight are cast as trios—number four for two sopranos and alto, number eight for alto, tenor, and bass. Movements five and seven also consist of variations on the chorale. And Bach made movement six, a jubilant fugue, keystone of the entire composition.

While it is comparatively simple to analyze the formal structure of *Jesu, meine Freude,* it is much more difficult to capture in words the range of expression that is found in this remarkable work. Overall, one is suffused with feelings of warmth, peace, and acceptance. Within this emotional ambiance, though, there are sections of great joy, faith, despair, devotion. Bach wrote *Jesu, meine Freude* to honor the memory of one specific, unknown Leipzig burgher, but its emotional impact is so universal and so beautifully expressed that it cannot fail to touch and move every one of us.

Jesu, meine Freude,
meines Herzens Weide,
Jesu, meine Zier,
ach wie lang, ach, lange
ist dem Herzen bange,
und verlangt nach dir?
Gottes Lamm, mein Bräutigam,
ausser dir soll mir auf Erden

nichts sonst Liebers werden.

Es ist nun nichts Verdammliches
an denen, die in Christo Jesu
sind, die nicht nach dem
Fleische wandeln, sondern
nach dem Geist.
Romans 8, v.1

Unter deinem Schirmen
bin ich vor den Sturmen
aller Feinde frei.
Lass den Satan wittern,
lass den Feind erbittern,
mir steht Jesus bei.
Ob es itzt gleich kracht und
blitzt,
ob gleich Sünd und Hölle
schrecken:
Jesus will mich decken.

Jesu, my joy,
pasture of my heart
Jesu, my treasure,
how long, oh how long
does my heart grieve
and long for Thee!
Lamb of God, my bridegroom,
apart from Thee nothing on
earth
shall be more dear to me.

There is now no condemnation
to them which are in Christ
Jesus, who walk not after the
flesh, but after the Spirit.

Under Thy protection
I am free from the raging
of all my foes.
Let Satan thunder,
let the foe rage,
Jesus is by my side!
Through thunder and lightning,

through the horrors of sin and
hell,
Jesus will protect me.

Denn das Gesetz des Geistes,
   der da lebendig machet in
   Christo Jesu, hat mich frei
   gemacht von dem Gesetz der
   Sünde und des Todes.
Romans 8, v.2

Trotz dem alten Drachen,
Trotz des Todes Rachen,
Trotz der Furcht dazu!

Tobe, Welt, und springe,
ich steh hier und singe
in gar sichrer Ruh.
Gottes Macht hält mich in acht;
Erd und Abgrund muss
   verstummen,
ob sie noch so brummen.

Ihr aber seid nicht fleischlich,
sondern geistlich, so anders
Gottes Geist in euch wohnet.

Wer aber Christi Geist nicht
hat, der ist nicht sein.
Romans 8, v.9

Weg mit allen Schätzen!
Du bist mein Ergötzen,
Jesu, meine Lust!
Weg, ihr eitlen Ehren,
ich mag euch nicht hören,
bleibt mir unbewusst!
Elend, Not, Kreuz, Schmach
   und Tod
Soll mich, ob ich viel muss
   leiden,
nicht von Jesu scheiden.

So aber Christus in euch ist, so
   ist der Leib zwar tot um der

For the law of the Spirit of life
   in Christ Jesus hath made me
   free from the law of sin and
   death.

Defiance to the old serpent,
defiance to the raging of death,
defiance to fear besides!

Rage, world, and leap,
I shall stand here and sing,
quite in safety and peace.
God's might watches over me;
Earth and the abyss must fall
   silent,
for all their roaring.

But ye are not in the flesh, but
in the Spirit, if so be that the
Spirit of God dwell in you.
   Now if
any man have not the Spirit of
Christ, he is none of his.

Away with all treasures,
Thou art my delight,
Jesu, my joy!
Away vain honours
I would hear nothing of you,
remain unknown to me!
Misery, need, crosses, disgrace
   and death
shall not, however much I have
   to suffer,
part me from Jesus.

And if Christ be in you, the
   body is dead because of sin;

Sünde willen; der Geist aber
ist das Leben um der
Gerechtigkeit willen.
Romans 8, v.10

but the Spirit is life because
of righteousness.

Gute Nacht, o Wesen;
das die Welt erlesen,
mir gefällst du nicht!
Gute Nacht ihr Sunden
bleibet weit dahinten,
kommt nicht mehr ans Licht!
Gute Nacht du Stolz und
    Pracht!
Dir sei ganz, du Lasterleben,
gute Nacht gegeben.

Good night, earthly being
that was given to the world,
you please me not!
Good night, sins,
get far behind me `
come no more into the light!
Good night, pride and pomp!

To you utterly, burdensome life,
be wished good night.

So nun das Geist des, der Jesum
    von den Toten auferweckt
    hat, in euch wohnet, so wird
    auch derselbige, der Christum
    von den Toten auferweckt
    hat, eure sterblichen Leiber
    lebendig machen, um des
    willen, dass sein Geist in euch
    wohnet.
Romans 8, v.11

But if the Spirit of him that
    raised up Jesus from the dead
    dwell in you, he that raised
    Christ from the dead shall
    also quicken your mortal
    bodies by his Spirit that
    dwelleth in you.

Weicht, iht Trauergeister,
denn mein Freudenmeister,
Jesus, tritt herein.
Denen, die Gott lieben,
muss auch ihr Betrüben
lauter Wonne sein.
Duld ich schon hier Spott und
    Hohn,
dennoch bleibst du auch im
    Leide,
Jesu, meine Freude.
Johann Franck, 1653

Yield, spirits of grief,
for the Master of my joys,
Jesus, has entered in.
For those that love God
even their troubles must
be pure bliss.
If I now endure scorn and
    mockery,
still thou art, even in suffering,

Jesu, my joy!

MASS IN B MINOR, BWV 232

1 hour, 50 minutes

At first glance, it is hard to understand why Bach wrote his magnificent *Mass in B minor*. Over the many years that he was working on the *Mass,* he was employed as cantor at the Lutheran St. Thomas Church in Leipzig, where it would have been inconceivable to present a complete Roman Catholic Mass. Nor could it have found a place in the Catholic liturgy because of its monumental size and conception.

Only when we consider that Bach completed the *Mass* within two years of his death do we glimpse a clue to the purpose of the *Mass.* For Bach, this was a time of summation, of culmination, in which he assembled what some have termed "specimen books" of various types of music. One splendid example is his very last composition, left unfinished at his death: *Die Kunst der Fuge* ("Art of the Fugue"), which was both a summary of the possibilities inherent in this style of composition and a powerful and arresting composition in its own right. Similarly, the *B minor Mass* might be considered both a crowning climax of the possibilities inherent in Bach's sacred choral music and one of the outstanding musical creations of all time. Some, though, including the late musicologist Paul Henry Lang, believe that Bach did not intend the *B minor Mass* to be played all at once.

Bach composed the *"Kyrie"* and *"Gloria"* parts of the *Mass* as a *Missa* to be performed at St. Thomas for some major church feast in 1733. It was an accepted practice to use the first two movements of the Catholic Mass in Lutheran churches. Bach subsequently wrote four other so-called Lutheran masses —in G major, G minor, A major, and F major—for this very purpose.

The B minor *Missa* was the largest in scale of his Lutheran masses: the Kyrie and Gloria alone last about an hour. On the death of August the Strong, elector of Saxony and king of Poland, on July 27, 1733, Bach sent a presentation copy of the two movements and a most humble letter to the king's successor, Friedrich August II, in the hope of being appointed court composer—an honor he finally received in November 1736.

The third part of the *Mass,* the *"Sanctus,"* was a revision of a *"Sanctus"* Bach had composed for performance in Leipzig on Christmas Day 1724 (or 1723, according to some). Many of the individual movements in the second and fourth parts of the *Mass,* however—which he composed between 1745 and 1748, just a few years before his death in 1750—were borrowings or reworkings of movements from earlier cantatas.

No evidence exists that the *Mass* was performed in its entirety during Bach's lifetime. Apparently, the first complete performance was given in Berlin on February 12, 1835, and the initial publication followed ten years later.

1. *"Kyrie eleison."* Noted choral conductor Helmuth Rilling once described the opening as a "banner headline." It is a brief, bold, homophonic statement by five-part chorus and orchestra of the theme that becomes the principal subject of the mighty fugue that follows. Many repetitions of the two-note descending half-step figure that Bach associated with sighs and pleading pervade this movement.

2. *"Christe eleison."* This movement, for two soprano soloists, presents a stark contrast to the preceding *"Kyrie."* Instead of the entreaties of the *"Kyrie,"* this movement bespeaks an almost joyous acceptance of Christ's mercy. Its strength and confidence come from both the vigor of the solo writing and the propulsive force of the forward-moving lines in the orchestra.

3. *"Kyrie eleison."* Rather than returning to the music of the first *"Kyrie,"* Bach creates a completely new fugue, written in sixteenth-century style, for the second *"Kyrie."* The broad principal subject deliberately moves up through the four-part choir. As the fugue continues, though, the entrances crowd closer together until, in the final statements, the entrances are syncopated, coming on accented offbeats, adding an intensity that to some extent presages the coming *"Gloria."*

4. *"Gloria in excelsis Deo."* Bach abruptly changes character

for the *"Gloria,"* replacing the restraint of the *"Kyrie"* with extroverted jubilation, focusing much more on the orchestra, and writing vocal parts that are more instrumental in conception. In addition, Bach adds trumpets and timpani to the orchestra, replacing the gentle oboe d'amores with the more powerful oboes and, particularly in the first part, writing in a brilliant, virtuosic style.

5. *"Laudamus te."* Set between two big choral movements, *"Laudamus te"* is a small-scale gem—the performing group limited to soprano II (or mezzo-soprano) soloist, solo violin, and string orchestra. The writing for the two soloists is highly melismatic and deeply expressive.

6. *"Gratias agimus tibi."* This fugal movement, for choir and full orchestra, represents a reworking of Bach's cantata *Wir danken dir, Gott, wir danken dir, und verkündigen deine Wunder,* BWV 29 ("We thank You, God, we thank You and proclaim Your wonders"). The words are remarkably close to the translation of the *Mass* text "We thank You for Your great glory." The style looks back to the strict counterpoint of sixteenth-century *stile antico.*

7. *"Domine Deus."* In this duet for soprano I and tenor with solo flute, the two voices symbolically represent God the Father and God the Son. While the tenor sings, *"Domine Deus, Rex coelestis, Deus Pater omnipotens"* ("O Lord God, King of heaven, God the Father Almighty"), the soprano sings, *"Domine Fili unigenite, Jesu Christe altissime"* ("O Lord, Jesus Christ, the only begotten Son, high above all"). Melodically, the vocal parts in this section are characterized by the descending pairs of notes first heard in the opening *"Kyrie."*

8. *"Qui tollis."* Following without pause is the *"Qui tollis,"* which Bach based on the first part of his cantata BWV 46, *Schauet doch und sehet* ("Behold and see if there be any sorrow like unto my sorrow"). That part is here transformed into a prayer for mercy. The composer divides the choir into four parts, with soprano II on top, giving the group a dark, veiled quality. Although not heard in the choral parts, the descending two-note figure is prominent in the orchestra.

9. *"Qui sedes ad dextram."* An aria for alto with an obbligato oboe d'amore, the *"Qui sedes"* is one of the most moving and affecting sections of the entire *Mass.* Once again Bach makes use of the descending two-note figure, often as an echo at the end of a phrase, strengthening the emotional power of the supplications expressed in *"Miserere nobis"* ("Have mercy on us").

10. *"Quoniam tu solus sanctus."* The writing in this aria, for bass soloist with obbligato parts for the low-pitched corno di caccia (hunting horn) and two bassoons, makes a strange setting of a text that reaches its climax with the words "You alone are high above all." Yet despite the low tessitura, the music most effectively projects the exultation of the adoration. Also, it provides a dramatic contrast to the brilliantly energetic *"Cum Sancto Spiritu"* that follows. A symbolic touch: the opening horn call is a musical palindrome (the notes are identical forward or backward). This compositional device is sometimes used to represent the perfection of the risen Christ.

11. *"Cum Sancto Spiritu."* This movement is both the conclusion and the culmination of the entire *"Gloria"* section of the *Mass.* At the end of the score Bach wrote, *"Fine—SDG"* (abbreviating *Soli Deo Gloria,* and meaning "The end—to God alone the glory.") In this powerful paean of praise to the Almighty, Bach unleashes all the strength of the choir and orchestra in an ecstasy of fugal wonder—which makes the brief homophonic section near the middle of the movement an absolutely magical moment.

12. *"Credo in unum Deum."* This opens the *"Credo,"* or Nicene Creed, the third major section of the *Mass.* Bach divides it into eight separate movements that form an arch shape, with the three central ideas of Christian belief—incarnation, crucifixion, and resurrection—at the apex. Using the Gregorian chant of the *"Credo"* as the subject (although accompanying it with a very un-Gregorian perpetual movement line in the bass), Bach fashions a highly complex seven-voice fugue for the entirety of this brief movement—the seven voices being soprano I, soprano II, alto, tenor, bass, violin I, and violin II.

13. *"Patrem omnipotentem."* Based on Bach's cantata *Gott,*

wie dein Name, so ist auch dein Ruhm, (God, as thy name, so is thy fame) BWV 171, this movement follows with barely any break. Bach maintains the same dense, contrapuntal texture of the preceding movement and even inserts jubilant exclamations of *"Credo in unum Deo"* over the first three statements of *"Patrem omnipotentem."*

14. *"Et in unum Dominum."* In this movement, set as a gentle duet for soprano and alto, Bach expresses the textual concept of the "Lord Jesus Christ, the only begotten Son of God" in musical terms. In the very first measure the first violins play a three-note motif marcato, with each note separate, representing the Father. Immediately the second violins follow, playing the identical motif, but with the second and third notes played legato, slurred smoothly together, giving the motif a gentler character representative of Christ, the Son. These two similar but different motifs reappear many times through the movement.

15. *"Et incarnatus est."* A five-note figure in the violins—which, Helmuth Rilling points out, is a literal representation of the cross—opens and pervades this movement for five-voice choir. One can see the cross by drawing a line connecting the second and fifth notes and another line connecting the third and fourth notes. Rilling adds that the cross is also the Greek letter *chi,* which is the first letter of *Christos.* The choir writing achieves great poise and reverence over the persistent violin motif.

16. *"Crucifixus."* Bach casts this movement, the anguished central piece of the *"Credo,"* as a passacaglia, a musical form in which a short bass melody is repeated thirteen times with continuous variations in the voices and instruments above. According to Rilling's conjecture, Bach chose the highly repetitious passacaglia form to symbolize the centrality of the crucifixion in Christian dogma. The passacaglia bass line, with its descending line, is not original to Bach but is the so-called *lamento bass,* which was popular among many composers of his time. The movement is a reworking of part of Bach's early cantata BWV 12, *Weinen, Klagen, Sorgen, Zagen* ("Weeping, lamentations,

pity, hopelessness"). Bach darkens the tonal ambiance by specifying that the choir consist of soprano II, alto, tenor, and bass.

17. *"Et resurrexit."* After the low, quiet conclusion to *"Crucifixus,"* the full choir and orchestra come in with a high-pitched burst of energy to launch *"Et resurrexit."* Exultantly they announce the resurrection of Christ in a powerful, symmetrical fanfare, in which the pitches, but not the rhythms, are the same forward and backward. The strength of the brilliant writing for both choir and orchestra leaves no question of Bach's full-hearted, joyful acceptance of the resurrection.

18. *"Et in Spiritum sanctum."* After the powerful emotional impact of the preceding movements, Bach establishes a welcome gentle lightness of mood with a bass aria accompanied by just two oboe d'amores and continuo.

19. *"Confiteor unum baptisma."* Bach divides this highly structured, contrapuntally dense movement for full choir and orchestra into three discrete sections. The first is based on two melodies—*"Confiteor, confiteor"* and *"in remissionem peccatorum"*—and the combination of the two along with hints of an old Gregorian chant. The tempo slows considerably for the middle section, a setting of the words *"et expecto resurrectionem mortuorum."* Bach then repeats this last line of text in a fast, bright tempo, which opens the triumphant concluding section based on a chorus from his cantata *Gott, man lobet dich in der Stille zu Zion* (God, one praises Thee in the stillness of Zion), BWV 120.

20. *"Sanctus."* Bach increases his performing forces for the *"Sanctus,"* adding a second alto part to the choir and a third oboe to the orchestra. In the massive first part of the *"Sanctus,"* he makes abundant use of all the performers, calling on them to play and sing virtually without stop during this entire grandiose, monumental section. With the words *"Pleni sunt coeli,"* Bach dramatically speeds up the tempo, reduces the texture to single voices introducing an extended fugue, and replaces the grandiosity with joyful jubilation.

21. *"Osanna."* The melody for this movement Bach borrowed from his cantata *Preise dein Glücke, gesegnetes Sachsen*

(Praise your good luck, blessed Saxony), BWV 215. One can speculate that Bach chose this source because its principal theme has the same motif of three repeated notes as the theme of the previous "Pleni sunt coeli et terra." The movement opens with a ringing unison declaration of faith that quickly adds various instruments to reach a twenty-voice climax, and it maintains that high energy level—except for two striking piano (soft), echolike passages near the end.

22. *"Benedictus."* If the only two ways to capture a listener's attention are to shout and to whisper, the *"Osanna"* is analogous to a shout, using the largest performing forces of the *Mass,* and the *"Benedictus"* may be likened to a whisper, using the smallest performing forces—solo tenor, solo flute (or sometimes a violin), and continuo. Quiet and meditative throughout, this movement projects a tranquil, though reverential, quality. Traditionally, the choir repeats *"Osanna"* at the end of *"Benedictus."*

23. *"Agnus Dei."* As in *"Benedictus,"* Bach limits himself here to a solo voice (alto), a single instrumental line (violin), and continuo to craft a movement of outstanding expressiveness and sensitivity. The composer based the music on his cantata BWV 11, which is known as the *Himmelfahrts-Oratorium.* Frequently performed apart from the *Mass,* this aria includes many chromaticisms, which add both poignancy and intensity, and numerous subtle imitations of the vocal line in the violin.

24. *"Dona nobis pacem."* Instead of borrowing from a previous composition, Bach based this movement on the "Gratias agimus tibi" section of the *"Gloria"* of this *Mass.* Here, though, he starts quietly and builds right through to the end, creating not a supplicant's prayer for peace, but a ringing affirmation of faith and devotion.

Standard Text (see Appendix)

MAGNIFICAT IN D MAJOR, BWV 243

30 minutes

When Bach became cantor of St. Thomas Church in Leipzig in 1723, his major obligation was to provide music for the various Sunday and feast day services, as well as to train and lead the choir and instrumentalists—a truly demanding schedule. At times, he would be required to compose a new work in just a few days, which forced him to work at top speed and to take shortcuts by borrowing from himself or others. In preparation for his first Christmas in Leipzig, though, Bach was excused from his other duties from the middle of November in order to have sufficient time to compose a Magnificat for Christmas Vespers.

The Magnificat, which received its first performance on Christmas Day 1723, was in the key of E flat and had four interspersed movements to tell the Nativity story. Years later— some suggest it was in the spring of 1732—Bach revised the work, changing the key to D major (his key to express jubilation), making some minor changes in the scoring, and eliminating the four Christmas interpolations. In this form it could also be used for the July 2 Feast of the Visitation.

The Magnificat is a song of praise for the Virgin Mary that dates far back in the Christian liturgy. Bach used the traditional text (Luke 1:46–55) plus two verses of the Lesser Doxology, and he wrote the music for a large performing group—five soloists (two sopranos, alto, tenor, and bass), five-part mixed choir (two sopranos, alto, tenor, and bass), and an orchestra of two flutes, two oboes (one playing oboe d'amore), three trumpets, timpani, strings, and continuo.

Surrounding the exuberant, highly ornamented choral section, which makes up the major part of the first movement, are brilliant opening and closing trumpet fanfares. After the uninhibited joy that has been projected, the second movement, an alto solo, sounds equally rapturous, although a little more re-strained. The soprano solo that follows introduces a note of solemnity and leads, without pause, to the vigorous, spirited chorus *"Omnes generationes."*

The bass solo that comes next is characterized by its confident air and reflective mood. Bach establishes a gentle, rocking motion for the alto and tenor duet *"Et misericordia,"* but he shatters the calm with the powerful chorus *"Fecit potentiam";* striking is the way Bach flings the word *"dispersit"* ("scattered") around the choir before reaching the slow, quiet ending of the movement. Next, an agitated, vigorous tenor solo leads to a light, tender alto solo, *"Esurientes implevit bonis."* After an expressive, emotional trio for two sopranos and alto, Bach moves to a fugal chorus, *"Sicut locutus est,"* and concludes the Magnificat with another chorus, *"Gloria Patri,"* a mighty ending that finishes with a brief reminder of the first-movement opening.

Standard Text (see Appendix)

PASSION ACCORDING TO ST. MATTHEW, BWV 244

3 hours

Some scholars hold, based on a list of compositions prepared after his death and the fact that he wrote five annual cycles of church cantatas, that Bach wrote a total of five Passions: *Passion According to St. Matthew* and *Passion According to St. John,* which are discussed here; a *Passion According to St. Mark* from 1731, for which only the libretto and a few musical fragments (mostly found in cantatas 54 and 198) still exist; a completely lost *Passion According to St. Luke;* and a missing, early, single-choir *Passion According to St. Matthew* that Bach replaced with the currently performed double-choir version.

Bach composed the *St. Matthew Passion* in Leipzig in 1728 and 1729. He drew the text from chapters 26 and 27 of the Gospel of St. Matthew, with additional text by Picander, the pen name of postal official and poet Christian Friedrich Henrici. Performance requires very considerable artistic forces: a tenor singing the role of the Evangelist and a bass singing the role of Jesus; at least four other vocal soloists (soprano, mezzo-soprano, tenor, and bass), and more if each only sings one part; a double choir and a boys' choir; and a double orchestra, including two separate continuo sections of organ, cello, bassoon, and double bass.

The composer directed the premiere at the Church of St. Thomas in Leipzig on Good Friday, April 15, 1729. The presentation was part of the afternoon service, Part I being performed before the sermon, and Part II afterward.

Bach made slight revisions in the music in 1736, 1739, and 1745, presumably for subsequent performances. This towering masterpiece was then not heard again for nearly a century, until March 11, 1829, when Felix Mendelssohn led the work in a famous Berlin concert—the event directly responsible for the rediscovery of the music of the Cantor of Leipzig. (An actor, Edward Devrient, sang the role of Jesus at the Berlin performance, which led to Mendelssohn's oft-quoted comment "Well, it takes a clown and a Jew to reintroduce the greatest Christian music to the people.")

After a brief orchestral introduction, choir I enters lamenting, followed by choir II, seeking to understand what is happening by crying out, "Who? How? What? Where?" As choir I answers, the pure voices of the boys' chorus waft above the adults, intoning the chorale *"O lamm Gottes unschuldig"* ("O Innocent Lamb of God"). (The use of boys' voices is customary; Bach only calls for "supplementary" sopranos.)

Now the dramatic account of the events leading up to the crucifixion begins with a recitative in which the Evangelist introduces Jesus, who prophesies His own death. Jesus' words, here and throughout, are sung amid an aura of soft, exquisite string sound, a sort of aural halo. This leads to a chorale that appears several times in the *Passion,* each time with different text.

The story continues: the plotting against Jesus, the resistance against having His capture occur on Passover, the anointing incident at the home of Simon the leper in Bethany, and the affecting alto recitative and aria in response. Judas then offers to betray Jesus, which leads to a highly emotional soprano aria.

The next several movements deal with the Last Supper. One of the most exciting, albeit brief, moments in the entire work comes with the emotional outburst as the choir (the Apostles) wildly shout out, *"Herr, bin ichs?"* ("Lord, is it I?") to find out who will betray Jesus. The soprano recitative and aria sum up the conflicting feelings—pain at the thought of Christ's death, and consolation in the legacy He will leave behind.

From the Last Supper, the action shifts to Gethsemane—the prayers of Jesus, the pain and grief of the disciples, the actual kiss of betrayal by Judas, the taking of Jesus, the anger of the crowd, and the desertion of His followers. The musical climax of this segment is the chorus *"O Mensch, bewein dein Sünde gross"* ("O mankind, bewail thy heavy sins"), which is the finale of Part I.

Instead of continuing immediately with the unfolding story, Part II opens with the alto soloist and choir II mourning the loss of Jesus. Only then does Bach pick up the narrative again with the testimony of the false witnesses, the questioning by the High Priest, the denial of Jesus by Peter, and the delivery of Jesus to Pontius Pilate. Judas, now filled with remorse, hangs himself.

As was the custom on a feast day, one prisoner is to be released. Pilate asks the crowd whether it should be Barabbas, a convicted murderer, or Jesus, who Pilate knows is innocent. The crowd shouts its desire—"Barabbas!"—and continues with the words *"Lass ihn kreuzigen!"* ("Let Him be crucified!")

The drama rushes forward with the scourging of Jesus, His walk to Golgotha, and His crucifixion. The alto recitative and aria that begins, *"Ach, Golgatha, unsel ges Golgatha!"* ("Ah, Golgotha, accursed Golgotha!") provides an especially touching and moving section as the choir rudely interrupts four times, asking *"Wo?"* ("Where?")—a reminder of the opening chorus of the *Passion*.

After further torture on the cross, Jesus dies, unleashing a mighty earthquake and throwing open the graves of the saints. The *Passion* then ends with each of the four soloists bidding Jesus farewell and both choirs coming together in a lullabylike double chorus, *"Wir setzen uns mit Tränen nieder"* ("We sit by Thee with tears overflowing").

PASSION ACCORDING TO ST. JOHN, BWV 245

2 hours, 10 minutes

Although it bears a higher BWV number than the *St. Matthew Passion* (and hence follows in this book), the *St. John Passion* was actually composed earlier, in about ten weeks during the winter of 1722–23, while Bach was still living in Cöthen. The text comes from chapters 18 and 19 of the Gospel According to St. John, plus some brief excerpts from St. Matthew and additional text from a *Passion* poem that the poet–town councillor of Hamburg, Barthold Heinrich Brockes, had written some years earlier. The composer led the first performance at the Good Friday services on April 7, 1724, in St. Nicholas Church, Leipzig, where he had moved in 1723. He subsequently made some revisions, probably for additional performances.

St. John is probably heard less often today than *St. Matthew*, perhaps because the former is in some ways a more stark and therefore more painful evocation of the anguish of the Passion, lacking the comforting sections found in *St. Matthew*.

The *St. John Passion* opens with a magnificent chorus that combines despair at the death of Jesus with faith in His triumph over death. The story of the Passion then begins dramatically with the betrayal and capture of Jesus, featuring the Evangelist as narrator, Jesus, and the choir as the crowd. Interspersed are chorales with their comments on the unfolding events.

Bach then introduces an alto aria, after which the Evangelist tells of Peter following Jesus, and the soprano sings an aria expanding on this idea. The movements detailing Peter's denial of Jesus ensue, and Part I ends with a tenor aria expressing Peter's pain and bewilderment and a chorale calling on Jesus to bring understanding.

After a chorale, Part II continues the story with the appearance of Jesus before Pilate, in which the choir now represents the crowd of Jews. When Pilate asks the mob whom to release, they ask not for Jesus, but for the convicted murderer, Barabbas, whereupon Pilate has Jesus scourged.

Two of the musical high points of the entire work follow—a pained arioso for solo bass and a comforting aria for solo tenor —which are made all the more moving by the mocking chorus of Roman soldiers that follows. Pilate now seeks the release of Jesus, but the crowd will not allow it.

The Evangelist relates how Jesus is being led to Golgotha for the crucifixion. Bach here inserts an exciting bass aria that is interrupted by frenzied cries of *"Wohin?"* ("Where?") from the upper voices of the choir. The crucifixion and death of Jesus follow, including the Evangelist's narration, the words of Pilate and Jesus, and the choir singing chorales or playing the part of the Roman soldiers.

The conclusion of the *Passion* includes arias for each soloist that, in effect, bids farewell to Jesus. Between the arias, the Evangelist continues his account of the events after the death of Jesus. Finally, Bach inserts an angelic chorus, *"Ruht wohl, ihr heiligen Gebeine"* ("May Your holy body rest in peace"), and ends the entire work with a chorale, *"Ach Herr, lass dein lieb' Engelein"* ("Ah, Lord, send Your dear angels").

CHRISTMAS ORATORIO, BWV 248

3 hours

During Bach's tenure as cantor of St. Thomas Church in Leipzig, Christmas was celebrated on six days—December 25, 26, and 27, January 1 (Feast of the Circumcision), the following Sunday, and January 6 (Feast of the Epiphany). Bach wrote his monumental *Christmas Oratorio,* consisting of six separate, large-scale, but related compositions, to provide music for each of the days. He completed the music, probably in October 1734, and gave the entire work its first performance on the six days of Christmas at St. Thomas at the end of 1734 and the beginning of 1735.

Although the *Christmas Oratorio* ranks high among Bach's most beloved compositions, some music scholars remain troubled by the fact that about a dozen of the total of sixty-four movements are parodies. ("Parody," from the Greek word meaning "imitated song," originally meant a serious reworking of an older musical composition; the word contained none of the satirical and comical elements that are now part of its definition.) Bach borrowed the parody movements from earlier, secular cantatas, mostly from works that were unlikely to be performed again because he wrote them to celebrate specific events.

How could Bach take music he had composed for various nonreligious purposes and use it in a sacred oratorio? Although there is no simple response to this concern, it is abundantly clear that, with the revisions he made in the old music and the substitution of new text, every single part of the *Christmas Oratorio* sounds absolutely fitting and appropriate in its place in the oratorio.

Another question bedeviling the scholars is whether to consider the *Christmas Oratorio* a single unified composition or six separate works meant to be performed independently over a two-week period. While there is no evidence that Bach ever performed it other than on the six individual occasions, the tonal relationships of the parts (D,G,D,F,A,D) show that the oratorio works perfectly well when played consecutively on one program.

Choral directors differ in their approach to this work. Some play it as one piece. Others, concerned that the entire oratorio runs too long, either perform just the first three parts, which constitute a good, complete group, or give the first three parts at one performance and the next three at another. A few directors prefer to make extensive cuts and perform all six parts in that way.

Commentators sometimes refer to the six parts of the *Christmas Oratorio* as six cantatas. The parts do, indeed, resemble cantatas in that they are made up of choruses and chorales, solo arias, duets, trios, and recitatives. But in other respects the work is more like other oratorios or Passions in that there is a narrator, the Evangelist, sung by a tenor, and roles for an Angel (soprano) and Herod (bass).

Bach took the texts for Parts I through IV from the Gospel of St. Luke, chapter 2, verses 1 through 21; Parts V and VI come from the Gospel of St. Matthew, chapter 2, verses 1 through 12. Additional nonbiblical text was provided by the Leipzig postal official and poet, Picander (pen name of Christian Friedrich Henrici), with whom Bach worked very closely in the preparation of the libretto.

The oratorio starts with a jubilant chorus, *"Jauchzet, frohlocket!"* ("Rejoice, exult!"), replete with brilliant high trumpets and stirring timpani. (This is one of the parody movements. It comes from Bach's cantata *Tönet, ihr Pauken, erschallet, Trompeten!,* BMV 214—"Sound Drums, Ring Out, Trumpets!"—which he had composed to honor Christine Eberhardine, queen of Saxony.) After the chorus, the Evangelist starts the story of the Nativity, which is taken up by the solo alto in a wondrously tender and gentle recitative and aria; the account continues with various musical numbers that reflect on and respond to what is happening, as well as what will be. The section then continues with a chorale, *"Ach, mein herzliebes*

Jesulein"—which is better known as the chorale and Christmas carol *"Von Himmel hoch da komm ich hier"*—before a return to the joyful spirit of the opening.

Part II begins with an extended orchestral introduction, a quietly rocking movement in pastoral style that brings to mind the shepherds coming to adore the newborn child. The Evangelist continues the gospel narrative, joined by the Angel announcing the birth and a solo tenor urging the shepherds to hurry to the infant. Bach demonstrates his fondness for the alto voice in the touching lullaby (*"Schlafe mein Liebster"*) which he assigns to her. The concluding chorale of this part, *"Wir singen dir in deinem Heer,"* uses the same basic melody as the one that ended Part I, but with different words.

After the comparative tranquility of Part II, Part III recaptures the force and brilliance of Part I, starting with an energetic choral fugue. The musical highlights of this section include the expressive soprano-bass duet and—again showing Bach's predilection for the alto voice—a most moving alto aria as Mary wonders at the miracle that has befallen her. The use of the solo violin in the accompaniment adds to the aria's emotional impact. Bach provides a strong ending for this section by calling for a repeat of the opening chorus.

The exceptionally devotional Part IV deals with the childhood of Jesus. Very striking is the soprano aria—*"Flösst, mein Heiland"* ("Ah, my Savior")—which is concerned with the naming of Jesus. Several times a second soprano echoes words of the solo soprano. This is another parody movement, coming from Bach's cantata *Hercules auf dem Scheidewege*, BMV 213, in which the echoes are the oracle's answers to Hercules' questions. The chorale that brings this section to a close is of special interest because of the lengthy orchestral interludes that come before, between, and after the lines of text.

Bach writes a mighty fugal choral movement to begin Part V. The Evangelist now turns to St. Matthew to continue the narrative, which deals with the arrival of the Wise Men. The section contains the one trio in the oratorio, called a terzetto—a highly dramatic, contrapuntal movement for solo soprano, alto, and tenor—to the words *"Ach, wann wird die Zeit erscheinen?"* ("Ah, when will the time come?"). A quiet but self-assured chorale brings the part to a close.

Perhaps the most forceful chorus in the entire work, the triumphant *"Herr, wenn die stolzen Feinde schnauben,"* introduces Part VI. The account then continues, with Herod calling for the Sages and the Wise Men making their offerings and leaving. Two outstanding arias are heard in the course of this part—*"Nur ein Wink von seinen Händen"* for soprano and *"Nun mögt ihr stolzen Feinde"* for tenor. And the *Christmas Oratorio* ends with a mighty chorus celebrating victory over death, the devil, sin, and hell.

LUDWIG VAN BEETHOVEN

Born December 16, 1770, in Bonn
Died March 26, 1827, in Vienna

"I must despise the world that does not know that music is a higher revelation than all wisdom and philosophy." With this pronouncement Beethoven, the revolutionary, clearly separated his musical purpose from that of his predecessors.

Beethoven considered himself a creative artist—a designation that Bach, Haydn, Mozart, and their contemporaries never even considered. Until Beethoven's time, most composers were in the employ of aristocrats or church officials, and to a large extent they regarded themselves as skilled craftsmen who produced music to fit the needs of their employers. While they turned out any number of glorious, enduring masterpieces, they essentially wrote music for specific occasions or purposes, with little thought of future performance.

By considering himself an artist, Beethoven expressed the belief that he was writing, not only for a single performance or to fulfill a particular commission, but for posterity. Contributing to this outlook was the rise of public concerts during his lifetime. Beethoven expected many copies of his music to be published so that different performing organizations could present the work over and over again in various concert halls. In this important respect, Beethoven and others of his time differed from their seventeenth- or eighteenth-century forebears, who expected their music to be played once and then, at best, to be deposited in the palace or church archives.

Beethoven's era—the decades just before and after the start of the nineteenth century—was a time of great foment and revolution. The French Revolution of 1789 had planted the seeds of a new social and political order in the Western world. The rise of the bourgeoisie gave birth to a transformed, more egalitarian economic system. And Beethoven, more than any other composer, was able to forge a music that expressed the spirit and substance of this new, radically altered world.

While Beethoven's early works were firmly rooted in the musical traditions of Haydn and Mozart, he soon began to strain and struggle against the limitations and restrictions of the older men's compositional practices. Vastly expanding the scope, emotional content, and overall dimensions of his compositions, he infused them with new force and flexibility. He was able to achieve sharp and forceful contrasts by exploding outward the range of pitches and dynamics. His music soared to powerful climaxes that far surpassed anything heard before. While never fully discarding the old, he bent and shaped the forms and organizing principles to his own musical imperatives. Above all, as the ultimate musical architect, he created large-scale compositions that surged forward, with note following note in inevitable succession.

Beethoven created his major choral compositions in two bursts of activity separated by more than a decade. During the first period, from about 1802 to 1808, he wrote Fantasia for Piano, Chorus, and Orchestra, *Christ on the Mount of Olives,* and Mass in C. This was also the time when he was becoming increasingly aware of his worsening deafness and raged against the cruel fate that was robbing him of his most valued sense. Although still under the influence of Haydn and Mozart, these early works already bear the hallmarks of Beethoven's unique musical personality—compelling tectonic sense, powerful emotions, intense passions, and arresting contrasts.

His last two choral works—*Missa solemnis* and Ninth Symphony—are inspired, sublime masterpieces. (Although a number of symphonies include choral sections, only a few, such as Beethoven's Ninth and Mahler's Eighth, fit comfortably in a book discussing choral masterpieces.) Composed between 1819 and 1824, they came at the very end of his life. By then he was totally deaf, but he had come to accept his terrible condition, and he realized that he was still able to write works that expressed the genius of his creative urge.

FANTASIA FOR PIANO, CHORUS, AND ORCHESTRA, Op. 80
(Choral Fantasia)

18 minutes

It was in 1800 that Beethoven first conceived the audacious idea of an instrumental composition crowned by a choral finale. But it was not until December 1808 that he realized his vision.

At the time, he was preparing an "academy," a concert that composers put on to introduce their new works and to earn money from ticket sales. The program already included the Fifth and Sixth Symphonies, Fourth Piano Concerto, three movements of the Mass in C, and the concert aria *"Ah! Perfido"*—more than enough music for one program. Tradition, however, demanded that the concert also include an extended improvisation. To fulfill this obligation, as well as to provide a particularly powerful finale to the evening, Beethoven wrote the Fantasia a few weeks before the December 22, 1808, performance at the Theater an der Wien in Vienna.

Beethoven planned to start the Fantasia with an extended piano introduction, bring in the orchestra, and then build to a climax that would combine piano, chorus, and orchestra. So rushed was he in composing the work, however, that he did not have time to write out the opening section. Instead, he improvised the piano part at the premiere and put it down on paper much later.

Present performances of the Fantasia open with Beethoven's lengthy, virtuosic, composed "improvisation." The orchestra then enters quietly, and a dialogue between orchestra and piano ensues. After a series of horn calls and oboe echoes, the piano states the principal theme, a simple, childlike melody that Beethoven borrowed from his 1796 song *"Gegenliebe"* ("Requited Love").

The composer then devotes the remainder of the Fantasia to free variations on this melody. Its naive simplicity makes it adaptable to any instrument or voice, allows it to take on any emotional quality or text, and permits embellishments and additional complexity in the course of the variations.

After putting the melody through its paces with just the piano and orchestra, Beethoven recalls the earlier dialogue and then introduces the chorus. The text (by either Christoph Kuffner or Friedrich Treitschke) presents a paean to art and has no relation to the original *"Gegenliebe,"* which had a text by Gottfried August Bürger.

Beethoven's attitude toward the text and the speed of composition can be learned from a letter he later wrote to his publisher: "Will you perhaps want to substitute other words, as the text, like the music, was the work of a very short time, so that I could not even write a score?" And, over the words "a very short time," Beethoven added the detail "of a night."

Schmeichelnd hold und
   lieblich klingen
  unsers Lebens Harmonien,

Und dem Schönheitssinn
   entschwingen
  Blumen sich, die ewig
   blühn.

Fried' und Freude gleiten
   freundlich
  wie der Wellen
   Wechselspiel;
Was sich drängte rauh und
   feindlich,
  ordnet sich zu Hochgefühl.

Wenn der Töne Zauber
   walten
  und des Wortes Weihe
   spricht,

Soft and sweet through ether
   winging
  sound and harmonies of
   life,
There immortal flowers
   springing
  when the soul is freed from
   strife.

Peace and joy are sweetly
   blended
  like the waves alternate
   play;
What for mastery contended,

  learns to yield and to obey.

When on music's mighty
   pinion
  souls of men to heaven
   rise,

Muss sich Herrliches
    gestalten,
  Nacht und Stürme werden
    Licht.

Äuss're Ruhe, inn're Wonne

  herrschen für den
    Glücklichen.
Doch der Künste
    Frühlingssonne
  lässt aus beiden Licht
    enstehn.

Grosses, das in's Herz
    gedrungen,
  blüht dann neu und
    Schönempor.
Hat ein Geist sich
    aufgeschwungen,
  hall't ihm stets ein
    Geisterchor.

Nehmt denn hin, ihr
    schönen Seelen,
  froh die Gaben schöner
    Kunst.
Wenn sich Lieb' und Kraft
    vermählen,
  lohnt dem Menschen
    Götter-Gunst.

Then both vanish earth's
    dominion,
  Man is native to the skies.

Calm without and joy within
    us
  is the bliss for which we
    long.
If the art of magic wins us

  joy and calm are turned to
    song.

With its tide of joy unbroken,

  music's flood our life
    surrounds.
What a mastermind has
    spoken,
  through eternity resounds.

Oh! receive ye joy invited,

  all its blessings without
    guile.
When in love and strength
    united,
  man earns the gods'
    approving smile.

CHRIST ON THE MOUNT OF OLIVES, Op. 85
(Christus am Oelberge)

45 minutes

As with the Fantasia, Beethoven composed *Christ on the Mount of Olives* within a few weeks for a concert known as an "academy" to be held on April 5, 1803, at Vienna's Theater an der Wien. The program also featured the First and Second Symphonies, the Third Piano Concerto, and assorted vocal selections. Although composed early in his life, it has a high opus number because it was not published until 1811, eight years later.

Christ on the Mount of Olives is Beethoven's sole oratorio. The text, written by the contemporary and popular Viennese poet Franz Xavier Huber, recounts the story from the prayers of Jesus on the Mount of Olives to His arrest in the Garden of Gethsemane. In addition to orchestra, the score calls for three solo voices—tenor (Christ), soprano (Seraph), bass (Peter)—and choir, which includes choirs of angels, soldiers, and disciples.

After its highly successful premiere, followed by four performances the same year and many more over the next few decades, *Christ on the Mount of Olives* was only occasionally heard, a situation that, for the most part, still exists today. Apparently, some people take offense at the role of Jesus being sung; others consider the text overly sentimental or object to the lack of fugues, a hallmark of most oratorios.

While *Christ on the Mount of Olives* may not be Beethoven's most inspired creation, it surely shows flashes of genius and contains many moments of heightened drama and expressiveness. Few can deny the intensity and poignancy of Jesus' aria *"Meine Seele"* ("All my soul"), in which he evinces the all-too-human fear of death. Nor can one fail to be stirred by the otherworldly mystical aura as the Seraph repeats the words of Jehovah, *"So spricht Jehova,"* ("Thus saith Jehovah"). And how wonderful is the suppressed energy of the celebrated chorus *"Wir haben ihn gesehen"* ("We surely here shall find Him").

MASS IN C MAJOR, Op. 86

45 minutes

Early in 1807, Beethoven's former student, Prince Nikolaus Esterházy, asked the composer to write a Mass to celebrate the September name day of Princess Marie Esterházy. Beethoven composed the music during July and August in Heiligenstadt, and he conducted the first performance at the prince's magnificent palace in Eisenstadt on September 13, 1807.

Accustomed to the Masses that Haydn, his former *Kapellmeister,* composed for the princess's name day every year from 1796 to 1802, the prince, at the end of the performance, reportedly asked, "But my dear Beethoven, what is it you have done now?" Johann Nepomuk Hummel, *Kapellmeister* to the Esterházys at the time, laughed loudly at the remark. Infuriated, Beethoven immediately left for Vienna—a departure that might have also been hastened by the very poor accommodations he had been given in the Esterházy palace. Still angry at the affront, Beethoven later changed the dedication to Prince Ferdinand Kinsky.

Clearly, Beethoven regarded the prince's comment as a malicious insult. But some place a kinder interpretation on the hapless quote. The prince and the others had never heard anything like the Mass in C before. Beethoven—a sincere believer, but not a practicing Catholic—had written a shocking work, intense and impassioned and filled with highly personal religious fervor. Beethoven's Romanticism was extremely rare for those days, and the variety of musical textures and dynamics he employed far exceeded the Classical traditions of the time. Perhaps, then, the prince's question was only a sincere effort to understand better this radically new kind of music.

Even Beethoven acknowledged that the *Mass* struck out in new directions. As he wrote in a letter to his publisher, who was showing some reluctance to put the score into print, "The reason for my having wished to bind you to publish this *Mass* is in the first place and chiefly because it is dear to my heart and in spite of the coldness of our age to such works. . . . I do not like to say anything about my *Mass* or myself, but I believe I have treated the text as it has seldom been treated."

Beethoven described the entire *Mass* as "gentle," with an "overall serenity." The character of the *"Kyrie,"* he said, was of "devout submission, truly profound religious feeling." Just as the solo voices (soprano, alto, tenor, and bass) grow out of the chorus parts in the opening *"Kyrie,"* the chorus later emerges from the solo lines in the *"Christe eleison."*

The *"Gloria"* shows Beethoven's full range of expression, moving from the burst of exultant brilliance with which the section opens, through the mostly quiet, deeply affecting middle section, to the cumulative power of the repeated "Amens" at the end. To represent the traditional custom of bowing the head at the words *"Adoramus te,"* Beethoven uses a giant leap down in both the soprano and bass, followed by an even bigger upward leap.

The *"Credo"* opens in a strikingly original way, starting with a whispered unison C in the chorus; then it speeds up and rises in dynamics to the full-voiced fourth repeat. Other points of special interest are the harsh outburst at the word *"Crucifixus"* and the touch of tone painting as the basses slither down a chromatic scale to the words *"sub Pontius Pilate"* ("under Pontius Pilate").

The simple, devotional *"Sanctus"* glimmers with its own special light. The *"Benedictus"* brings the soloists and chorus together for the first time in the *Mass*, with telling effect. Interestingly enough, the extended *"Benedictus,"* which lasts several minutes, uses only six words, *"Benedictus qui venit in nomine Domini"* ("Blessed is He that cometh in the name of the Lord").

The fervent *"Agnus Dei"* starts with a nervous throbbing in the orchestra but ends with a serene, confident reprise of the

"Kyrie" melody to the words *"Dona nobis pacem"* ("Grant us peace").

Standard Text (see Appendix)

MISSA SOLEMNIS, Op. 123

1 hour, 25 minutes

On many occasions, Beethoven exhibited two sides of his personality in apparent opposition. Often he would perform magnificently at the piano, casting a magical spell over his listeners, and then, at the end, slam his fist down on the keyboard and break out in raucous laughter, completely shattering the mood he had just so masterfully created.

Beethoven's feelings about religion, too, were conflicted. Although Catholic by birth, he did not generally observe the practices of the church, nor was he a regular churchgoer. Nonetheless, he was deeply devout. When he was preparing to compose *Missa solemnis* he wrote, "God above everything! For an eternal, all-knowing Providence guides the fortune and misfortune of mortal men."

Missa solemnis ("Solemn Mass," distinguished from *Missa brevis,* "Short Mass," for liturgical use) epitomizes the reconciliation that Beethoven sought to effect between the styles of church music and concert music. To be sure, *Missa solemnis* is a musical setting of the most sacred rite of the Catholic church. Yet, in Beethoven's realization, the Mass lasts for well over an hour and calls for huge performing forces—four soloists, a large mixed choir, and a full-sized orchestra—which are much too large for an ordinary church service.

Furthermore, even though Beethoven does not organize any sections of *Missa solemnis* into traditional instrumental forms, he treats the melodic material symphonically. The *"Kyrie,"* for example, is in the traditional ternary or three-part form—*"Kyrie eleison"* ("Lord have mercy") first, then the contrasting

"Christe eleison" ("Christ have mercy"), and finally a return of *"Kyrie eleison."* But Beethoven builds the entire movement on five short, distinctive motifs, which he states, expands, varies, transposes, and restates just as he does in his purely instrumental works.

Beethoven also departs from the more usual settings of the Mass in the way he uses soloists, chorus, and orchestra. Effortlessly and seamlessly, he interweaves the three groups, instead of giving entire sections to one or the other. Everyone shares equally in the unfolding of the music.

As is his wont, Beethoven infuses the music with many sharp contrasts. Most effective are the various abrupt, unexpected changes from very loud to very soft or vice versa. Also, since the Mass contains prayers for peace, Beethoven saw fit to include a few bellicose sections that stand in stark relief to the more pious passages.

Beethoven called the *Missa solemnis* "the *greatest* work that I have composed." Nevertheless, he was willing to degrade and besmirch the work by dragging it through a series of tawdry business deals. He sold "original manuscripts" of *Missa solemnis*—actually prepared by copyists—to various admirers, including composer Luigi Cherubini and poet Johann von Goethe, for fifty ducats each. Then he sold the publication rights, first to Simrock in 1820 for nine hundred gulden and then to Peters in 1821 for one thousand gulden, before submitting it to Schott for publication for another thousand gulden!

The period when Beethoven was completing *Missa solemnis*, however, was an extremely trying one for the composer. Legal battles with his widowed sister-in-law over guardianship of his nephew, difficulties in hiring and firing servants, and runaway inflation that had greatly diminished the value of his pension forced him to search desperately for money to pay his many debts.

Beethoven began work on this profound and moving masterwork in 1819 in preparation for the March 20, 1820, installation of his loyal patron and former student, Archduke Rudolph, son of Emperor Leopold II, as archbishop of Olmütz. "The day when a solemn mass by me is performed as part of the ceremonies for Your Imperial Highness will be the happiest day of my life and God will inspire me so that my poor gifts may contribute to the glorification of this solemn day." So wrote Beethoven to the archduke in June 1819 when he first learned of his appointment.

For four years, long past the date of Rudolph's enthronement, Beethoven struggled to realize his musical vision. During that period the scope, length, and breadth of conception of the music continued to grow and expand. The work moved far beyond his original intention—music for a specific occasion—and became instead a very personal testament to Beethoven's feelings on life and religion and a universal statement of faith in humanity.

Although Beethoven finally delivered a copy of the score to the archduke on March 19, 1823, the premiere was given in St. Petersburg, Russia, on April 7, 1824. Three movements—"Kyrie," "Credo," and "Agnus Dei"—had a hearing in Vienna on May 7. This performance was the only one, incomplete as it was, of Missa solemnis that Beethoven ever witnessed, since he was completely deaf by then. The work was presented in this abbreviated form because church officials forbade the presentation of sacred music in secular venues.

Many consider Missa solemnis the most difficult of all the major choral works. The orchestra part, in all its variety, requires especial attention to the details of rhythm and balance. The solo parts are extremely demanding, and the violin solo in the "Sanctus" is the equivalent of the slow movement of a violin concerto.

Still, the choir faces the greatest challenge of all. The piece requires rock-solid tenors and sopranos able to reach and sustain notes at the very top of their range. Critic John Steane points out that, after singing "Et vitam venturi" on a high B flat, the sopranos "begin to wonder whether the life to come may not be more imminent than previously supposed."

Choristers need supernatural breath control—or a director who knows trick ways to keep up the tone—to hold out the impossibly long notes. Finally, the composition demands a conductor who understands the music, can penetrate Beethoven's intent, and is able to give the work a convincing musical shape. A tall order indeed!

Standard Text (see Appendix)

SYMPHONY NO. 9, Op. 125, "CHORAL SYMPHONY"

Allegro, ma non troppo, un poco maestoso
Molto vivace
Adagio molto e cantabile
Allegro assai

1 hour, 6 minutes

From a 1793 letter written by Beethoven's friend Fischenich to Charlotte von Schiller, we learn that the twenty-three-year-old composer was proposing to write music to Friedrich von Schiller's epic poem, *"An die Freude"* ("Ode to Joy"). Beethoven's own notebooks show that years later, in 1798 and 1811, he was still searching for a way to achieve his goal. We know that he considered making the poem into a concert aria for a solo voice or introducing the words as an interlude in an orchestral overture.

Finally, in 1822, Beethoven found a place for the "Ode"—as the last movement of his ninth symphony. He simply added four vocal soloists and choir to the orchestra that had played the first three movements.

Commentators differ sharply in their evaluation of this symphony. They debate the value of the choral finale: is it a "crime or a crown" (in the words of musical scholar Donald Tovey)? Some say it is an artistic blunder and a major miscalculation on Beethoven's part. Others dismiss the significance of the lyrics in this abstract piece of music. After all, they point out, Beethoven used only about one third of Schiller's ninety-six-line poem and freely changed the order to suit his musical needs. Since Schiller was only twenty-five when he wrote it, and he suggested that it be read by friends "around the festive board," some hold that the "Ode" is little more than a German student drinking song.

For most listeners, however, the "Ode" is indeed the "crown" of the ninth symphony. Viewed in this light, the first three movements of the symphony are but an extended preparation for the choral finale.

Richard Wagner, an enthusiastic admirer of the Ninth, traced the meaning of the symphony's four movements as he heard it:

I. A struggle, conceived in the greatest grandeur, of the soul contending for happiness against the oppression of that inimical power that places itself between us and the joys of earth. . . .

II. Wild delight seizes us at once. . . . It is a new world that we enter, one in which we are carried away to dizzy intoxication.

III. How differently these tones speak to our hearts! How pure, how celestially soothing they are as they melt the defiance, the wild impulse of the soul harassed by despair into a soft, melancholy feeling!

IV. A harsh outcry begins the transition from the third to the fourth movements, a cry of disappointment at not attaining the contentment so earnestly sought. Then, with the beginning of the Ode, we hear clearly expressed what must appear to the anxious seeker for happiness as the highest lasting pleasure.

Beethoven forges the first movement's principal theme out of evanescent flickers of sound, building it up to a rhythmically charged melody based on a descending D minor chord. After expanding this subject, Beethoven introduces a contrasting quiet, lyrical melody, along with a number of varied subsidiary ideas. The remainder of the movement works through the different melodies, then brings them back for a condensed, but complete, recapitulation before summarizing the entire movement with a climactic coda.

Several groups of vigorous hammerlike blows introduce the arresting, rhythmic motto of the Scherzo. Very quickly, though, they evolve into a light, tripping tune that passes fugally through the strings. (The premiere audience was so taken with this movement that it burst into applause and demanded a repetition.) Beethoven bases the central contrasting trio on a flowing cantilena melody before repeating the Scherzo and adding a coda to conclude the movement.

For the Adagio molto, Beethoven creates two themes with a perfection of line, depth of emotion, and sublime nobility that seem to transcend human invention. He treats these melodies in free, leisurely variation form, giving the movement a profound, spiritual quality that Beethoven rarely, if ever, surpassed.

The finale opens with two ferocious outbursts in the winds, answered by brief recitative-like passages in the cellos and double basses. The remainder of the strings then enter and recall the first-movement theme, which is interrupted by another recitative in the lower strings. Fragments of the second- and third-movement themes present themselves, too, each time cut short by a recitative. Finally the cellos and basses state the fourth-movement theme, a disarmingly simple, folk song–like melody —which Beethoven arrived at only after creating and discarding over two hundred preliminary versions!

Beethoven varies the melody, adding more instruments and increasing the complexity and volume until the full orchestra explodes into an enormous, raging dissonance. At this point, the baritone soloist enters with the only words by Beethoven (the rest of the text is from Schiller's "Ode"): *"O Freunde, nicht diese Töne! Sondern lasst uns angenehmere anstimmen, und freudenvollere!"* ("O friends, not these sounds! Let us sing something more pleasant, full of gladness.") Beethoven set the "Ode," which follows, as a gigantic set of free and wide-ranging variations that involve soloists, choir, and orchestra.

Beethoven completed the symphony in February 1824, after about a year and a half of concentrated work. The premiere was given in Vienna on May 7, 1824, with Beethoven seated on the stage, back to the audience, to help the conductor with the tempi. The composer, now totally deaf, could not hear the audience's tumultuous applause at the end, but thanks to one of the singers, who turned him around, he was able to see and enjoy the fervid response his music had evoked.

BASS SOLO

O Freunde, nicht diese Töne!	O friends, not these sounds!
Sondern lasst uns angenehmere	Let us sing something more
anstimmen, und freudenvollere.	pleasant, full of gladness.

BASS SOLO AND CHORUS

Freude, schöner Götterfunken	Joy, thou source of light immortal,
Tochter aus Elysium,	Daughter of Elysium,
Wir betreten feuer-trunken,	Touched with fire, to the portal
Himmlische, dein Heiligtum!	Of thy radiant shrine we come.
Deine Zauber binden wieder	Thy pure magic frees all others
Was die Mode streng geteilt;	Held in custom's rigid rings;
Alle Menschen werden Brüder,	Men throughout the world are brothers
Wo dein sanfter Flügel weilt.	In the haven of thy wings.

QUARTET AND CHORUS

Wem der grosse Wurf gelungen,	He who knows the pride and pleasure
Eines Freundes Freund zu sein,	Of a friendship firm and strong,
Wer ein holdes Weib errungen,	He who has a wife to treasure,
Mische seinen Jubel ein!	Let him swell our mighty song!
Ja, wer auch nur eine Seele	If there is a single being
Sein nennt auf dem Erdenrund!	Who can call a heart his own,
Und wer's nie gekonnt, der stehle	And denies it—then, unseeing,
Weinend sich aus diesem Bund!	Let him go and weep alone.
Freude trinken alle Wesen	Joy is drunk by all God's creatures
An den Brüsten der Natur;	Straight from earth's abundant breast;
Alle Guten, alle Bösen	Good and bad, all things are Nature's,
Folgen ihre Rosenspur.	And with blameless joy are blessed.
Küsse gab sie uns und Reben,	Joy gives love and wine; her gladness

Einen Freund, geprüft im Tod;
Wollust war dem Wurm
  gegeben,
Und der Cherub steht vor Gott.

Makes the universe her zone,
From the worm that feels
  spring's madness
To the angels near God's
  throne.

TENOR SOLO AND CHORUS

Froh, wie seine Sonnen fliegen

Durch des Himmels prächt'gen
  Plan,
Laufet, Brüder, eure Bahn,

Freudig, wie ein Held zum
  Siegen.

Glad, as when the suns run
  glorious
Through the deep and dazzling
  skies,
Brothers, run with shining
  eyes—
Heroes, happy and victorious.

CHORUS

Freude, schöner Götterfunken,
  usw.
Seid umschlungen, Millionen!

Diesen Kuss der ganzen Welt!
Brüder, über'm Sternenzelt
Muss ein lieber Vater wohnen.

Ihr stürzt nieder, Millionen?
Ahnest du den Schöpfer, Welt?

Such' ihn über'm Sternenzelt!
Über Sternen muss er wohnen.

Joy, thou source of light
  immortal, *etc.*
Millions, myriads, rise and
  gather!
Share this universal kiss!
Brothers, in a heaven of bliss
Smiles the world's all-loving
  Father.
Do the millions, his creation,
Know him and his works of
  love?
Seek him! In the heights above
Is his starry habitation!

HECTOR BERLIOZ

Born December 11, 1803, in La Côte-St.-André, France
Died March 8, 1869, in Paris

Most great composers come from musical families, show their talent at a very early age, and are outstanding performers on one or more instruments. Berlioz had none of these attributes. His father was a physician; his mother came from a family of landowners. Other than the most rudimentary skill on the guitar and flute, Berlioz never learned to play a musical instrument very well. In fact, Berlioz's first strong inclination toward a career in music came after he fled his first dissection at the medical school his father insisted he attend. And he was nearly twenty years old at the time!

Because of this nonmusical background—or perhaps in spite of it—Berlioz became one of the great innovators in the history of music. Lacking the innate musical instincts or foundation that is common among composers, Berlioz had to find his own way. Well endowed with imagination, zeal, and yes, genius, Berlioz struck out in wholly new directions—establishing new concepts of melody, harmony, and form, representing people, places, and events in compositions (program music), and identifying a musical motif with a person (idée fixe). These are among the primary defining elements of Romanticism in music, an artistic movement in which Berlioz played a seminal role. Despite his recognized deficiencies—an excess here, an awkward transition there, a technical weakness here, a lack of inspired melody there—the force of his musical personality swept aside these problems, and he was able to produce a limited number of compositions of striking beauty and lasting value.

REQUIEM, Op. 5
(Grande Messe des morts)

1 hour, 20 minutes

That Berlioz began the composition of his *Requiem* in March 1837 is quite certain. Less sure is his reason for undertaking the work in the first place. His *Mémoires* states that Count Adrien de Gasparin, minister of the interior, commissioned a Requiem Mass to commemorate the seventh anniversary of the July 1830 revolution. But Berlioz's *Lettres* indicates that Gasparin requested the music for a service to memorialize the innocent victims of the July 1835 attempt to kill the unpopular King Louis Philippe.

No matter the inspiration, Berlioz started to plan a monumental, grandiose composition. In keeping with the style of many artists of the time, Berlioz sought to express the ideals of the 1789 French Revolution in a colossal creation symbolic of a strong, united nation. The score calls for a tenor soloist, a chorus of 210 (80 sopranos and altos, 60 tenors, 70 basses), and an orchestra of 140, which is augmented by 50 players in four brass bands seated at the four corners of the hall. Also, Berlioz asked that, if space permitted, the chorus be doubled or tripled in number and that the orchestra be proportionately increased.

Initially, Berlioz struggled to grasp the traditional French text of the Requiem Mass and mold it to his purposes. But once he began to compose, the work proceeded quickly. In fact, Berlioz's thoughts came so fast that he could not set them down rapidly enough. Finally, he hit on a shorthand approach in which he penciled the sketches on the score paper and then wrote the final version in ink over the pencil markings.

By the beginning of July 1837, Berlioz had completed most of the *Requiem*. He had just started rehearsals when Count Gasparin's successor informed the composer that his music was not needed! The work languished until October of the same year, when word came to Paris that the governor-general of the French colony of Algiers, a General Damrémont, had been killed at the battle of Constantine.

Accounts vary as to what happened next. Either the new minister asked Berlioz to produce the already completed *Requiem* for Damrémont's memorial service or Berlioz petitioned his friend, author Alexandre Dumas, to arrange a performance. In any case, the *Requiem* finally received its premiere at the memorial service in the huge, domed St.-Louis des Invalides chapel on December 5, 1837—to both popular and critical approbation.

Many listeners sense that Berlioz drew his inspiration less from religious fervor than from artistic imperative. Rather than present a highly inspired adoration of the Almighty, Berlioz offers a very exciting and dramatic musical dialogue between opposites—the hellish and the celestial, the personal and the universal.

In spite of the vast musical forces at his disposal, Berlioz uses them sparingly, only to underscore individual moments of paralyzing terror or incredible wonder. The most astounding such occasion comes at the *"Tuba mirum,"* the fateful call to the Day of Judgment and the portentous opening of the gates of hell. The climax occurs in the *"Dies irae,"* when all sixteen timpani begin a fearsome roll that leads to the amazing sound of the choir, full orchestra, and four surrounding bands. Berlioz himself described this section as "overwhelming . . . of a horrifying grandeur."

For the most part, however, the *Requiem* maintains a quiet, melancholy character. In fact, Berlioz dramatically reduces the number of performers in two short, quiet movements—number three, *"Quid sum miser,"* for men's voices, English horn, bassoon, cello, and string bass only, and number five, *"Quaerens me,"* for six-part a cappella choir. Another example of Berlioz's restraint occurs in the *"Offertorium,"* where the composer focuses interest in the orchestra and essentially confines the choir to just two notes!

Throughout, Berlioz achieves many stunning effects of

orchestral color. To cite but two: Between the chantlike choir phrases in number eight, *"Hostias,"* he introduces a chord played by eight trombones on a low unison note and three flutes playing harmony high in their register. (Is the huge gap between these instruments symbolic of the distance from "death to life" as described in the text?) Number ten, *"Agnus Dei,"* opens with a woodwind chord that disappears into a viola echo, a magical effect that might be described as undertones emerging from the chord.

The many joys and splendors to be found in the *Requiem* have helped it earn a secure place in today's repertoire. Evidence that the composer recognized its special quality is found in a letter to his friend, Humbert Ferrand, dated January 11, 1867. Berlioz wrote, "If everything I had ever written was to be burned except for a single work, I would plead for my *Grande Messe des morts.*"

Standard Text (see Appendix)

TE DEUM, Op. 22

45 minutes

In 1832, after a visit to Milan, Berlioz conceived the idea of writing a major orchestral work to commemorate Napoléon's victory over the Italians and his triumphant return to France. The composer prepared some preliminary sketches but then abandoned the project.

Some seventeen years later, in 1849, Berlioz rededicated himself to the task. He decided to expand the original concept into a vocal and orchestral work, and he used some sections of his early draft to compose the *Te Deum* for tenor soloist and three choirs. Choir I consisted of first sopranos, tenors, and basses; choir II of second sopranos or altos, tenors, and basses; and choir III of children's or boys' choir of sopranos and altos. On the score, however, the composer notes that the third choir may be omitted, "although it greatly enhances the effect."

Completed in 1849 or 1850, the *Te Deum* had to wait until April 30, 1855, for its first performance, which was held at the Church of St. Eustache, Paris, in connection with the opening of the Industrial Exhibition. The performers numbered 950—100 in each of the adult choirs, 600 in the children's choir, and an orchestra of 150. At the composer's request, the choirs and orchestra were located as far from the organ as possible.

As was his wont, Berlioz freely reordered and cut the traditional text of the *Te Deum*. When he expected his *Te Deum* to be performed at a ceremony honoring Napoléon's military successes, Berlioz added two purely orchestral sections—number three, "Prelude," and number eight, "March." But he chose to omit them at the premiere; his notes suggest that they only be played "for a Thanksgiving after a victory or for any other service of a military character."

Patriotism and ceremony characterize the *Te Deum* much more than religiosity. Most performances of the work today take place either in concert halls or in connection with an important civic celebration, seldom as part of a church worship service.

Four of the movements—numbers one, two, five, and seven—Berlioz designates as hymns. These epic movements of great sweep and splendor range from the complexities of the double fugue in the opening, *"Te Deum,"* to the increasingly horrific musical visions of the Last Judgment in the final *"Judex crederis."*

Berlioz designates two of the movements—numbers four and six—as prayers. In the hushed and solemn number four, *"Dignare Domine,"* the composer holds together the wispy, elusive bits of melody with unceasing, low pedal tones in the cellos. The lyrical tenor aria—number six, *"Te ergo quaesumus"*—largely confines the chorus to chanting on a single pitch.

The *Te Deum* is much better heard in a live performance—preferably in a large church—than on a CD. Berlioz's magical spatial and tonal effects—especially when he juxtaposes one section of choir I against a section of choir II, or when he plays the orchestra off against the distant sound of the organ—make for a thrilling aural experience, even with fewer than 950 performers.

Standard Text (see Appendix)

LA DAMNATION DE FAUST, Op. 24

2 hours, 15 minutes

"The marvelous book fascinated me from the very first moment. I could not put it down. I read it incessantly, at meals, in the theater, in the street, everywhere."

So wrote Berlioz in 1827 on reading the first translation into French (by Gérard de Nerval) of Goethe's *Faust*. In fact, the book affected Berlioz so deeply that, only one year later, he wrote his Op. 1, *Eight Scenes from Faust* for chorus and orchestra, based on the Goethe play. Berlioz, however, later considered it an immature work, asked that it be withdrawn, and destroyed all the copies he could locate.

Late in 1845, Berlioz again started to write music based on the Faust legend. This time, though, he cast it as what he variously called a dramatic legend or a concert opera. Like an opera, it requires soloists, chorus, and orchestra, is highly dramatic, and has many scenic and stage directions. But, like an oratorio, it is made up of choruses, recitatives, and arias, as well as orchestral selections, and is often performed without sets or costumes. *La Damnation de Faust,* however, has been performed as a fully staged opera in theaters around the world, including New York's Metropolitan Opera (premiere December 7, 1906).

From Berlioz's *Mémoires* we learn that he wrote "nearly the whole of the book" and the music while on a leisurely concert tour through Austria, Hungary, Bohemia, and Silesia. He completed the composition back in Paris on October 19, 1846, and at his own expense he presented the first performance there on

December 6 of that year. The hall was only half full at the premiere, and the few people who attended received the work with ill-concealed hostility. One leading critic quipped, "The audience was more composed than the music."

With the help of his friend, Almire Gandonnière, Berlioz made two basic changes in rewriting the story of the learned philosopher Faust selling his soul to the devil in return for magical powers and love on earth. First, Berlioz set the first part in Hungary instead of Germany. There was a very practical reason for this decision. Early in 1846, Berlioz had orchestrated a well-known Hungarian military march, the *Rakoczy March*, which scored an overwhelming triumph when he conducted it in Budapest. Since Berlioz wanted to include the crowd-pleasing march in his Faust piece, he set the opening in Hungary.

The second and more basic plot change was to condemn Faust to hell in the final scene, instead of allowing him to be redeemed and ascend to heaven, as recounted by Goethe. Here, too, Berlioz had good justification; musically speaking, hell is much more interesting than heaven, and Berlioz knew that he could paint a wonderfully exciting tonal picture of Faust plunging into the raging inferno.

La Damnation de Faust consists of four major sections, which Berlioz further divides into twenty set pieces; of the twenty, about twelve include chorus parts. The role of the choir keeps alternating among citizens, students, soldiers, tavern guests, gnomes, sylphs, peasants, the damned in hell, and spirits in heaven.

Part I. The work opens with Faust wandering in the fields, musing on nature's beauties. His reveries are interrupted by a bright, happy chorus of peasants. Into this scene Hungarian soldiers parade to the stirring strains of the *Rakoczy March*.

Part II. The scene shifts to Germany, where Faust, bemoaning the futility of existence and about to drink poison, hears a distant chorus singing an Easter hymn, which turns his thoughts to God. Mephistopheles suddenly appears and lures Faust to a wine cellar, where a male choir of carousers sings the famous "Amen Chorus," a parody of the learned Baroque fugal style.

Next, Mephistopheles leads Faust to a beautiful garden on the banks of the Elbe River. The old man falls asleep to the music of a chorus of sylphs and gnomes, and he dreams of the fair Marguerite, whom he has not yet met. Faust awakens when a troop of soldiers appears, singing of their victories. Groups of students and citizens follow with songs of love and wine.

Part III. A number of stirring arias and duets are heard as Faust greets Marguerite in her room, they fall in love, and they swear eternal devotion to each other. At the sound of an approaching chorus of villagers, Mephistopheles forces Faust to leave.

Part IV. Choirs of soldiers and students sing their merry songs outside Marguerite's window as she sits alone, burdened with longing for her departed lover. Mephistopheles, meanwhile, confronts the equally desolate Faust and tells him that Marguerite has been imprisoned for giving her mother a fatal sleeping potion. The evil Mephistopheles convinces Faust to sign a paper that he believes will free Marguerite, but it really gives Mephistopheles control over his soul. As Mephistopheles and Faust leave, Faust assumes they are heading off to rescue Marguerite. Instead, he follows Mephistopheles on what becomes a wild descent into the dark realms of hell, where he hears the ghastly choir of the damned. At the same time, a choir of angel voices can be heard guiding Marguerite on her ascent to heaven.

L'ENFANCE DU CHRIST:
A SACRED TRILOGY, Op. 25
(The Infant Christ)

1 hour, 30 minutes

Berlioz was attending a rather dull party in September 1850 when the guests started playing cards. Disinclined to play, Berlioz acceded to the request of his friend and host, the architect

Pierre Leduc, to write a short parlor piece in his guest album. Drawing the five lines of the staff by hand, the composer quickly sketched in a brief melody.

Berlioz later decided that the music had "a certain character of primitive, pastoral mysticism," and he invented an appropriate program—the melody represented the shepherds' farewell to the Holy Family as they departed Judea for Egypt. He also added words to the melody.

When the composer was done, he told Leduc, "Now I am going to put your name to this. I want to compromise you."

Leduc objected. "That's absurd! Everybody knows that I know nothing about music."

"That is indeed a brand-new reason for not composing" was Berlioz's riposte. "But wait! Since vanity prevents your adopting my piece, I am going to make up a name out of yours. I shall call the author Pierre Ducré, whom I hereby appoint music master of the Sainte Chapelle in Paris during the seventeenth century. My manuscript thus acquires enormous antiquarian value."

Pleased with what he had created so quickly, Berlioz added an overture before the "Shepherds' Farewell," added some music to depict the travels of the Holy Family to Egypt, and gave the work the title *La Fuite en Égypte* ("The Flight into Egypt"). The composer introduced this piece in Paris on November 12, 1850, claiming that he had discovered the manuscript in a cupboard during renovations of Sainte Chapelle and even complaining how hard it was to decipher the "old notation"!

Why did Berlioz continue the charade? Did he mean to poke fun at the Parisian audiences who often lacked an appreciation of his music? Was he attempting to trick the critics?

Berlioz finally confessed his duplicity in 1852 and soon thereafter decided to expand the work. In 1853, he completed *L'Arrivée à Saïs* ("The Arrival of Saïs") to follow *La Fuite en Égypte*, and the next year he added *Le Songe d'Hérode* ("Herod's Dream") as a prelude. Calling the entire composition *L'Enfance du Christ: A Sacred Trilogy*, the composer gave the Paris premiere on December 10, 1854, the day before his fifty-first birthday. The work calls for mixed choir, orchestra, and seven soloists—soprano, two tenors, two baritones, and two basses (though often it is performed with but one each of tenor, baritone, and bass).

L'Enfance du Christ was perhaps the best received of any Berlioz work. The audience was much taken with the purity, simplicity, restraint, and transparency of the writing. In this retelling of an imaginary incident in the childhood of Christ, the audience sensed Berlioz's yearning to return to the faith he had known as a child. Listeners also realized that the composer was not portraying idealized religious figures so much as he was representing parents trying to save their infant son.

The first part, *Le Songe d'Hérod,* opens in Jerusalem. After a narrator (tenor) and two Roman soldiers (tenor and bass) establish the setting and situation, Herod (baritone) tells of dreaming that he will be destroyed by a child. A choir of soothsayers advises him to protect himself by ordering the death of all newborns. The scene then shifts to a stable in Bethlehem, where a choir of angels warns Mary (soprano) and Joseph (baritone) to escape to Egypt to save their son.

Part II, *La Fuite en Égypte,* consists of an extended fugal orchestral overture, the "Shepherds' Farewell" chorus—the germ from which the entire work grows, and the best-known section of the piece—an exquisite solo for the narrator ("The Peace of the Holy Family"), and a concluding chorus of angels softly singing, "Alleluia, alleluia."

The narrator opens *L'Arrivée à Saïs* by relating the difficult journey to Egypt. The chorus of "cruel and haughty" people of Saïs turns the Holy Family away from the places where they seek shelter. Finally, the Patriarch of an Ishmaelite family (bass) takes them in, and a choir of family members helps them feel welcome. In the concluding epilogue, the narrator and choir look ahead to Christ's return to His birthplace to fulfill His mission of salvation, and the oratorio concludes with chorus softly intoning, "Amen, amen."

LEONARD

BERNSTEIN

Born August 25, 1918, in Lawrence, Massachusetts
Died October 14, 1990, in New York City

Famed musicologist Nicolas Slonimsky very aptly described Leonard Bernstein as "a singular, if not a unique, phenomenon in music history."

Bernstein first came to prominence on November 14, 1943, when he stepped in at the last minute to conduct the New York Philharmonic for the ailing Bruno Walter. By 1958 Bernstein was appointed music director of that orchestra, the first American-born conductor to be so honored, and he quickly gained recognition as one of the leading conductors of his time.

While Bernstein was winning accolades on the podium, he was also garnering praise for a number of major compositions, noted as much for their high quality as for their wide range. From his pen flowed symphonies and other works for the concert hall, *West Side Story* and *Wonderful Town* for the Broadway stage, the ballet *Fancy Free*, the film score for *On the Waterfront*, and *Candide*, a cross between an opera and a musical.

Bernstein infused his compositions with amazing energy and vitality, at the same time displaying his incredible ability to synthesize and combine elements of classical music with the rhythms and melodies of modern jazz and pop music. In addition, he managed to imbue every note with expressiveness and emotional impact, to craft memorable melodies, and to transcend the accepted rules and strictures of musical composition while finding his own, distinctive musical voice. His Young People's Concerts, television appearances, and outstanding books on music brought new understanding and appreciation of music to people of all ages.

Besides his musical accomplishments, Bernstein also distinguished himself as a leader in the struggle for world peace, racial equality, and other social causes.

Chichester Psalms and *Mass* are Bernstein's best-known choral works; his symphony *Kaddish,* for narrator, chorus, and orchestra, is less familiar.

CHICHESTER PSALMS

20 minutes

In describing the genesis of *Chichester Psalms,* Bernstein wrote that in 1964 and 1965, he had a sabbatical from the New York Philharmonic, which he used only to compose. During that year he decided to write some pieces that he called "less old fashioned." He wrote a lot of avant garde music, which he discarded. "And" as he wrote, "what I came out with at the end of the year was a piece called *Chichester Psalms,* which is simple and tonal and tuneful and as pure B-flat as any piece you can think of . . . because that was what I honestly wished to write."

The Very Reverend Walter Hussey, dean of Chichester Cathedral in England, commissioned the *Chichester Psalms* for the Southern Cathedrals Festival, which brought together the choirs of Chichester, Winchester, and Salisbury cathedrals. Bernstein completed the composition on May 7, 1965, and conducted the official premiere in Chichester on July 31, 1965, preceding it with a performance in New York on July 15, 1965.

Bernstein scored the work for a male alto soloist (or a countertenor, but not a woman), a choir of boy sopranos, male altos, tenors, and basses (or a regular choir of sopranos, altos, tenors, and basses), and a large orchestra minus the woodwinds. He used obsessive repetitions of the Hebrew text, drawn from the Book of Psalms, as well as distinctive scales and rhythms to create the aura of ancient ritual.

The work explodes into being with a powerful summons, a sort of ferocious chorale, "Awake, psaltery and harp!" (The psaltery is an ancient instrument played by plucking a number of strings stretched over a flat soundboard.) The compelling cry quickly gives way to the jazzy, dancelike body of the movement, "Make a joyful noise unto the Lord," which ends with a reminder of the opening chorale.

To a harp accompaniment, the solo boy alto sings the simple, naive "The Lord is my shepherd," suggesting David as a shepherd boy to Bernstein's friend Jack Gottlieb. The treble voices pick up the melody until the men interrupt fiercely with "Why do the nations rage?" The section concludes with the return of the movement's initial childlike serenity.

After an intense orchestral introduction, the choir enters with the touchingly tender melody "Lord, my heart is not haughty." An a cappella echo of the opening chorale ends this section and leads to the peroration, the yearning for peace in the words "Behold how good, and how pleasant it is, for brethren to dwell together in unity."

I.

Psalm 108:2

Urah, haneval, v'chinor!	Awake, psaltery and harp!
A-irah shahar!	I will rouse the dawn!

Psalm 100

Hariu l'Adonai kol haarets.	Make a joyful noise unto the Lord all ye lands.
Iv'du et Adonai b'simha.	Serve the Lord with gladness.
Bo-u l'fanav bir'nanah.	Come before his presence with singing.
D'u ki Adonai Hu Elohim.	Know ye that the Lord, he is God.
Hu asanu, v'lo anahnu.	It is he that hath made us and not we ourselves.
Amo v'tson mar'ito.	We are his people and the sheep of his pasture.

Bo-u sh'arav b'todah,	Enter into his gates with thanksgiving.
Hatseirotav bit'hilah,	And unto his courts with praise.
Hodu lo, bar'chu sh'mo.	Be thankful unto him, and bless his name.
Ki tov Adonai, l'olam has'do,	For the Lord is good, his mercy is everlasting,
V'ad dor vador emunato.	And his truth endureth to all generations.

II

Psalm 23:1–4

Adonai ro-i, lo ehsar.	The Lord is my shepherd, I shall not want.
Bin'ot deshe yarbitseini,	He maketh me to lie down in green pastures,
Al mei m'nuhot y'nahaleini,	He leadeth me beside the still waters,
Naf'shi yy'shovev,	He restoreth my soul,
Yan'heini b'ma'aglei tsedek,	He leadeth me in the paths of righteousness,
L'ma'an' sh'mo.	For his name's sake.
Gam ki eilech,	Yea, though I walk
B'gei tsalmavet,	Through the valley of the shadow of death,
Lo ira ra,	I will fear no evil
Ki Atah imadi.	For thou art with me.
Shiv't'cha umishan'techa	Thy rod and Thy staff
Hemah y'nahamuni.	They comfort me.

Psalm 2:1–4

Lamah rag'shu goyim	Why do the nations rage,
Ul'umim yeh'gu rik?	And the people imagine a vain thing?
Yit'yats'vu malchei erets,	The kings of the earth set themselves,
V'roznim nos'du yahad	And the rulers take counsel together

Al Adonai v'al m'shiho.

Against the Lord and against his anointed,

N'natkah et mos'roteimo,

Saying let us break their bands asunder,

V'nashlichah mimenu avoteimo.

And cast away their cords from us.

Yoshev bashamayim
Yis'hak, Adonai
Yil'ag lamo!

He that sitteth in the heavens
Shall laugh, and the Lord
Shall have them in derision!

Psalm 23:5–6

Ta'aroch l'gfanai shulchan

Thou preparest a table before me

Neged tsor'rai
Dishanta vashemen roshi

In the presence of mine enemies,
Thou anointest my head with oil,

Cosi r'vayah.
Ach tov vahesed
Yird'funi kol y'mei hayai,

My cup runneth over.
Surely goodness and mercy
Shall follow me all the days of my life,

V'shav'ti b'veit Adonai

And I will dwell in the house of the Lord

L'orech yamim.

Forever.

III

Psalm 131

Adonai, Adonai,
Lo gavah libi,
V'lo ramu einai,
V'lo hilachti
Big'dolot uv'niflaot
Mimeni.
Im lo shiviti
V'domam'ti,
Naf'shi k'gamul alei imo,

Lord, Lord,
My heart is not haughty,
Nor mine eyes lofty,
Neither do I exercise myself
In great matters or in things
Too wonderful for me.
Surely I have calmed
And quieted myself,
As a child that is weaned of his mother,

Kagamul alai naf'shi.

My soul is even as a weaned child.

Yahel Yis'rael el Adonai	Let Israel hope in the Lord
Me'atah v'ad olam.	From henceforth and forever.

Psalm 133:1

Hineh mah tov,	Behold how good,
Umah nayim,	And how pleasant it is,
Shevet ahim	For brethren to dwell
Gam yahad.	Together in unity.

MASS: A THEATRE PIECE FOR SINGERS, PLAYERS, AND DANCERS

1 hour, 50 minutes

After eleven years as music director of the New York Philharmonic, Bernstein resigned in 1969 to devote more of his time to composing. The first major piece to emerge was his *Mass*. It was composed at the request of Jacqueline Kennedy, widow of President John F. Kennedy, who asked that Bernstein be commissioned to write a work to inaugurate Kennedy Center, the new performing arts complex in Washington, D.C. Because of his close friendship with the Kennedy family, Bernstein was delighted to accept, and he composed the *Mass* without fee, although he did retain future performing rights.

In creating his *Mass*, Bernstein set himself exceedingly high goals. To reflect Kennedy's strong religious background, he structured the entire work around the Roman Catholic Mass; to be ecumenical, he infused elements of Jewish liturgy into the chorale's structure; and, to extend its reach and make it more of a "people's Mass," he interpolated sections of jazz, rock, blues, and southern folk-song idioms. Helped by lyricist Stephen Schwartz, Bernstein fashioned the words from sources as diverse as the letters of St. Paul and St. John and the statements of a conscientious objector and his wife. His text explored the role of religion in relation to the problems plaguing our modern world.

Few doubt the work's bold, brilliant conception, although opinions differ widely on Bernstein's success in achieving his lofty aims. Some call the piece blasphemous; others call it cheap and tawdry; still others find it an incredibly moving testament to the depth and intensity of the composer's fervor and faith. Undeniable, though, is its widespread popularity. Since its premiere at the Kennedy Center on September 8, 1971, the *Mass* has been heard all over the world, and in the summer of 1972 it was even performed daily for an unprecedented one-month run by New York's Metropolitan Opera Company.

Bernstein conceived *Mass* exclusively for the theater, not the church. A presentation requires some two hundred performers —about twenty solo singers, a mixed choir, a boys' choir, thirty-five stage musicians, an orchestra, and two organs, plus dancers who play the roles of acolytes.

After a startling opening, voices on tape emerge from the four corners of the hall in the *"Kyrie eleison."* A young Celebrant, dressed in blue jeans and simple shirt, stops the cacophony with a single loud chord on his guitar and sings his praise of God in "A Simple Song." Gradually the believers clothe him in liturgical garments, and he begins to perform the Mass as a priestly Celebrant.

Gradually, the believers surround the Celebrant and begin to express many questions and doubts as to his divinity. At first, he is able to keep them true to their faith. But in the *"Agnus Dei"* the crowd begins to turn against the Celebrant. Finally, at the climactic opening of "Things Get Broken," he flings the sacraments to the floor, destroys the altar cloth, rips off his vestments, and performs a wild dance on the altar. The transformation back into the young man he was at the beginning conveys the message that everyone is part of God and that God is within each of us. As the *Mass* concludes, the boys' choir walks down the aisles, warmly shaking the hands of audience members and whispering, "Pass it on."

ERNEST BLOCH

Born July 24, 1880, in Geneva
Died July 15, 1959, in Portland, Oregon

"It is the Jewish soul that interests me, the complex, glowing, agitated soul that I feel vibrating throughout the Bible."

With these words Ernest Bloch identified a major component of his creative impulse and the inspiration for some of his best-known compositions, including *Schelomo* (cello and orchestra), *Baal shem* (violin and piano), and *Sacred Service* (baritone, choir, and orchestra or organ).

Soon after starting violin lessons and his first efforts at composing, Bloch made a vow that someday he would become a composer. To lend weight to his decision, the ten-year-old boy wrote out his pledge, placed the paper on a mound of stones, and burned it—symbolically setting the direction for his life's work.

Although he did, in fact, write music throughout his life, the career of composer was not an easy one for Bloch to follow. For most of his life, he had to find the time to compose while involved with other work—helping in the family business in Geneva (1904–16), teaching at the Mannes School in New York (1917–20), founding and directing the Cleveland Institute of Music (1920–25), and directing the San Francisco Conservatory of Music (1925–30).

In 1930 the Jacob and Rose Stern Musical Fund offered Bloch an annual grant for ten years if he would devote himself exclusively to composition. Bloch, of course, was delighted to accept; he left for the small village of Roveredo in his native Switzerland and began full-time composing, working first on his *Sacred Service*. At the conclusion of the grant period, the Stern Fund endowed a chair for Bloch at the University of California, Berkeley, where he taught from 1940 until his retirement in 1952.

SACRED SERVICE
(Avodath hakodesh)

50 minutes

In 1927, while director of the San Francisco Conservatory, Bloch began speaking to Cantor Reuben Rinder of Temple Emanuel, a Reform temple in San Francisco, about his plans to write the music for a temple service. A few years later, when Gerald Warburg offered the composer a commission to compose just such a work and the grant from the Stern Fund freed him from his administrative duties, Bloch was finally able to envelop himself completely in the project.

And envelop himself Bloch did. According to his own estimates, he prepared himself by doing nearly two thousand counterpoint exercises over a six-month period. He also spent about three months carefully studying the text of the Sabbath Morning Service (as found in the *Union Prayer Book for Jewish Worship*) in three languages: the original Hebrew, his native French, and his acquired English. Then he moved to Roveredo, Switzerland, to start work.

In a letter to the codirectors of the San Francisco Conservatory, Ada Clement and Lillian Hodgehead, written shortly after his arrival in Roveredo, Bloch said, "I have now memorized entirely the whole Service in Hebrew. I know its significance word by word. But what is more important, I have absorbed it to the point that it has become mine, as if it were the very expression of my soul. It has become the very text I was after since the age of ten . . . a dream of stars, of forces. I do not wish it for the Jews—who will probably fight it—not for the critics, nor for the 'Tradition'! It has become a private affair between God and me."

Despite his strong feelings about the text—or perhaps because of them—the composing did not go easily. "I am battling against notes, sounds, rhythms," he wrote in November 1930 to Cantor Rinder, "to extirpate out of my soul all the unexpressed music which is latent—since centuries—which was awaiting this marvelous text." Although it took three years, from the summer of 1930 to June 7, 1933, to complete the work, Bloch complained that it took him two years just to write the final twenty-five measures!

The following description is based on the composer's comments on the work. The composition is a setting of the texts—from Psalms, Deuteronomy, Isaiah, Proverbs, and other sources—used in the services of the Reform Temples in the United States. Bloch feels that, "in its great simplicity and variety, it embodies a philosophy acceptable to all men."

Sacred Service is divided into five parts that are performed without interruption. Part I opens with a short orchestral prelude entitled *Meditation,* which presents the six note motive (G, A, C, B, A, G) that is fundamental to the entire composition. Bloch considers "How goodly are Thy tents" *(Ma tovu)* as a "kind of invocation," which is followed by "Sing His Praise" *(Borechu es Adonoy),* a "more liturgical section." A short interlude leads to "Oh hear, Israel" *(Shema Yisroel),* which Bloch describes as "cosmic," and the "tragic accents" of "Rock of Israel" *(Tzur Yisroel)* bring Part I to a mournful conclusion.

"Kodosh, Kodosh, Kodosh" ("Holy, Holy, Holy"), the source of the *Sanctus* of the Catholic service, begins Part II, followed by "One is He, our God" *(Echod hu Eloheinu),* an "affirmation of the unity of the world." This part ends joyfully with "Thou shalt reign, Adonoy, evermore" *(Yimloch Adonoy le'olom).*

During Part III the Scroll, representing law, is taken from the Ark and carried through the congregation. The music expresses the composer's "wish that man may free himself from hate, from dark instincts and all that prevents him from rising above himself and seeing the truth."

In Part IV the Scroll is returned to the Ark but, as Bloch says, "it must remain alive in the hearts of men." The consoling "Tree of Life" *(Etz chayim he lamachazikim boh)* ends the fourth part.

Part V, the Epilogue (Adoration), "expresses the peace and solemnity of the Sabbath." After the Cantor addresses the people, this section projects the central idea of the service, "the eternal contribution of Israel to humanity." *Adon Olom* ("Eternal God") follows, which Bloch interpreted as the idea of accepting death as one accepts life, "with serenity and confidence." The service ends with the *Three Benedictions* and the *Three Amens*.

The premiere of *Sacred Service* was given in Turin, Italy, on January 12, 1934.

Part I

MAH TOVU

Mah tovu oholecho Yaakov, mishkenosecho Yisroel. Vaani berov chasdecho, ovo veisecho, eshtachaveh, eshtachaveh, el heichal kodshecho beyirosecho. Adonoy, Adonoy, ohavti meon beisecho, umekom mishkan kevodecho; vaani, eshtachaveh, veechrooh, evrecho lifnei Adonoy, Osi. Vaani sefilosi lecho Adonoy eis rotzon Elohim berov chasdecho, Aneini, aneini, beemes yishecho, beemes yishecho.

How goodly are thy tents, Yaakov, goodly thy dwellings, Israel. Through Thy great compassion, O Lord, I come to worship, to praise Thy Name, to praise Thy Name in Thy temple; I bow in reverence before Thee. Adonoy, Adonoy, I love the place where Thou dwellest, and the house wherein dwelleth Thy glory, there I bow worshipping Thee, O Lord my God, pow'r divine, creator of life and all! May my prayer, humbly upraised, seem good, Adonoy in Thine eyes, Elohim! I come in weakness. Answer Thou, answer Thou, in mercy grant me, O Lord, Thy salvation.

BORECHU

Borechu es Adonoy hamevoroch. Boruch Adonoy hamevoroch leolom voed.

Sing His praise, sing to the Lord, praise and adore! Sing praise to the Lord, praise and adore for evermore.

Shema Yisroel

Shema Yisroel Adonoy
Eloheinu, Adonoy echod!
Boruch shem kevod malchuso
leolom voed.

O hear, Israel, our God, our
creator, our God is One! O
praised be His name whose
Kingdom shall never end.

Veohavto

Veohavto eis Adonoy Elohecho,
bechol levovcho, uv'chol
nafshecho, uv'chol meodecho.
Vehoyu hadvorim hoeileh asher
onochi metzavcho hayom al
levovecho. Veshinantom
levonecho, vedibarto bom,
beshifte cho beveisecho,
uv'lechtocho vade rech,
uv'shochbecho, uv'kumecho.
Uk'shartom leos al yodecho,
vehoyu letotofos bein eineicho,
uch'savtom al mezuzos
beisecho, uvishorecho.

And thou shalt love Him, thou
shalt love Him, thy Lord God,
with all thy heart, and all thy
soul, shalt love Him with all thy
might. Thou shalt love him,
thou shalt love Him, the Lord
thy God, with all thy heart,
with all thy soul, shalt love him
with all thy might. And these
words which I command thee,
these words shall be on thy
heart this day, be on thy heart
this day. And thou shalt teach
thy children, and of them shalt
speak, when by thy hearth thou
sittest, and when thou walkest
on the way, and when thou
liest, and when thou risest up.
Thou shalt bind a sign on thy
hand, and as frontlets they shall
be between thine eyes. On the
doorposts of thy house be
written, also upon thy gates.

Mi Chomocho

Mi chomocho, mi chomocho
boelim Adonoy, mi komocho
nedor bakodesh, noro sehilos
oseh fele. Malchusecho rou vo
necho, Seh Eli onu veomru!
Adonoy yimloch, Adonoy
yimloch, leolom voed.

Who is like Thee, Who is like
Thee of the mighty, O Lord?
Who is like Thee, O Lord all
glorious? Thy works we
proclaim; Thy marvels praise!
And when Thy children were
shown Thy wonders, they cried,
behold, this is my God! And the
Lord shall reign forever and
ever.

TZUR YISROEL

Tzur Yisroel, Kumo beezras Yisroel, Goaleinu Adonoy, tzevo os shemo. Kedosh Yisroel, Boruch atoh Adonoy, Goal Yisroel. Amen.	Rock of Israel, arise to the help of Israel! Our deliv'rer Adonoy, O bless and praise his Name, O blessed Israel; O blest be Thou O Lord, O praise him and His holy Name, redeemer of Israel. Amen.

Part II

KEDUSHAH

Nekadesh es shimcho boolom, Keshem shemakdishim oso bishemei morom, Kakosuv al yad neviecho, vekoro zehelzeh veomar: Kodosh, Kodosh, Kodosh, Adonoy, tzevoos, melo chol hooretz kevodo, kevodo. Adir adirei nu, Adonoy, Adononei nu, moh adir, shimcho bechol hoorretz. Boruch kevod Adonoy mime komo. Echod hu, eloheinu. Huovinu. Hu malkeinu. Hu moshieinu, vehu yashmieinu berachamov l'einei kolchoi. Echod hu, elo heinu, hu ovi nu, hu malkeinu, hu moshieinu. Vehu yashmieinu, berachamov, l'einei kol choi. Yimloch Adonoy leolom! Elohayich Ziyon, ledor vodor. Halaluyah!	Sanctified be Thy name evermore on earth as it is sanctified at Thy throne on high, and we hallow Thy Name as the prophets wrote, Thy name we glorify, proclaiming: Kodosh, kodosh, kodosh, Adonoy, tzevoos, heaven and the earth are filled with His glory. O God ever mighty, make us like unto Thee, Lord. How glorious is Thy name in all the earth. We praise Thy name, Lord our God, in Thy Dominion. One is the Lord our God. He our Father, He our Ruler, He our Redeemer. And He, and He shall answer us in His might in the sight of all men. For One, One is the Lord God, He our Father, He our Ruler, He our Redeemer. Shalt reign, Adonoy evermore. Zion, Zion, thy God, the Lord shall reign evermore. Halleluja!

Part III

YIHYU LEROZON

Yihyu lerozon imrei fi, yihyu
lerozon imrei fi, Vehegyon libi
lefonecho, vehegyon libi
lefonecho, Adonoy tzuri vegoali,
Adonoy tzuri vegoali, Amen,
Amen.

O Lord, may the words of my
mouth, O Lord, may the words
of my mouth and the
meditations of my heart be
acceptable before Thee,
Adonoy, my Rock and
Redeemer. Adonoy, my Rock
and Redeemer, Amen, Amen.

SEU SHEORIM

Seu sheorim rosheichem!
Useupischei olom! Veyovo
melech hakovod. Mihu ze
melech hakovod? Adonoy,
tzevoos, hu melech hakovod.
Selah, Selah, Selah.

Lift up your heads, O ye
portals! Lift, ye everlasting
doors! That the King of glory
may enter! Who is this King of
Glory? Adonoy of Sabaoth, He
is the King of Glory! Selah,
Selah, Selah.

TOROH TZIVOH

Toroh tzivoh lonu Moshe
morosho kehilas Yaakov. Beis
Yaakov lechu veneilecho, beor
Adonoy.

Torah, which God gave thro'
Moses, is the Law of the house
of Jacob. O house of Jacob,
come ye, walk in the light, the
light of the Lord.

SHEMA YISROEL

Shema Yisroel Adonoy
Eloheinu, Adonoy echod!

O hear Israel, our God, our
Creator, our God is One!

LECHO ADONOY

Lecho Adonoy hageduloh,
vehagevuroh, vehatiferes,
vehaneitzach, vehahod! Ki chol
bashomayim uvooretz, Lecho
Adonoy hamamlocho,
vehamisnasehlechol, lerosh.
Lecho, Adonoy hamamlocho
vehamisnaseh lechol lerosh!

And Thine, Adonoy, is the
greatness and all dominion and
Thine the majesty and the glory
and the pow'r, for all things in
heaven and on earth, in heaven
and earth are Thine, Adonoy,
and Thine, Thine the Kingdom,
be Thou, Lord, exalted, exalted
o'er all. And Thine, the
Kingdom, O Lord, our God,
and be Thou exalted, O Lord,
o'er all!

Part IV

GADELU LADONOY
Gadelu ladonoy iti,
un'romamoh shemo yachdov.

Praise the Lord, praise the Lord
with me, let us exalt His name
in one voice.

HODO AL ERETZ
Hodo al eretz veshomayim,
vayorem keren leamo, tehiloh
lechol chasidov livnei Yisroel,
livnei Yisroel amk'rovo,
amk'rovo. Halaluyah.

Earth sees His glory, and the
heavens, and He is the strength
of His people, the glory and
praise of all the just, of Israel,
that came before His presence.
Halleluja!

TORAS ADONOY
Toras Adonoy temimoh,
meshivas nofesh; Eidus Adonoy
neemonoh, machkimas pesi;
pikudei Adonoy yeshorim,
mesamchei leiv, mesamchei leiv!
Yiras Adonoy tehoro, tehoro,
omedes load. Kilekach tov
nosati lochem. Torosi, torosi, al
taazovu, al taazovu.

The Law of the Lord is perfect,
it doth restore the soul. His
precepts are sure and enduring,
and teach the simple. The laws
giv'n by the Lord are just Laws.
Rejoicing the heart, rejoicing
the heart. The Law of the Lord
is holy, is holy. Enduring
forever. Behold these precepts
the Lord hath shown thee;
regard them, regard them, do
not forsake them, do not
forsake them.

ETZ CHAYIM
Etz chayim he, lamachachazikim
boh, vesomecheho meushor;
d'rochehe darchei noam, vechol
nesivoseho sholom.

Tree of Life, life to them that
shall receive it, and its
preservers are happy, for its
ways are ways of beauty, and
all its paths are paths of peace.

Part V

VAANACHU
Vaanachnu koreim
umishtachavim umodim, Lifnei

We adore Thee and bow the
head and humble our hearts

melech malchei ham'lochim, Hakodosh boruch hu. [Minister, speaking in English:] May the time not be distant, O God, when Thy Name shall be worshipped in all the Earth, when unbelief shall disappear and error be no more. May the day come when all men shall invoke Thy Name, when corruption and evil shall give way to purity and goodness, when superstition shall no longer enslave the mind, nor fetichism blind the eye! O may all men recognize that they are brethren, so that one in spirit and one in fellowship they may be forever united, forever united before Thee. Then, shall Thine kingdom be established on Earth and the word of Thine ancient seer be fulfilled! [Chorus:] Bayom hau yihyeh Adonoy Echod, ushemo Echod! [Minister:] And now, ere we part, let us call to mind those who have finished their earthly course and have been gathered to the eternal home. Though vanished from bodily sight, they have not ceased to be, and it is well with them; they abide in the shadow of the Most High. Let those who mourn for them be comforted. Let them submit their aching hearts to God, for He is just and wise and merciful in all His doings, though no man, no man, can comprehend

before Thee. Before the King of King of Kings! The Lord God be praised! The Lord God be adored! Praise the Lord! Praise, praise Him! [Minister, see left.] [Chorus:] And on that day the Lord shall be One, be One, His name be One! [Minister.] God of Israel! Arise to the help of Israel! Our Redeemer, Adonoy Sabaoth, our God. Arise to the help of Israel!

His ways. . . . In the divine
order of nature both life and
death, joy and sorrow, serve
beneficent ends, and in the
fulness of time we shall know
why we are tried and why our
love brings us sorrow as well as
happiness. Wait patiently all ye
that mourn, and be ye of good
courage, for surely your longing
souls shall be satisfied. [Chorus
and baritone soloist:] Tzur
Yisroel! Kumo beezras Yisroel!
Goaleinu, Adonoy tzevoos
shemo. Kumo beezras Yisroel!

Adon Olom

Adon Olom asher molach,
Beterem kol yetzir nivro; lees
naasoh, vecheftzo kol, Asay
melech shemo nikro. Veacharey
kichlos hakol, levado . . .
yimloch no roh. Vehu hoyoh,
vehu hoveh, vehuh yih' yeh,
besiforo roh! Vehu echod veayn
sheini; lehamshil lo, lehach
biroh; Beli reishis, beli sachlis,
velo hoos vehamisroh! Vehu Eli,
Vechay goali, vetzur chevli,
beeis tzoroh. Vehu nissi,
umonosli, menos kosi, beyom
ekro. Beyodo afkid ruchi, Beeis
ishan veoiroh; veim
ruchigeviyosi, Adonoy le, velo
iro.

Eternal God who reigned
supreme while all was yet a
formless void, in sovreign pow'r
ordained this world, and His
name then as King was
proclaimed. And after this, if
chaos come, the Lord God will
rule alone, and One He was,
and One He is, and One shall
be in pow'r supreme! For he is
One, and One shall be. To our
God none can be compared! He
ne'er began, He never will end;
to Him the might, and glory
and pow'r! He is my God, my
God, my living God, my God,
my refuge in my distress. And
He is my sign, and my refuge,
my cup of salvation, when e'er I
call. In His hand my soul shall
rest, shall rest when I sleep and
when I wake, and with my soul,
my body, He is with me. I shall
not fear.

BENEDICTION

Yevochecho Adonoy
veyishmerecho. Amen. Yoeir
Adonoy ponov eilecho,
veyichoneko. Amen, Amen. Yiso
Adonoy ponov eilecho, veyosem
lecho. Sholom. Amen, Amen,
Amen.

Now may the Lord bless you
and guard you. And shine upon
you the light of His
countenance and be gracious
unto you. Amen, Amen. And
lift up to you His face and give
you, and give you peace.
Sholom. Amen, Amen, Amen.

JOHANNES
BRAHMS

Born May 7, 1833, in Hamburg
Died April 3, 1897, in Vienna

When Boston's Symphony Hall was being built in 1900, one wag suggested that the signs should read, "Exit—in case of Brahms." This comment reflected the wide schism that divided much of the musical world at the time. The Wagnerites, who were then dominant in Boston, believed that Richard Wagner had pointed out vital new directions for all future composers to follow. The Brahmsians, on the other hand, regarded Johannes Brahms as the capstone of the great musical traditions from the past, as evidenced in the famous listing of the three Bs—Bach, Beethoven, Brahms.

Few can deny that Brahms's music was solidly wed to the music of the past. The result was a wonderful synthesis, a blending together of Classical ideals with the advanced melodic, harmonic, and rhythmic vocabulary of nineteenth-century Romanticism. It was music that came at the end of an era and served more as a summary of what had come before than as a harbinger of the new and different.

A slow, extremely self-critical composer, Brahms nevertheless turned out a remarkable amount of music. In the realm of vocal music alone, he wrote six large-scale and sixty smaller choral works, along with some two hundred songs. *Ein deutsches Requiem,* by far his best-known choral composition, remains a staple of the modern choral repertoire. Two other outstanding choral works, the *Alto Rhapsody* and *Schicksalslied,* are heard frequently; they suffer some neglect because their short lengths present problems of programming. Only rarely performed are *Song of Triumph, Nänie,* and *Song of the Fates.*

EIN DEUTSCHES REQUIEM, Op. 45
(A German Requiem)

1 hour, 10 minutes

One evening Brahms was asked how he spent the day. "I was working on my symphony," the composer replied. "In the morning I added a note. In the afternoon I took it out."

Apocryphal as this story might be, it does point up the slow, careful pace at which Brahms fashioned his music. Few of his compositions, though, took as long to compose as his *Requiem*.

The *Requiem*'s origin dates back to 1854 when Brahms was composing his First Symphony. After much work, Brahms decided to recast the symphony as a piano concerto, and he discarded the symphony's original slow movement. Later, Brahms adapted this discarded music, much altered, to become the opening section of the *Requiem*'s second movement.

The specific idea of writing a Requiem first took hold in Brahms's mind in 1856, on the death of his dear friend and great advocate, the composer Robert Schumann. At age 23, Brahms was probably the youngest composer ever to contemplate writing music that dealt with death: Berlioz was 34, Mozart 35, Fauré 43, Dvořák 49, and Verdi 61 when they composed their Requiems. As a preparatory first step, Brahms composed a four-movement cantata, which he completed in 1861.

On February 2, 1865, Brahms received a telegram from his brother Fritz urging the composer to rush to Hamburg (from his home in Vienna) if he wanted to see his mother alive. Unfortunately, Brahms arrived too late. The failed effort to reach his mother before she died pained Brahms greatly and turned his thoughts back to his Requiem. Clara Schumann, widow of Robert and a close friend of Brahms, later wrote, "We all think he wrote in her memory, though he never expressly said so."

By August 1866, Brahms had completed a six-movement Requiem. According to several contemporary reports, the first three movements received a very poor performance in Vienna on December 1, 1867, and were adjudged a complete failure. The composer then reworked the music and led a performance of all six movements in Bremen on Good Friday, April 10, 1868. This presentation scored a resounding success, winning for Brahms his first international acclaim.

Nevertheless, Brahms was still dissatisfied with the work, and he consoled himself with a visit to his mother's grave on the day following the concert. Not long thereafter, in May 1868, Brahms wrote the soprano solo *"Ihr habt nun Traurigkeit"* ("And ye now therefore have sorrow"). The deeply moving aria, probably memorializing his mother, was inserted into the *Requiem* and became its fifth movement. In this final form the *Requiem* received its third premiere on February 18, 1869, in Leipzig.

Brahms himself compiled the text of this *Requiem* from Martin Luther's German translation of the Bible. The words convey feelings of hope and consolation; they are more concerned with comforting the living than praying for the soul of the departed.

Theodore M. Finney discerns what he believes to be the true message of the *Requiem* in a paragraph made up of the first lines of each movement: "Blessed are they that mourn. For all flesh is as grass. Lord, make me to know mine end. How lovely is Thy dwelling. And ye now therefore have sorrow: but I will see you again. For here have we no continuing city. Blessed are the dead."

Brahms's decision to use a German text, instead of the more traditional Latin, may have come from an entry Brahms found in Schumann's notebook, which expressed the older composer's hope of composing such a work one day. Some commentators, though, believe *Protestant Requiem* would have been a more appropriate title than *German Requiem*. Brahms, however, wrote in a letter, "As regards the title, I will confess I should gladly have left out 'German' and substituted 'Human.'"

Siegfried Ochs, a famed choral conductor and friend of Brahms, related that the composer once told him that "the whole work was, essentially, founded on the chorale, '*Wer nur den lieben Gott lässt walten.*' " The melody of this old Lutheran hymn (the title translates as "Who all his will to God resigneth") has an arch shape, with a rising-falling contour. The curved melodic line is heard at the opening of the first movement, at the choral entrance in the second movement, and in the final movement.

Brahms also casts most of the individual movements in ternary form—an opening section, a contrasting middle section, and a return of the opening. In effect, this gives each movement an up-and-down shape similar to the Lutheran hymn melody. Finally, the affinities between movements one and seven (seven actually develops material from one), two and six (the funereal march of number two complemented by the vision of the Last Judgment in number six), and three and five (grief followed by consolation)—with four, "How lovely is thy dwelling," standing alone as the keystone—give the entire composition the same rising-falling form.

After completing his monumental masterpiece—by far the largest work he ever composed—Brahms eloquently expressed his deep satisfaction: "Now I am consoled. I have surmounted obstacles that I thought I could never overcome and I feel like an eagle, soaring ever higher and higher."

I. Chorus

Selig sind, die da Leid tragen,	Blessed are they that mourn;
denn sie sollen getröstet werden.	for they shall be comforted.

MATTHEW 5:4

Die mit Tränen säen,	They that sow in tears
werden mit Freuden ernten.	shall reap in joy.
Sie gehen hin und weinen,	He that goeth forth and weepeth,
und tragen edlen Samen,	bearing precious seed,
und kommen mit Freuden	shall doubtless come again with rejoicing,
und bringen ihre Garben.	bringing his sheaves with him.

PSALMS 126:5–6

II. Chorus

Denn alles Fleisch es ist wie Gras	For all flesh is as grass,
und alle Herrlichkeit des Menschen	and all the glory of man
wie des Grases Blumen.	as the flower of grass.
Das Gras ist verdorret	The grass withereth,
und die Blume abgefallen.	and the flower thereof falleth away.

1 PETER 1:24

So seid nun geduldig, lieben Brüder,	Be patient therefore, brethren,
bis auf die Zukunft des Herrn.	unto the coming of the Lord.
Siehe ein Ackermann wartet	Behold the husbandman waiteth
auf die köstliche Frucht der Erde	for the precious fruit of the earth,
und ist geduldig darüber,	and hath long patience for it,
bis er empfahe den Morgenregen und Abendregen.	until he receive the early and latter rain.
So seid geduldig.	Be patient, therefore.

JAMES 5:7

Aber des Herrn Wort bleibet in Ewigkeit.	But the word of the Lord endureth for ever.

1 PETER 1:25

Die Erlöseten des Herrn werden widerkommen,	And the ransomed of the Lord shall return,
und gen Zion kommen mit Jauchzen;	and come to Zion with songs
Freude, ewige Freude wird über ihrem Haupte sein;	and everlasting joy upon their heads:
Freude und Wonne werden sie ergreifen,	they shall obtain joy and gladness,
und Schmerz und Seufzen wird weg müssen.	and sorrow and sighing shall flee away.

ISAIAH 35:10

III. Baritone and Chorus

Herr, lehre doch mich,	Lord, make me to know mine end,
das ein Ende mit mir haben muss,	and the measure of my days,
und mein Leben ein Ziel hat,	what it is;
und ich davon muss.	that I may know how frail I am.
Siehe, meine Tage	Behold, thou hast made my days
sind einer Handbreit vor dir,	as an handbreadth;
und mein Leben ist wie nichts vor dir.	and mine age is as nothing before thee:
Ach, wie gar nichts sind alle Menschen,	verily every man at his best state
die doch so sicher leben.	is altogether vanity.
Sie gehen daher wie ein Schemen,	Surely every man walketh in a vain shew:
und machen ihnen viel vergebliche Unruhe;	surely they are disquieted in vain;
sie sammeln und wissen nicht,	he heapeth up riches,
wer es kriegen wird.	and knoweth not who shall gather them.
Nun Herr, wes soll ich mich trösten?	And now, Lord, what wait I for?
Ich hoffe auf dich.	My hope is in thee.

Psalms 39:4–7

Der Gerechten Seelen sind in Gottes Hand	But the souls of the righteous are in the hand of God,
und keine Qual rühret sie an.	and there shall no torment touch them.

Wisdom of Solomon 3:1

IV. Chorus

Wie lieblich sind deine Wohnungen,	How amiable are thy tabernacles,
Herr Zebaoth!	O Lord of hosts!

Meine Seele verlanget und sehnet sich	My soul longeth, yea, even fainteth
nach den Vorhöfen des Herrn;	for the courts of the Lord:
mein Leib und Seele freuen sich	my heart and my flesh crieth out
in dem lebendigen Gott.	for the living God.
Wohl denen, die in deinem Hause wohnen,	Blessed are they that dwell in thy house:
die loben dich immerdar!	they will be still praising thee.

PSALMS 84:1–2, 4

V. Soprano and Chorus

Ihr habt nun Traurigkeit;	And ye now therefore have sorrow:
aber ich will euch weider sehen,	but I will see you again,
und euer Herz soll sich freuen,	and your heart shall rejoice,
und eure Freude soll niemand von euch nehmen.	and your joy no man taketh from you.

JOHN 16:22

Ich will euch trösten,	As one whom his mother comforteth,
wie einen seine Mutter tröstet.	so will I comfort you.

ISAIAH 66:13

Sehet mich an: ich habe eine kleine Zeit	Behold with your eyes,
Mühe und Arbeit gehabt	how that I laboured but a little,
und habe grossen Trost funden.	and found for myself much rest.

ECCLESIASTICUS 51:27

VI. Baritone and Chorus

Denn wir haben hie keine bleibende Statt,	For here have we no continuing city.
sondern die zukünftige suchen wir.	but we seek one to come.

HEBREWS 13:14

Siehe, ich sage euch ein Geheimnis.	Behold, I shew you a mystery;

Wir werden nicht alle entschlafen,	we shall not all sleep,
wir werden aber alle verwandelt werden;	but we shall all be changed,
und dasselbige plötzlich in einem Augenblick	in a moment, in the twinkling of an eye,
zu der Zeit der letzten Posaune.	at the last trump;
Denn es wird die Posaune schallen	for the trumpet shall sound,
und die Toten werden auferstehen unverweslich,	and the dead shall be raised incorruptible,
und wir werden verwandelt werden.	and we shall be changed.
Dann wird erfüllet werden	Then shall be brought to pass
das Wort, das geschrieben steht:	the saying that is written:
Der Tod ist verschlungen in den Sieg.	Death is swallowed up in victory.
Tod, wo ist dein Stachel?	O death, where is thy sting?
Hölle, wo ist dein Sieg?	O grave, where is thy victory?

1 Corinthians 15:51–2, 54–5

Herr, du bist würdig,	Thou art worthy, O Lord,
zu nehmen Preis und Ehre und Kraft,	to receive glory and honour and power;
denn du hast alle Dinge erschaffen,	for thou hast created all things,
und durch deinen Willen haben sie das Wessen	and for thy pleasure
und sind geschaffen.	they are and were created.

Revelation 4:11

VII. Chorus

Selig sind die Toten,	Blessed are the dead
die in dem Herren sterben,	which die in the Lord
von nun an.	from henceforth:
Ja, der Geist spricht,	Yea, saith the Spirit,
dass sie ruhen von ihrer Arbeit;	that they may rest from their labours;

| denn ihre Werke folgen ihnen nach. | and their works do follow them. |

REVELATION 14:13

ALTO RHAPSODY, Op. 53 (Rhapsody for Alto, Men's Chorus, and Orchestra)

13 minutes

As a young man, Brahms contributed to the family income by playing piano in the brothels of Hamburg. Later, he commented that these early experiences with the ladies of the night ("those who turned me against marriage") were responsible for his life-long inability to sustain normal relationships with women.

One of Brahms's failed romances affected the creation of the *Alto Rhapsody.* Unable to express his affection for Clara Schumann, widow of composer Robert Schumann, because of social restraints, Brahms transferred his attention to the Schumanns' daughter, Julie. When Brahms received the news, in July 1869, that Julie had become engaged to Count Viktor Radicati di Marmorito, the disappointed suitor reacted angrily and bitterly. He later wrote to publisher Simrock, "Here I have written a bridal song for the Schumann Countess—but I do this sort of thing with concealed wrath—with rage!"

The "bridal song" to which Brahms refers is the *Alto Rhapsody,* which he composed in late 1869. The composer chose the text from the middle three verses of Goethe's poem *"Harzreise im Winter"* ("Winter Journey Through the Harz Mountains"). The song tells of a lonely, moody misanthrope who wanders through the snow-covered mountains until he finally finds some degree of comfort and tranquility.

The one-movement *Alto Rhapsody* opens with the orchestra creating the melancholy mood that permeates most of the work. The solo voice enters to tell of the unhappy youth's pain and longing. In the second section, which follows without pause, the alto continues the litany of despair but presents some hope of solace. In the final section, the wanderer's sorrowful spirits lift as the men's choir enters for the first time, adding its voice in support and supplication.

The premiere of the *Alto Rhapsody* was given in Jena on March 3, 1870, with Pauline Viardot-Garcia as the alto soloist.

ALT

Aber abseits, wer ist's?
Ins Gebüsch verliert sich sein
   Pfad,
hinter ihm schlagen
die Sträuche zusammen,
das Gras steht wieder auf,
die Oede verschlingt ihn.

Ach, wer heilet die Schmerzen
des, dem Balsam zu Gift ward?

Der sich Menschenhass

aus der Fülle der Liebe trank!
Erst verachtet, nun ein
   Verächter,
zehrt er heimlich auf
seinen eigen Wert
in ungnügender Selbstucht.

ALT UND MÄNNERCHOR
Ist auf deinem Psalter,
Vater der Liebe, ein Ton
seinem Ohre vernehmlich,
so erquicke sein Herz!
Oeffne den umwölkten Blick
über die tausend Quellen

neben dem Durstenden
in der Wüste.

ALTO

Who is that, wandering alone?
He loses his way in the brush,

behind him the branches
close together again,
the grass springs back again,
emptiness swallows him.

Ah, who can heal the pain
of one who finds poison in
   balsam?
He has drunk the hate of
   mankind
from the cup of love!
First scorned, now scorning,

he secretly wastes
his own merit
in useless searching for himself.

ALTO AND MALE CHORUS
If there is in your Psalter,
Father of Love, a melody
that can reach his ear,
revive his heart!
Turn your unclouded light
down on the thousand
   fountains
beside the thirsting soul
in the wasteland.

SCHICKSALSLIED, Op. 54
(Song of Destiny)

17 minutes

Schicksalslied is Brahms's setting of the poem "Hyperion's *Schicksalslied*" from Friedrich Hölderlin's novel *Hyperion*. The poem can be divided into two parts: the first deals with the bliss, beauty, tranquility, and divine repose of the gods and heavenly spirits; the second describes the despair, confusion, and blind destiny that rob humans of their peace and contentment.

In his setting for four-part choir and orchestra, Brahms starts with an extended orchestral prelude of the utmost serenity and calmness. The music sustains this mood throughout the first two verses, which focus on the idyllic lives of the gods. Then, suddenly, the tempo, meter, and character change as the choir and orchestra start to rail and rage against cruel fate.

In his original draft, following the section that depicts the turmoil on earth, Brahms repeated the opening, thus ending the work with a sense of comfort rather than the "uncertainty" with which Hölderlin's verse concludes. Later, Brahms scaled down the recapitulation, only bringing back a variation of the orchestral introduction.

At first, some speculated that Brahms had missed the point of the Hölderlin poem by bringing back the heavenly character. Now, most everyone agrees that it was Brahms's strong sense of form and order that led to the seeming lapse. Brahms, following Classical ideals and traditions, felt that every musical journey must return to its point of origin. This is most simply realized in ternary form—an opening section, a contrast, and a repeat of the opening.

Thus, Brahms's deep need to balance the form compelled him to bring back the opening. His musical skill and vision allow us to feel the full impact of Hölderlin's poem, despite the apparent inconsistency of the ending.

Brahms first began to consider composing *Schicksalslied* early in 1869, soon after the premiere of his *Ein deutsches Requiem.* Not completed until May 1871, *Schicksalslied* received its first performance in Karlsruhe on October 18 of that year, with the composer conducting.

Ihr wandelt droben im Licht	You wander above in light,
Auf weichen Boden, selige Genien!	On forgiving soil, blessed immortals!
Glänzende Götterlüfte	Sparkling divine breezes
Rühren Euch leicht,	Touch you gently,
Wie die Finger der Künstlerin	Like the fingers of the player
Heilige Saiten	On sacred strings.
Schicksallos, wie der schlafende	No destiny awaits the holy ones
Säugling atmen die Himmlischen;	They breathe like sleeping babies;
Keusch bewahrt	Chastely guarded
In beschneidner Knospe	In modest bud,
Blühet ewig	Their spirit blooms eternally
Ihnen der Geist,	And their blissful eyes
Und der seligen Augen	See only quiet,
Blicken in stiller	Still eternity
Ewiger Klarheit.	In utmost clarity.
Doch uns ist gegeben	But to us is given
Auf keiner Stätte zu ruhn;	No resting place;
Es schwinden, es fallen	We, suffering mankind,
Die leidenden Menschen	Fall headlong
Blindings von einer	Blindly descending
Stunde zur andern,	From one hour to another,
Wie Wasser von Klippe	As water thrown
Zu Klippe geworfen,	From rock to rock,
Jahrlang ins Ungewisse hinab.	Through the years into uncertainty.

BENJAMIN BRITTEN

Born November 22, 1913, in Lowestoft, England
Died December 4, 1976, in Aldeburgh, England

Benjamin Britten grew up in a house on the east coast of England, facing the North Sea. But Britten's earliest memory was not the roar of the crashing waves or the shrill calls of the circling gulls. Instead it was the sound of a bomb, dropped by a German plane during World War I, falling and exploding in a nearby field. Equally vivid was the horror and terror etched into his heart and mind at that moment.

The sound and sensation of that childhood memory stayed with Britten his whole life. Moreover, it played a major part in shaping his very powerful antiwar feelings and the great concern he felt for all humanity.

Two major factors helped to shape Britten's musical style. One was his great admiration for the seventeenth-century English composer Henry Purcell, who Britten said was his strongest influence and the composer from whom he learned the most. Britten especially singled out the "clarity, brilliance, tenderness and strangeness" of Purcell's music, characteristics that accurately describe Britten's own work as well.

The clean, sharp, economical sound of Britten's music derives also from the first position he held after graduating from London's Royal College of Music in 1933. Britten was hired to write the scores for the documentary films being produced by the British Post Office. "The film company I was working for," Britten wrote, "had very little money. I had to write scores, not for large orchestras, but for six or seven players, and to make these instruments make all the effects that each film demanded." The discipline imposed by the limited resources helped Britten learn to avoid all excesses and overblown rhetoric, and it contributed to the lean, incisive style of his music.

A CEREMONY OF CAROLS, Op. 28

20 minutes

Due perhaps to his early memory of a German bomb exploding near his childhood home, Britten became a deeply committed pacifist and conscientious objector. Despite his patriotic fervor, Britten's antiwar beliefs dictated that he leave England the summer before World War II and go to the United States. Conflicted by his pacifist feelings and his love of England, however, Britten decided to return home in the spring of 1942, while the war was still being fought. And it was during the one-month Atlantic crossing on a Swedish freighter that Britten composed *A Ceremony of Carols*.

In this moving work, Britten shows his amazing ability to achieve all sorts of musical effects with minimum means and great economy by writing for just treble voices (he envisioned a choir of boys, but the work is usually performed by women's voices) with a single harp accompaniment (he sanctioned the use of a piano when a harp is not available). The texts come from medieval Christmas carols. The nine carols are preceded and followed by a processional and recessional.

1. *"Procession."* The choristers enter and walk to the stage or front of the church, singing in unison and without accompaniment a setting of the traditional Latin hymn *"Hodie Christus natus est."*

2. *"Wolcum Yole!"* A joyous fifteenth-century carol sung, in the opening and closing sections, over a repeated, two-note ostinato figure in the harp.

3. *"There Is No Rose."* A quiet fifteenth-century carol with origins in the Latin liturgy; these origins explain the mixture of English and Latin in the text.

4. *"That Yongë Child."* A melancholy melody sung by a solo voice to an anonymous text.

5. *"Balulalow."* A cradle song written by three Scottish

brothers—James, John, and Robert Wedderburn—around 1567. Britten accompanies the song by alternating major and minor chords.

6. *"As Dew in Aprille."* A gay, lively carol that is chordal in the opening and closing verses, with the three-part choir divided into two parts in the middle verses.

7. *"This Little Babe."* A poem by Robert Southwell is the text for this energetic, highly rhythmic carol, which continues its fast tempo even when the voice parts move more slowly near the end.

8. *"Interlude."* A section for harp alone that maintains the same ingenuous, light tone as the carols.

9. *"In Freezing Winter Night."* A setting of another poem by Robert Southwell in which the altos repeat an ostinato phrase under the two upper voices, helping Britten convey the icy cold of the scene.

10. *"Spring Carol."* With utter simplicity, Britten gives the words of William Cornish's poem to two solo voices.

11. *"Deo Gracias."* In this challenging carol—which compares Adam and Eve, who brought sin into the world, with Mary, through whom sin could be overcome—Britten effectively captures the exotic sound of medieval music.

12. *"Recession."* A literal repeat of the procession, sung as the choir files out.

A Ceremony of Carols received its first performance in Norwich, England, on December 5, 1942.

WAR REQUIEM, Op. 66

1 hour, 30 minutes

On November 15, 1940, German bombers scored a direct hit on the fourteenth-century St. Michael's Cathedral in Coventry, England. The air strike was particularly significant because it was one of the first times that a church building in an unarmed city of no military or strategic importance was bombed, presumably for the sole purpose of frightening and demoralizing the population.

It took over sixteen years to build a new cathedral, which was placed right next to the shattered skeleton of the old one. The church authorities then asked Benjamin Britten to write a large-scale composition for the consecration of the new cathedral. They requested that it focus on both the need to put an end to the cruelty and inhumanity of war and the urgency of moving toward reconciliation.

The composer was happy to accept the commission, since it would allow him to express some of his most fervently held views. As Britten scholar Peter Evans explained, "It represented not only an effort to mark worthily a triumphant recovery from the ashes of war, but also a conscious resolve on the composer's part to put the experience of his entire creative activity to that date at the service of a passionate denunciation of the bestial wickedness by which man is made to take up arms against his fellow."

At first, Britten contemplated writing a Requiem. Then he decided to expand his conception, interspersing nine powerful antiwar poems by the British poet Wilfred Owen (1893–1918) between the sections of the Latin Requiem. Owen was a particularly fitting choice as librettist: he was an army officer who had been awarded the Military Cross for bravery but was killed at age twenty-five, one week before the armistice that ended World War I.

On the title page of the score, Britten inscribed Owen's words: "My subject is War, and the pity of War. The Poetry is in the pity. All a poet can do is warn." The composer aimed to have the ageless universals of the traditional Requiem engage and confront the poet's personal cry of anger and pain at the horrors of modern warfare. Britten also wanted to call for reconciliation (particularly in the last poem used in the *War Requiem,* which begins, "It seemed that out of battle I escaped.").

To accomplish his conception, Britten organized the performing forces on three musical planes—both literally and symbolically. In front are the tenor and baritone soloists and a small chamber orchestra that together present Owen's poems. In general, the tenor stands for a British soldier or the poet; the baritone is a German soldier. (For the premiere, Britten arranged that the tenor part be sung by Peter Pears, a Briton, and the baritone by Dietrich Fischer-Dieskau, a German.)

Behind them looms the mixed choir, soprano soloist, and large orchestra that are concerned with the presentation of the Latin Mass. And in the background stands a boys' choir of treble voices accompanied by either an organ or harmonium. Their role is largely confined to the Mass, especially when the text deals with death and the beyond.

Musically, Britten uses a variety of styles and textures, often in striking juxtaposition. The total effect, though, is of organic unity and growth as the music unfolds. At a few places, the ironic effect of Britten's placement of Owen's poetry within the sequence of the Requiem text has a powerful impact. Two examples: In the *"Dies irae,"* right after *"Salva me, fons pietatis"* ("Save me, O fountain of goodness"), Owen's poem begins, "Out there, we've walked quite friendly up to Death." And in the *"Offertorium,"* Owen's very different version interrupts the Requiem's account of Abraham's sacrifice.

One musical device that appears throughout the piece is the interval of the tritone, in notes, from C to F sharp. The frequent appearances of this strange, stark interval, one that medieval theorists labeled *diabolus in musica* ("the devil in music"), add to the highly dramatic impact of this very eloquent and moving diatribe against the horrors of war.

Britten finished the composition of the *War Requiem* on December 20, 1961, and the first performance was given at the consecration of St. Michael's Cathedral in Coventry on May 30, 1962.

ANTON BRUCKNER

Born September 4, 1824, in Ansfelden, Upper Austria
Died October 11, 1896, in Vienna

Born to a village schoolmaster in rural Austria, Bruckner led a life as uneventful as his personality was unassuming. He received his first musical instruction from Augustinian monks as part of his training to follow his father's career as a schoolteacher. His special talent in music, though, led him to the more serious study of the organ and composition, and the decision to become a composer. And compose he did, even while spending several years as schoolteacher and then as church organist before becoming a professor at the Vienna Conservatory from 1868 to 1891.

In the highly sophisticated musical world of late nineteenth-century Vienna, people considered Bruckner a naive country bumpkin. He was not especially well-read or educated; his personal library was largely confined to books on either religion or music. Attired as he usually was in ill-fitting clothes—shirt and jacket that were overly large, trousers that were too short, and with a very close, peasant-style hairdo—Bruckner was hardly an imposing figure.

Throughout his life, Bruckner maintained an unswerving belief in Catholicism and a profound devotion to God. His faith was so deep that he even kept a daily list of the prayers he recited, and if the Angelus sounded while he was lecturing, he would stop, kneel, and pray before continuing.

Knowing of Bruckner's twin loves—the Catholic church and music—one would expect an affinity for sacred choral music, which he did indeed pursue. In fact, he turned out a rather considerable body of such works, totaling some eighty-six separate compositions. Of these, a few maintain important places in today's repertoire: the Mass in E minor, the lesser-known Masses in D minor and F minor, the *Te Deum* (which is Bruckner's most beloved sacred choral work), and *Psalm 150*.

MASS NO. 2 IN E MINOR

30 minutes

Although Bruckner wrote seven Masses, only three are played at all today—No. 1 in D minor, No. 2 in E minor, and No. 3 in F minor. He composed all three while organist at the Linz (Austria) Cathedral from 1856 to 1868.

The Mass in D minor (D major might be more fitting, since most of the movements are in the major mode) is a magnificent festival Mass for four soloists, mixed choir, and orchestra. Composed in 1864, the D minor finds Bruckner very much under the musical influence of Richard Wagner in his use of chromatic harmonies and even of leading motifs, which he introduces and brings back several times in the course of the work.

The Third Mass in F minor is the most massive of the three, lasting over an hour. Bruckner began the composition in 1867 after a mental breakdown and while still a patient in a clinic treating nervous disorders; he completed it in September of the following year. Features of the F minor are the homophonic choral writing, the importance of the orchestra, and the cyclical form, in which melodies heard earlier reappear later. The impassioned shouts of *"Credo!"* ("I believe!") interrupting the fugue near the end of the *"Credo"* section give some indication of the intensity of Bruckner's religious fervor.

Composed for the dedication of the Votive Chapel in the Cathedral of the Immaculate Conception in Linz, Mass No. 2 in E minor is now perhaps the most frequently performed of Bruckner's Masses. Bruckner probably began writing the work in September 1866 and finished on November 25, 1866.

Bruckner composed the E minor Mass for mixed choir (with no soloists) and a sparsely used orchestra of oboes, clarinets, bassoons, trumpets, four horns, and three trombones, without strings, percussion, or organ. The result is to focus most of the attention on the choir, which might have been Bruckner's intention from the start. Or the scoring may have been in response to a practical concern, since the dedication ceremony was held outdoors—where the sound of vocal soloists and strings could be lost, and where no organ was available.

Although he used a nineteenth-century vocabulary, it is obvious that Bruckner found his inspiration in sixteenth-century vocal polyphony. The greater use of counterpoint and fugal textures in this Mass indicates Bruckner's obeisance to Giovanni da Palestrina. To underscore this relationship, Bruckner bases the canon at the start of the *"Sanctus"* on a theme from a *Missa Breve* by Palestrina—the only known example of Bruckner using a nonoriginal theme. Further, several of the other themes suggest plainsong origins.

Clearly Bruckner conceived this Mass for liturgical use. Evidence for this belief is that he omits the words *"Gloria in excelsis"* and *"Credo in unum Deum,"* since traditionally they are spoken by the officiating priest.

The largely a cappella *"Kyrie"* uses only the horns and trombones to lend support at the climactic moments. The melody seems derived from plainsong, with the choir divided into eight parts, and the writing essentially polyphonic.

The style changes for the *"Gloria,"* in which the choral writing is in four parts, is much more chordal, and is accompanied throughout.

The *"Credo"* has one principal theme, which is transformed for *"Et incarnatus"* and for *"Et in Spiritum."*

After opening with a dialogue between the women's voices and the men's, the *"Benedictus"* continues with a flowing line in the orchestra supporting the slow-moving melody of the choir.

Although the choir sings in eight parts for the *"Agnus Dei,"* each statement of those words is presented in striking unison, using a melody that is reminiscent of plainsong. After building to a climax, the movement—and Mass—come to a quiet close.

Bruckner conducted the premiere of his Mass in E minor in the outdoor Cathedral Square in Linz on September 29, 1869— a day he called "one of the greatest days of my life." Over the following years, he put the score through four revisions (in 1876, 1882, 1885, and 1896), making, as he said, "rhythmic modifications" and "tightening up [the] structure."

Standard Text (see Appendix)

TE DEUM

25 minutes

Early in 1881, Joseph Hellmesberger, court conductor in Vienna, suggested to Bruckner that he write a Te Deum. The composer started making preliminary sketches around Easter of that year, but he then interrupted himself to compose his Seventh Symphony. He resumed work on the *Te Deum* in September 1883, completing it on March 7, 1884.

When Bruckner submitted the manuscript to Hellmesberger, the conductor deemed it "too long" and refused to perform it when Bruckner refused to make any cuts. The first performance came on May 2, 1885, in Vienna, with the composer conducting, but with the orchestra part played on two pianos. The first complete performance was given in Vienna by the Wagner Society on January 10, 1886, under the baton of Hans Richter. Both performances were huge successes, and the work was soon taken up in other cities in Europe and America; the 1892 United States premiere was given in Cincinnati by Theodore Thomas with a choir of 800, an orchestra of 120, and an audience of 7,000!

Written for four soloists, mixed choir, and large orchestra, the work was cast in five movements that divided the stanzas of the *Te Deum* text unequally:

Movement I: stanzas 1–19
Movement II: stanza 20
Movement III: stanza 21
Movement IV: stanzas 22–28
Movement V: stanza 29

Bruckner's *Te Deum,* a glorious and reverent hymn of praise to the Almighty, opens with a puissant outbreak in the orchestra and an equally forceful unison choir entrance. The excitement soon gives way to a quiet section for the soloists, after which the choir returns in an expansion of its opening measures.

The second movement, *"Te ergo,"* uses only the solo voices, with a solo violin adding a delicate tracery over the warm melody they sing. The hushed atmosphere of *"Te ergo"* is smashed by the violent start of *"Aeterna fac,"* which recalls the opening of the work, albeit with a relentless downward melodic movement in the orchestra. The choir sings largely in unison.

A solo tenor dominates most of *"Salvum fac."* Echoes from earlier sections—the solo violin from *"Te ergo"* and a literal quote of the opening of the *Te Deum*—tie this movement to what has come before. The final movement, *"In te, Domine, speravi,"* crowns the entire *Te Deum.* Of special interest is the theme Bruckner uses for the choir presentation of *"Non confundar"*: he borrows the theme from the Adagio movement of his Seventh Symphony. Bruckner explains that he conceived the melody when he learned, early in 1883, that Richard Wagner was very sick. "The thought had crossed my mind that before long the Master would die, and then the C sharp minor theme of the Adagio came to me," Bruckner wrote. The composer follows *"Non confundar"* with an incredible fugue on two themes and a monumental concluding section that includes several references to music already heard.

Evidence that Bruckner considered the *Te Deum* an outstanding accomplishment is found in his famous quote: "When God calls me to Him one day and asks what I have done with the talent He gave me, I'll show Him the score of my *Te Deum* and He is bound to judge me mercifully."

Standard Text (see Appendix)

PSALM 150

10 minutes

Bruckner was asked to compose a choral work for a major musical and theatrical exhibit to be held in Vienna in 1892. For his text, the composer chose the final psalm—No. 150, "Praise ye the Lord"—with its several musical references: "Praise Him with the sound of the trumpet; praise Him with the psaltery and harp. Praise Him with the timbrel and dance; praise Him with the stringed instruments and organs. Praise Him upon the loud cymbals; praise Him upon the high sounding cymbals."

Completed on June 29, 1892, Bruckner's setting of *Psalm 150* uses a mixed choir and large orchestra, plus a brief solo soprano part. Filled with jubilation and fire, the work resembles Bruckner's *Te Deum* in character. The piece starts with rapturous cries of "Hallelujah!" followed by a contrasting quiet section that includes the soprano solo. After a reminder of the opening, Bruckner introduces a fugal section characterized by big octave leaps, both up and down, in the melodic line. From here the work builds to a forceful and brilliant conclusion.

The premiere of *Psalm 150* was given in Vienna on November 15, 1892.

Halleluja!	Alleluia.
Lobet den Herrn in seinem Heiligtum.	Praise God in His sanctuary:
Lobet ihn in der Feste seiner Macht.	Praise Him in the firmament of His power.
Lobet ihn in seinen Taten!	Praise Him for His mighty acts:
Lobet ihn in seiner grossen Herrlichkeit!	Praise Him according to His excellent greatness!
Lobet ihn mit Posaunen.	Praise Him with the sound of the trumpet:

Lobet ihn mit Psalter und Harfen.	Praise Him with the psaltery and harp.
Lobet ihn mit Pauken und Reigen.	Praise Him with the timbrel and dance:
Lobet ihn mit Saiten und Pfeifen.	Praise Him with stringed instruments and organs.
Lobet ihn mit hellen Zymbeln,	Praise Him upon the loud cymbals:
Lobet ihn mit wohlklingenden Zymbeln!	Praise Him upon the high sounding cymbals.
Alles, was Odem hat, lobe den Herrn.	Let every thing that hath breath praise the Lord.
Halleluja!	Alleluia!

FREDERICK DELIUS

Born January 29, 1862, in Bradford, England
Died June 10, 1934, in Grez-sur-Loing, France

Since Frederick Delius showed considerable musical interest and ability as a child, his parents arranged for violin lessons. His wealthy father, however, was determined that his son take over the family wool export business and not make music his career. Eventually, the young man agreed, but he fared so poorly—Harold Schonberg called Delius "the worst businessman since the invention of money"—that his father encouraged him to leave by buying a Florida orange plantation for the twenty-two-year-old to take over.

Delius was equally unsuccessful in the orange business and soon abandoned his share to an older brother. At the same time, he started the serious study of music, first in Florida and New York and then at the Leipzig Conservatory. After a visit to Paris, he decided to settle in France, making his permanent home in Grez-sur-Loing in 1897.

Through his writings, we get some idea of Delius's approach to music. "I don't believe in learning harmony or counterpoint," he wrote. "Learning kills instinct. For me, music is very simple. It is the expression of a poetical and emotional nature."

He expands this last point in other writings: "Music does not exist for the purpose of emphasizing or exaggerating something which happens outside its own sphere. Musical expression only begins to be significant where words and actions reach their uttermost limits of expression. It is only that which cannot be expressed otherwise that is worth expressing in music."

Scholars find it difficult to categorize Delius's music. Most often they classify him as an Impressionist, although his music differs very considerably from that of Claude Debussy, the leading Impressionist composer. Delius's music is characterized by great refinement and delicacy, and by elegance and subtlety, yet it is capable of soaring to moments of overwhelming drama, passion, and power.

In the early years of the twentieth century, music lovers, particularly in England and Germany, considered Delius one of the most important contemporary composers. Over the following decades, the distinguished English conductor Sir Thomas Beecham was an enthusiastic advocate of his music. In recent years, although Delius has fallen somewhat from favor, his music is still well represented on records and is heard with some frequency on the concert stage.

A MASS OF LIFE

1 hour, 40 minutes

Frederick Delius expressed some views that were strongly antichurch and antireligious. He placed his faith, not in God, but in the individual, setting as his ideal individuals who were strong, callous, and able to triumph over fear and suffering. In the writings of the German mystical philosopher Friedrich Nietzsche, Delius discovered an outlook on life and humanity that corresponded very closely with his own predilections.

The attraction to Nietzsche's ideas made it almost inevitable that Delius would find inspiration in his writings. The first occasion was in 1898 when Delius composed *Das Mitternachtslied Zarathustras* ("The Night Song of Zarathustra") for solo baritone, male choir, and orchestra, drawing the text from Nietzsche's monumental work *Also Sprach Zarathustra* ("Thus Spoke Zarathustra").

Then, in August 1904, while on a cycling trip in Brittany with conductor Fritz Cassirer, Delius had the idea of composing a major work based on Nietzsche's *Zarathustra*. Cassirer helped the composer choose the sections of text to be set, and within a few months Delius started to work on the score, keeping *Das Mitternachtslied Zarathustras* as the final section of the new work. He chose the title, *A Mass of Life,* as a contrast to the Christian Requiem Mass, which is a Mass of death—although he, of course, had no thought that this *Mass* would ever be used for liturgical purposes.

Delius composed *A Mass of Life* for four soloists, double choir, and large orchestra. He finished the composition in November 1905, and Sir Thomas Beecham conducted the premiere in London on June 7, 1909.

When Delius was asked for a brief analysis of the *Mass*, Fritz Cassirer suggested, and the composer accepted, the following reply: "As *Zarathustra* is absolutely not composed thematically, a brief analysis is impossible. The pure and simple rendering of the *mood* of the Zarathustra poem has been my aim."

The *Mass* opens with a resplendent, impassioned choral prayer to the will. The following sections, for soloists and choir, deal with the joy of laughter and dance and with the glory of life itself. The basses interrupt with a preview of "The Night Song," which is followed by the doubts and misgivings of "The Riddle." The first part ends with "The Night Song" for baritone and choir, an amazing evocation of the eerie stillness of the night.

The second part finds Zarathustra, represented by the baritone, alone in the mountains. As he wanders around, he comes upon young girls dancing; many commentators consider this section the musical high point of the entire composition. He then enters a meadow where he dozes off to the sound of the shepherd's pipes. The work ends with all the performers joining in ecstatic paeans to joy and rapture.

Despite the magnificence and sweep of *A Mass of Life*, some feel that Delius did not succeed in maintaining a uniformly high level of inspiration throughout. Many more, however, agree with Sir Thomas Beecham that this is indeed a "monumental masterpiece!"

MAURICE DURUFLÉ

Born January 11, 1902, in Louviers, France
Died June 16, 1986, in Paris

The names of such composers as Bach, Haydn, Mozart, Beethoven, Schubert, and so on, who wrote considerable numbers of outstanding works, fill the annals of music history. Much more limited is the list of composers who are remembered not so much for a body of work as for one or two compositions that people generally consider masterworks.

Maurice Duruflé belongs on the second list. The only composition by Duruflé with a secure place in the current repertoire is his *Requiem*, Op. 9. Less popular, but still occasionally played, are his *Motets on Gregorian Chants*, Op. 10, *Messe cum jubilo*, Op. 11, and some organ pieces. It should be mentioned, however, that he wrote very slowly and subjected every work to countless revisions, so that his entire output is limited to the three choral works and a small number of organ and orchestral pieces.

Duruflé began his music studies at the choir school of the Rouen Cathedral, then spent several years at the Paris Conservatoire, where he earned prizes in virtually every subject on his graduation in 1930. That same year he became organist at the Church of St. Étienne-du-Mont, and in 1942 he was appointed professor of harmony at the Paris Conservatoire, all the while continuing his career as a virtuoso organist.

Although Duruflé was a product of the twentieth century, he was not at all interested in the new directions struck by contemporary music. In his words, "[I] am incapable of adding anything significant to the piano repertoire, view the string quartet with apprehension, and envisage with terror the idea of composing a song after the finished examples of Schubert, Fauré, and Debussy." As major influences, he cites the French composers Debussy, Ravel, Fauré, and Paul Dukas (his teacher at the Paris Conservatoire), as well as Gregorian chant.

REQUIEM, Op. 9

40 minutes

The end of World War II found Duruflé working on a suite of organ pieces based on Gregorian chant melodies from the Mass for the Dead. While he was engaged in this project, his publisher, Durand, asked him to compose a Requiem.

Considering the timing of Durand's commission fortuitous, Duruflé decided to adapt some of the music he had already written for the *Requiem*. In creating the *Requiem*, though, he went far beyond the original Gregorian chants, treating them very freely, adding countermelodies and imitative sections, and making good use of the advanced harmonies and unique orchestral effects that he had learned from studying the music of Debussy, Ravel, Dukas, and Fauré (particularly Fauré's *Requiem*). Duruflé completed the work in 1947, and it received its first performance on Paris Radio in November of that year.

Duruflé based his *Requiem* on the Gregorian themes from the Mass for the Dead. Sometimes he kept the text intact, with the orchestral part only supplying support or comment. At other times, he simply found his inspiration in the Gregorian chants. Throughout he strove, as he put it, "to reconcile, as far as possible, Gregorian rhythm as it has been established by the Benedictines of Solesmes with the exigencies of modern meter."

The musical form of each piece follows the same form as the liturgy. The episodic organ part underlines certain accents and occasionally replaces the too-human sonorities of the orchestra. To Duruflé, the organ "represents the idea of peace, of faith and hope."

Such adjectives as "restrained," "tranquil," and "spiritual" accurately describe the Duruflé *Requiem*. While this description might sound limiting in expressive content, the very opposite is true. The music throbs with emotion and feeling, providing moments of thrilling excitement and sections of great poignancy that audiences find very moving and uplifting.

The first movement, "Introit," is of the utmost simplicity, presenting the Gregorian melody in a way that successfully combines its traditional setting with more modern elements.

Duruflé employs imitative counterpoint throughout the following *"Kyrie,"* which is also based on authentic Gregorian melody. It conveys an earnest plea for mercy, which is the true spirit of this section.

The level of visceral excitement reaches a great height in the "Offertory," which starts with a quiet orchestral introduction, builds to a perfervid climax, and then gradually returns to the quiet of the opening.

The flowing figure in the orchestra for the *"Sanctus"* supports the choir as it builds to triumphant shouts of *"Osanna,"* after which the intensity falls away, creating a symmetrical arch shape of intensity.

"Pie Jesu" stands at the center of the *Requiem*'s sequence of movements, and the poignancy and depth of emotion Duruflé expresses in this rich, impassioned section are equally pivotal.

A rocking rhythmic figure underlies the wonderfully gentle, yet marvelously evocative, melody of the *"Agnus Dei."* In the course of the movement, Duruflé weaves a highly expressive countermelody around the original Gregorian theme.

Another emotional high point comes in the *"Lux aeterna,"* where Duruflé uses all of his considerable skill to convey the intensity of this prayer for those who have departed this earth.

In *"Libera me,"* the composer again builds the music up to a powerful and utterly convincing climax, reaching the apex on the words *"Dies illa."*

The ethereal and airy concluding movement, *"Paradisum,"* effectively evokes visions of the beauties and glories of the afterlife for true believers.

Duruflé originally composed the *Requiem* for mezzo-soprano and baritone soloists, mixed choir, and large orchestra, including organ. In 1961, the composer rescored the accompaniment for a chamber orchestra of strings, harp, trumpet, and organ. In addition, he prepared a version for organ alone, though he wrote, "The reduction for organ (and choir) may prove inadequate in certain parts of the Requiem where the expressive timbre of the strings is needed."

Standard Text (see Appendix)

ANTONIN DVOŘÁK

Born September 8, 1841, in Nelahozeves, near Prague
Died May 1, 1904, in Prague

"God, love, motherland," Dvořák's motto, succinctly summed up the values he held in his music, as well as in his life. The sincerity and devout nature of his religious music leave no doubt that Dvořák wholeheartedly embraced God and the church. The warm and affectionate qualities of his personality come through clearly in all his music. And the strong folk influence one hears in his compositions confirms the enormous pride he took in his native Bohemia.

Most photos show Dvořák with furrowed brow and a bristling, ferocious beard, features that belie his sweet and gentle nature—despite his reputation for a nasty temper when aroused. Uncharacteristically absent from his personality was the angst or bitterness that bedeviled other great composers, leading scholars to group Dvořák with Handel and Haydn as composers who enjoyed particularly good mental health.

Dvořák's bright and sparkling music, rife with delightful melody, conveys the sound of a composer at peace with himself, radiating qualities of grace and spontaneity that have delighted audiences from his day to ours. Not an intellectual or especially well read according to his biographers, Dvořák nevertheless brings a considerable musical intelligence to bear on all his compositions.

In his choral music, Dvořák displays the same skills that have made his instrumental works—such as the "New World Symphony"—audience favorites. The themes in the choral works are just as attractive, well developed, and expanded as in his symphonies, and the orchestra plays a major role in accompanying the choir.

Dvořák wrote close to twenty choral works. The best known are *Stabat Mater*, Op. 58, and *Requiem*, Op. 89.

STABAT MATER, Op. 58

1 hour, 20 minutes

It is hard to imagine worse times than those Dvořák endured in the mid-1870s. The first disaster occurred on September 21, 1875, when Dvořák's two-day-old daughter, Josefa, died. The following January, still mourning her passing and seeking a way to express his sorrow, Dvořák began composing music to the standard text of Stabat Mater, which describes Mary's grief when confronted with the death of her Son. Dvořák worked on the composition until May 7, 1876, when the press of several commissions forced him to turn to other projects.

For over a year, Dvořák neglected work on the *Stabat Mater*. Then two more terrible tragedies followed in rapid succession. On August 13, 1877, his eleven-month-old daughter, Rose, passed away after swallowing a phosphorous compound used to make matches. Less than one month later, on September 8, 1877—Dvořák's thirty-sixth birthday—his three-year-old son and last surviving child, Otakar, died of smallpox.

As though to assuage his pain, Dvořák picked up the *Stabat Mater* once again, and he completed it on November 13 of that year. Curiously enough, although the composer was already well established with a large and enthusiastic following, the composition did not receive its premiere until December 23, 1880, in Prague.

The obviously heartfelt and penetrating music clearly personalizes Mary's grief and conveys Dvořák's great suffering at this time. Writing mournful music did not come easily to the genial and generally cheerful composer, so it seems natural that he would somewhat temper the gloominess with the optimism of many folk-tinged melodies.

The *Stabat Mater* opens with some magnificent examples of tone painting. First, the rising octaves in the orchestra suggest a stretching or reaching up to Christ on the cross. The brief, doleful descending melodic figure that follows brings to mind an image of Mary weeping below.

The first movement for soloists and orchestra without choir, the *"Quis est homo,"* starts with a poised, spacious fugue. Eventually the theme that has been taken up successively and developed by the various parts in counterpoint gives way to great independence in the four voices.

The following movements, with approximately equal time for soloists and choir, present the subsequent verses of the text. Dvořák treats the words, which come from a medieval poem, quite freely, repeating, cutting, and rearranging the text to suit his musical requirements. Sometimes he even ignores the normal meter and accentuation of the Latin words. As an instrumental composer, Dvořák may have willingly sacrificed the prosody to the musical line, or it may be that he was merely unfamiliar with Latin.

Mention must be made of the especially beautiful alto solo movement, *"Inflammatus et accensus."* Here the driving rhythm of the orchestra creates a sharp contrast to the dignity and serenity of the vocal line.

The last section, *"Quando corpus morietur,"* which is thematically related to the opening movement, presents the same upward stretching octaves in the orchestra. The descending motif associated with Mary's grief follows, except that the tempo nearly doubles the speed of the first movement. This section builds to a powerful climax before coming to a hushed, reverential close.

Standard Text (see Appendix)

REQUIEM, Op. 89 (Missa pro defunctis)

1 hour, 35 minutes

Dvořák scored a resounding success when he conducted his *Stabat Mater* at a mammoth music festival celebrating the eight hundredth anniversary of the Worcester Cathedral in September 1884. As he wrote to his wife, "The *Stabat Mater* made a tremendous impression in a huge, magnificent church (4,000 people)."

The performance firmly established Dvořák's reputation in England and immediately led to commissions for two new choral works—*The Spectre's Bride* for the Birmingham Festival and *St. Ludmilla* for the Leeds Festival. In 1887 R. Harding Milward, secretary of the triennial Birmingham Festival, asked Dvořák to compose "a great oratorio" for the 1888 festival, showing the composer Cardinal John Henry Newman's "The Dream of Gerontius" as a possible text. (Sir Edward Elgar set the same words some years later.) However, Dvořák's busy composing and conducting schedule, along with a lack of enthusiasm for Cardinal Newman's poem, kept the composer from undertaking the commission at that time.

Nevertheless, Dvořák probably had the Birmingham Festival in mind when, on January 1, 1890, he began composing his *Requiem*. With but a short break for a trip to Russia, England, and Germany in the spring, Dvořák wrote the *Requiem* without stop, finishing on October 31. He conducted the premiere at the next Birmingham Festival, on October 9, 1891.

Dvořák divided the huge *Requiem* into two large sections. The first part, running through "*Lacrimosa*," projects prayerful feelings of great sadness and melancholy. The sharply different second part begins with the "*Offertorium*" and suggests acceptance of death and spiritual consolation.

A motif played at the very opening by unison muted strings runs through the entire *Requiem*. In words it can be described as note, note above, note below, starting note. (In actual pitches the notes are F, G flat, E, F.) This motto appears in virtually every movement, not as a principal theme, but as a unifying factor. By continually varying its mood, character, rhythm, and starting pitch, Dvořák maintains interest in the motto through all its appearances.

Jarmil Burghauser, Dvořák biographer and author of the thematic catalog of Dvořák's music, posits that the opening motto is a "mournful question on the meaning and purpose of human existence and death." Also, one hears the same notes—although a half step higher and in a slightly different rhythm—at the opening of the second *"Kyrie"* in Bach's B minor Mass. The question remains open on the true meaning of Dvořák's motto theme: is it Dvořák's speculation on the meaning of life—or is it his way of paying homage to Bach?

A particularly striking use of the motif appears at the opening of *"Tuba mirum,"* the trumpet call to the Last Judgment. Many composers set this text with brilliant, ringing brass fanfares. But Dvořák—by having two trumpets play the motto softly three times, and capping each repetition with a chord of pain and yearning—creates a wondrous effect of awe and reverence.

Another borrowed theme becomes the subject of the joyous, exuberant fugue in the last part of the *"Offertorium."* Dvořák wrote the music to the words *"Quam olim Abrahae"* and derived the melody from a fifteenth-century Czech hymn of praise, *"Vesele spivejme"* ("Let us sing joyfully"), which churchgoers still sang in Dvořák's time.

In this work, Dvořák does not strive for the overwhelming power and dramatic impact heard in the Requiems of Berlioz and Verdi. Rather, he focuses on feelings of devotion and fidelity, creating an especially eloquent and moving contemplation of the mystery of human existence.

Standard Text (see Appendix)

EDWARD ELGAR

Born June 2, 1857, in Broadheath, England
Died February 23, 1934, in Worcester, England

From the birth of Henry Purcell in the middle of the seventeenth century to Elgar's birth two hundred years later, England did not produce one composer of international fame. Elgar's success helped to set the stage for the flowering of English music in the twentieth century, including the great contributions of such outstanding figures as Ralph Vaughan Williams, William Walton, Michael Tippett, and Benjamin Britten.

In his early years, Elgar was a musical factotum in the city of Worcester, England. He conducted the Worcester Glee Club, was bandmaster at the County Lunatic Asylum, served as concertmaster of the Worcester Philharmonic, led the Worcester Amateur Instrumental Society, and was organist at St. George's Roman Catholic Church.

Although Elgar lacked formal training as a composer, he wrote music all the while he was following his various other musical pursuits. By the 1880s, his compositions were being performed around England, and he had gained some recognition as a composer. But life was still a struggle, and despite his calm, tweedy, mustachioed look, he was extremely bitter and cynical.

It was not until the turn of the century that Elgar finally won international fame with his *Enigma Variations* of 1899, *The Dream of Gerontius* (his choral masterpiece) from 1900, and his most famous work—albeit heard more at graduation ceremonies than in the concert hall—the first *Pomp and Circumstance March* of 1901.

In addition to *The Dream of Gerontius*, Elgar composed a good number of other major choral works: the oratorios *The Light of Life,* Op. 29, *The Apostles,* Op. 49, and *The Kingdom,* Op. 51; the cantatas *The Black Knight,* Op. 25, *Scenes from the Saga of King Olaf,* Op. 30, *Caractacus,* Op. 35, *Coronation Ode,* Op. 44, and *The Music Makers,* Op. 69; and for choir and orchestra, *Star of the Summer Night (Spanish Serenade)*, Op. 23, *Scenes from the Bavarian Highlands*, Op. 27, and *The Spirit of England*, Op. 80. Although a few of these pieces do occasionally appear on choral programs and in CD catalogs, it is only *The Dream of Gerontius* that has fully won the affection of music lovers throughout the world.

THE DREAM OF GERONTIUS, Op. 38

1 hour, 40 minutes

On the occasion of his wedding in 1889, Edward Elgar—a devout Catholic—received as a gift a copy of the poem "The Dream of Gerontius" by Cardinal John Henry Newman. The poem made a strong impression on the composer; he was particularly taken with the cardinal's vision of purgatory as taught by the Catholic church, and he dreamed of one day setting the poem to music. As Elgar later said, "The poem has been soaking in my mind for at least eight years. All that time I have been gradually assimilating the thoughts of the author into my own musical promptings."

The immediate impetus to start composing came in November 1898 when Elgar was asked to write a major choral work for the 1900 Birmingham Festival. He started work early in 1900 and completed the score on August 3, 1900. A friend who visited Elgar on the day he finished quoted the composer as saying, "I do not know what fate has in store for this work, but this much I can tell you, it is GOOD."

The first performance, given in Birmingham on October 3, 1900, and led by Hans Richter, proved to be an absolute disaster, cited by some as the biggest failure in the entire history of British music. The three soloists could not sing their roles, the choristers found the music far beyond their abilities (they "floundered pitifully," in Elgar's words), and the conductor had not fully mastered the score.

A number of perceptive listeners, including George Bernard

Shaw, recognized the quality of the score despite the poor performance, and they praised the work. But Elgar was devastated, especially since he had invested so much of himself and his feelings about his Catholicism in the music. "I always said God was against art," he wrote to a friend. "I have allowed my heart to open once—it is now shut against every religious feeling and every soft, gentle impulse forever."

Just two years later, though, a good performance in Germany redeemed *Gerontius* and helped win for it a rightful place as one of the staples of the international choral repertoire. In Great Britain, *Gerontius* ranks just behind Handel's *Messiah* and Mendelssohn's *Elijah* in frequency of performance.

Usually classified as an oratorio, *Gerontius* is perhaps better identified as a dramatic cantata, since the text is not from Scripture. Elgar divided the work into two big sections—the first dealing with the death of the elderly Gerontius, the second with the journey of his soul, guided by his Guardian Angel, past the evil spirits and ugly demons to arrive at the feet of the Almighty.

The figure of Gerontius is neither religious nor historical. The name comes from *Gerontes,* the general name for the wise old men who stood at the side of the kings of ancient Greece offering counsel.

Elgar composed *The Dream of Gerontius* for three soloists—mezzo-soprano, tenor, and bass—mixed choir and semichoir (which Elgar defined as no more than five sopranos, five altos, four tenors, and four basses), and large orchestra.

Several elements of the musical style of *Gerontius* recall the music of Richard Wagner. Two general areas of similarity are the use of rich, lush harmonies and the outstanding color and brilliance of the orchestral writing.

A more specific likeness is found in Elgar's use of leitmotifs, or leading motives, which are usually short, easily recognized phrases of melody. Like Wagner, Elgar used these leitmotifs to represent various feelings, situations, characters, and ideas.

In the orchestral prelude to *Gerontius,* Elgar introduces many of the leitmotifs that will be heard in the course of the work. His good friend August Jaeger prepared, with the composer's approval, a summary of the major themes in the prelude. He says the first slow theme is "Judgment," and the following agitated subject is Gerontius's "Fear." "The work now proceeds," writes Jaeger, "in a restless, undulating manner, rising to a passionate outburst, being the appeal for mercy. This dies away and is succeeded by an eloquent passage, full of poignant feeling. It rises to a great fortissimo statement of Prayer. This, too, dies away and soon a lovely, soothing melody is heard, later used as the theme of the Priest and Assistants sending the soul on its journey from earth."

Elgar avoids being overly rigorous and consistent in his use of leitmotifs. As the composer wrote to Jaeger, "You may be inclined to lay too great stress on the *leitmotiven* plan because I really do it without thought—intuitively, I mean." The composer also eliminates the division of the music into separate solos and choruses. The music flows seamlessly from soloist to choir to semichoir without break or interruption.

Among the musical high points of *The Dream of Gerontius* are the a cappella entrance of the semichoir singing *"Kyrie eleison"*; the radiant stillness of the introduction and the song of the Soul of Gerontius at the opening of Part II; the orchestral evocation of the demons of hell; the extended choral paean of praise in the middle of Part II; and the best-known section of *Gerontius,* the concluding pages, starting with the words "Praise to the Holiest in the height."

GABRIEL FAURÉ

Born May 12, 1845, in Pamiers, France
Died November 4, 1924, in Paris

Gabriel Fauré's career is simply described. His musical talent was first noted when he was a boy of nine, and he was sent from his small town to a special music school in Paris. On graduation at age twenty-one, although he was already composing, he supported himself as organist in a succession of churches in Paris. His most prestigious church appointment came at age fifty, when he was made organist at La Madeleine. At the same time, he began teaching at the Paris Conservatoire, becoming director in 1905 and continuing until 1920, when increasing deafness forced his resignation.

Fauré's music, also, invites easy depiction. Although his life spanned a remarkable period in musical history—Berlioz and Chopin were still composing in his youth, Wagner and Debussy came in the following generations, and Stravinsky and Schoenberg were active in his final decades—Fauré maintained an essentially conservative and traditional course. His elegant, graceful, and sensitive compositions are largely restricted to the smaller forms—songs, piano pieces, and chamber works; his two large-scale compositions are the opera *Pénélope* and his incredible *Requiem*.

Perhaps Aaron Copland best summed up Fauré's music when he wrote that "those aware of musical refinements cannot help admire the transparent texture, the clarity of thought, the well shaped proportions. Together they constitute a kind of Fauré magic that is difficult to analyze but lovely to hear."

REQUIEM, Op. 48

40 minutes, although Fauré insisted the duration should be
"30 minutes, 35 at the outside"

Gabriel Fauré once reacted very strongly to an article on religious faith in a Catholic journal. He wrote, "How nice is this self-assurance! How nice is the naivete, or the vanity, or the stupidity, or the bad faith of the people for whom this was written, printed, and distributed!"

Knowing of Fauré's cynical attitude helps us to realize that Fauré's *Requiem* was not composed with the burning fervor of a religious zealot. Familiarity with his thinking also provides an insight into the possible reason that Fauré chose not to focus on the wonder, fear, and threat of torture and damnation that are so powerfully evoked in other well-known Requiems. Written by a religious skeptic, this *Requiem* can be considered a contemplative work that strives to comfort and assuage the grief of the mourners while holding out the promise of eternal rest and surcease from suffering for the departed.

In their Requiems, Berlioz and Verdi erected huge, overwhelming cathedrals of sound designed to overcome doubt and deepen faith. By comparison, Fauré fashioned an exquisite, intimate, candlelit side chapel where warmth and deeply felt emotion are allowed to bring peace and solace. Although smaller in scope, Fauré's *Requiem* ranks just as high as the more grandiose essays in the form.

Fauré composed most of the *Requiem* in 1887, completing it in time for the funeral of one Joseph Le Soufaché at La Madeleine on January 16, 1888, with the composer conducting. Although Fauré dedicated the composition to his father, who died in 1885, and had nearly completed it when his mother died on December 31, 1887, he was eager not to associate the work too closely with his parents. "My Requiem," he wrote in a 1910 letter to Maurice Emmanuel, "was written for no reason, for pleasure, if I may be permitted to say so."

In its first version the *Requiem* consisted of five movements—"*Introit et Kyrie*," "*Sanctus*," "*Pie Jesu*," "*Agnus Dei*," and "*In Paradisum*." The work required a soprano solo, mixed choir (with boys singing the solo and treble choir parts), and an instrumental ensemble of solo violin (only in "*Sanctus*"), divided violas, divided cellos, double basses, harp, timpani, and organ.

Over the following years, Fauré expanded the original score for the second version. He added two movements—"*Libera me*," which he had originally composed in 1877, and the "*Offertoire*," composed in stages between 1887 and the late 1880s —making a total of seven movements. Also, he arranged the accompaniment for a more or less conventional orchestra: two each of flutes, clarinets, and bassoons, four horns, two trumpets, three trombones, timpani, two harps, organ, and the usual strings.

If the makeup of the orchestra is standard, Fauré's spare, minimal use of the instruments is surely not conventional. Rarely does the entire orchestra play together; the first and second violins play in unison and are heard only in four of the seven movements; the flutes and clarinets play only in "*Pie Jesu*"—the second clarinet for less than four measures. No one is certain whether Fauré made the additions to satisfy his own artistic imperatives, to make the work suitable for grander occasions and concert performances, or to satisfy his publisher's requests to put the score into more saleable form.

The opening movement, "*Introit et Kyrie*," majestic in character and chordal in texture, presents a very human prayer for eternal rest for the deceased. Fauré sets its tone in the introductory measures: the orchestra (without violins) sounds a powerful chord, which the choir answers with the mournful words "*Requiem aeternam*," and this is followed by two more descending chords and similar responses. The traditional second movement, "*Dies irae*"—a section that usually calls for some of the most dramatic and awesome music of the Requiem—did not fit comfortably into Fauré's conception of the work, and he did not set it at all.

Fauré cast the deeply affecting "Offertoire" in three parts. The first part has the choir singing without sopranos. A baritone dominates the slightly faster middle section over a gently rocking viola accompaniment and a brief organ solo. The final segment resembles the opening, but this time including the sopranos.

In the *"Sanctus,"* a miniature gem of a movement, the sopranos sing the highly expressive melody, echoed by the male voices, with the harp providing a foundation and the solo violin (or all the violins in the later version) gracefully weaving the voices and harp together.

The simple, prayerful *"Pie Jesu"* is sung by a solo soprano, with the orchestra murmuring discreetly in the background and coming forward only between the lines of text. Fauré took the text from the conclusion of the Sequence part of the Requiem.

The *"Agnus Dei,"* which also includes "Communion," emerges warm and tender and ends with an echo of the music from the introduction to the opening movement.

Fauré gently alludes to the horrors of the Last Judgment in *"Libera me,"* sending a shudder of fear through the choir, but the allusion does not seem to disturb the noble tranquility and confidence of the baritone soloist who opens and closes the movement.

Projecting a feeling of serenity and peace, *"In Paradisum,"* with text from the Burial Service, offers essentially a long, eloquent melody for the sopranos, with only occasional support from the other voices. This part of the *Requiem* has been described as the perfect musical representation of the flight of the soul to heaven.

A fitting close to a discussion of Fauré's *Requiem* is the composer's words on the composition: "They say that my Requiem does not express the terror of death; someone has called it a lullaby of death. But that is how I see death: as a happy deliverance, as a yearning for the joy that lies beyond, rather than as a sorrowful passing."

Standard Text (see Appendix)

CHARLES GOUNOD

Born June 18, 1818, in Paris
Died October 18, 1893, in Paris

While in Italy after winning the Prix de Rome (a prize offered to young composers by the Institut de France for four years of study in Rome) in 1839, Charles Gounod first recognized his strong attachment to the Catholic church and his great appreciation of the Renaissance composer Giovanni da Palestrina. Although he later came to fame as the composer of *Faust* and a few other operas, at the time Gounod was convinced that his true calling was to enter the priesthood, or at least to compose only sacred music.

On his return to Paris, Gounod spent two years at a theological seminary and took a position as organist at the Chapel for Foreign Missions, where he wore clerical garb and asked to be addressed as Abbé Gounod. For the following five years Gounod did indeed compose exclusively for the church.

In 1850 Gounod set off in a new direction, writing his first opera, *Sapho*. This departure was due, in part, to Gounod's realization that he could not build a career limited to church music. In addition, the composer wanted to express the earthy, sensual side of his personality—a style that had no place in religious music. He spent the remainder of his life writing both sacred and secular music, including a Requiem that was left unfinished at his death.

ST. CECILIA MASS
(Messe solennelle de Sainte Cécile)

45 minutes

Gounod composed the *St. Cecilia Mass* in the French country-side near Avranches during the summer of 1855. His profound faith led him to approach the project with great awe and humility. "There is only one difficulty," he wrote. "It is to match in music the demands of this incomparable and inexhaustible subject, the Mass! In music! By a paltry man! My God, take pity on me!"

St. Cecilia Mass, with its superb melodies, its dramatic use of various operatic devices, and the devout, reverential tone that springs from the depths of Gounod's religious faith, is a popular favorite. Of the hundred or so major sacred works, including nearly twenty Masses, which Gounod produced over his lifetime, only the *St. Cecilia Mass* has survived in the modern repertoire.

Gounod composed the *St. Cecilia Mass* for soprano, tenor, and bass soloists, mixed choir, organ, and orchestra. He uses all the performers throughout, save in the "Offertory," which Gounod scores for orchestra alone. The vocal parts are chordal in texture—there is not one fugue!—and they easily predominate over the orchestra.

Each movement is distinctive in some way. The *"Kyrie"* reflects Gounod's admiration for the choral writing of Palestrina. In the opening of the *"Gloria,"* the solo soprano line gently floats over the humming chorus to stunning effect. The spicy, swaggering melody of the *"Credo"* stays with the listener long after the *Mass* is done. So, too, does the yearning theme in the *"Sanctus"* linger in the memory. And the concluding *"Agnus Dei"* projects a wonderful mood of enormous compassion and tenderness.

St. Cecilia Mass received its premiere at the Church of St. Eustache, Paris, on November 29, 1855, probably with Gounod conducting.

Standard Text (see Appendix)

GEORGE FRIDERIC HANDEL

Born February 23, 1685, in Halle, Germany
Died April 14, 1759, in London

Despite the fact that Johann Sebastian Bach and George Frideric Handel were born within one month of each other in Germany, and the fact that we recognize both as the outstanding composers of the age, their lives were as different as could be. Bach remained in Germany his entire life, working as cantor in a number of German churches and turning out a succession of masterpieces that were little known outside the particular city in which he worked. Handel was a true cosmopolite and was widely hailed as the greatest composer of the age in Italy, England, and Germany.

Handel was born in Halle, a provincial German city, where he received his only instruction in music—organ, harpsichord, violin, and oboe, plus some instruction in fugue and counterpoint—and also began his career as a church organist. At age eighteen, seeking greater opportunities, Handel went to Hamburg to play violin in the opera orchestra and to compose his first operas.

After four years in Hamburg, Handel left for a three-year sojourn in Italy. It was a time of significant learning and development for him; he absorbed the lyrical vocal style of Italian opera and began to earn fame as a composer of operas in that style.

Handel came back to Germany when Elector Georg Ludwig of Hanover offered him a position as *Kapellmeister*. Over the next couple of years the composer visited London briefly, returned to Hanover, and asked leave for another trip to London —where he remained for the rest of his life. Elector Georg Ludwig, though, followed him, becoming King George I of England a few years later!

London, when Handel arrived, was a center of intellectual activity. Among the more illustrious figures of the time were Alexander Pope, Jonathan Swift, Isaac Newton, Joseph Addison, Richard Steele, John Gay, and John Arbuthnot. Handel's arrival into this milieu has been compared to the explosion of a brilliant Roman candle. The Italian operas that he was composing and presenting were the rage of the city—attracting huge throngs of fervent admirers among the nobility, the intellectuals, and the growing middle class.

Proving himself as adept in business as he was brilliant at composing, Handel put on season after season of immensely popular Italian opera (earning and losing several fortunes in the process). The 1720s, though, saw his success start to wane. A rival company presenting Italian opera opened, under political pressure some influential nobles turned against him, and the public showed a lessened interest in Italian opera. Also, *The Beggar's Opera*, the immensely popular ballad opera of 1728, became a particularly potent factor in turning audiences away from serious Italian opera. By 1737, Handel's opera company was out of business.

Before starting his career as an operatic composer in England, Handel had written *La Resurrezione* and *Il trionfo del Tempo e del Disinganno* while in Italy. These works are oratorios—extended works on religious themes, usually for soloists, choir, and orchestra. In 1717 he composed *Esther*, his first English oratorio; in the 1730s, as opera occupied him less and less, he turned his attention to a series of oratorios with English texts.

In addition to *Esther* and the six masterpieces discussed in this book, Handel's oratorios include:

> *Deborah* (1733)
> *Athalia* (1733)
> *Saul* (1738)
> *Joseph and His Brethren* (1743)
> *Belshazzar* (1744)
> *Occasional Oratorio* (1746)
> *Joshua* (1747)

Alexander Balus (1747)
Susanna (1748)
Theodora (1749)

Through his many oratorios, Handel established a style and tradition of oratorios that lasted in England through the nineteenth century, and the choral tradition that sprang from these oratorios endures until today. England's long-held passion for choral music led George Bernard Shaw to note, rather cynically, "The British public takes a creepy kind of pleasure in Requiems."

ISRAEL IN EGYPT

1 hour, 38 minutes

Israel in Egypt is distinguished from other Handel oratorios in that it has no real plot and the six soloists (two sopranos, alto, tenor, two basses) do not represent individual characters, but are used for strictly musical purposes. Further, since *Israel in Egypt* is the story of an entire people—the Israelites—the choir plays a bigger role here than in any other Handel oratorio. For example, *Israel in Egypt* contains twenty-eight choral numbers; *Messiah* contains only fifteen, and *Judas Maccabaeus* has only twenty-two.

Handel composed some of his most programmatic and pictorial music for this oratorio. The seven plagues, which occupy the middle movements of Part I, give the composer a wonderful opportunity for musical description. In "They loathed to drink of the river," Handel depicts the horror of the rivers turned to blood with two wrenching downward leaps (major sevenths) to start the melody of the fugal chorus. In "Their land brought forth frogs," we hear the violins vigorously leaping and hopping about. The orchestral buzzing makes vivid the text in "He spake the word, and there came all manner of flies and lice." Handel whips up an orchestral storm for "He gave them hailstones."

And in "He sent a thick darkness over the land," the music becomes dark, heavy, and oppressive. Another chance for tone painting comes in the chorus "But the waters overwhelmed their enemies," where the music suggests the roiling, rolling sea.

Handel himself probably chose the text of *Israel in Egypt,* perhaps with the help of his friend and later librettist, Charles Jennens. The selections, all from the Bible, come from Psalms 78, 105, and 106 and the Book of Exodus. The libretto traces the story of the Israelites, subjugated and in despair, struggling to achieve victory over their oppressors. Although specifically dealing with the enslavement of the Jewish nation by the Egyptians, the story applies with equal validity to any downtrodden people fighting for their freedom.

Handel divides the oratorio into two parts—*Exodus* and *Moses' Song.* He actually composed *Moses' Song* first, in the incredibly short period from October 1 to 11, 1738. After a four-day break, he wrote *Exodus* from October 15 to 28.

In composing the music for *Israel in Egypt,* Handel borrowed and completely reworked entire sections from at least three other composers—Dionigi Erba, Francesco Urio, and Alessandro Stradella—who are now largely forgotten. While such wholesale appropriation of one composer's music by another was a common and accepted practice in Handel's time, by most accounts he took greater advantage of the custom than most of his contemporaries.

The tenor recitative and chorus that follow the overture tell of the succession of a new pharaoh and the suffering of the Jewish people under his rule. After these come Handel's vivid descriptions of the horrors of the seven plagues that God visited on the Egyptians. The mood then lightens considerably: Handel devotes the remainder of the first part to the choir's recounting, over several movements, the story of the Jews' departure from their slavery in Egypt. Part I ends with what conductor Kurt Pahlen describes as a "devout, monumental song of triumph."

Part II, *Moses' Song,* offers thanks to God for the Israelites' miraculous rescue from the clutches of their Egyptian captors. Hymns of praise, vows of devotion, prayers of thanksgiving, and reminiscences of the flight to freedom pour forth in a glorious series of choral movements, with but a few interruptions for solo or duet movements. The section concludes with the magnificent "Sing ye to the Lord" for soprano and double choir (in this case, the choir divided into eight parts).

Handel led the first performance of *Israel in Egypt* in London on April 4, 1739. Accounts from the time suggest that the choir and orchestra were about the same size, each with approximately thirty members, a necessary balance to ensure that neither group was subservient to the other.

The response at the premiere and at the few performances that followed was rather tepid. The explanation is probably that London audiences loved compositions that featured florid vocal display, so they were disappointed in *Israel in Egypt,* which emphasized the choir, giving little opportunity for virtuoso vocalizing. *Israel in Egypt* has only four arias, compared with fifteen in *Messiah* and twenty-two in *Judas Maccabaeus.*

Despite the early lack of enthusiasm, *Israel in Egypt* has gone on to become one of the most popular of Handel's oratorios. The French writer Romain Rolland, who was trained as a musicologist, once expressed the modern appreciation of *Israel in Egypt* by calling the work "the greatest choral epic that exists."

Part I   EXODUS

1. RECITATIVE: TENOR
   Now there arose a new king over Egypt, which knew not Joseph; and he set over Israel taskmasters to afflict them with burthens, and they made them serve with rigour.   Exod. 1: 8, 11, 13

2. SOLO ALTO AND DOUBLE CHORUS (Largo)
   And the children of Israel sighed by reason of the bondage, and their cry came up unto God. They oppressed them with burthens, and made them serve with rigour; and their cry came up unto God.   Exod. 2: 23

3. RECITATIVE: TENOR
   Then sent He Moses, His servant, and Aaron whom He had cho-

sen; these shewed His signs among them, and wonders in the land of Ham. He turned their waters into blood.   Ps. 105: 26, 27, 29

4. FUGUE: CHORUS (Largo)
They loathed to drink of the river. He turned their waters into blood.   Exod. 7: 18, 19

5. ARIA: ALTO (Andante)
Their land brought forth frogs, yea even in their king's chambers.   Ps. 105: 30

He gave their cattle over to the pestilence; blotches and blains broke forth on man and beast.   Exod. 9: 9, 10

6. DOUBLE CHORUS (Andante larghetto)
He spake the word, and there came all manner of flies and lice in all their quarters. He spake; and the locusts came without number, and devoured the fruits of the ground.   Ps. 105: 31, 34, 35

7. DOUBLE CHORUS (Allegro)
He gave them hailstones for rain; fire mingled with the hail ran along upon the ground.   Ps. 105: 32; Exod. 9: 23, 24

8. CHORUS (Largo)
He sent a thick darkness over the land, even darkness which might be felt.   Exod. 10: 21

9. DOUBLE FUGUE: CHORUS (A tempo giusto)
He smote all the first-born of Egypt, the chief of all their strength.   Ps. 105: 36

10. CHORUS (Andante)
But as for His people, He led them forth like sheep: He brought them out with silver and gold; there was not one feeble person among their tribes.   Ps. 78: 52; 105: 37

11. DOUBLE FUGUE: CHORUS (A tempo giusto)
Egypt was glad when they departed, for the fear of them fell upon them.   Ps. 105: 38

12. RECITATIVE: DOUBLE CHORUS (Grave)
He rebuked the Red Sea, and it was dried up.   Ps. 106: 9

13. DOUBLE FUGUE: CHORUS (A tempo giusto)
He led them through the deep as through a wilderness.   Ps. 106: 9

14. CHORUS (A tempo giusto)
But the waters overwhelmed their enemies, there was not one of them left.   Ps. 106: 11

15. DOUBLE CHORUS [Transition] (Grave)
And Israel saw that great work that the Lord did upon the Egyptians: and the people feared the Lord.   Exod. 14: 31

16. FUGUE: CHORUS (Larghetto)
And believed the Lord and His servant Moses.   Exod. 14: 31

Part II   MOSES' SONG

17. DOUBLE CHORUS (A tempo giusto)
Moses and the children of Israel sang this song unto the Lord, and spake saying: Exod. 15: 1

18. DOUBLE CHORUS (Andante)
I will sing unto the Lord, for He hath triumphed gloriously: the horse and his rider hath He thrown into the sea.   Exod. 15: 1

19. DUET FOR TWO SOPRANOS (Larghetto)
The Lord is my strength and my song; He is become my salvation.   Exod. 15: 2

20. DOUBLE CHORUS (Grave)
He is my God, and I will prepare Him an habitation: my father's God.   Exod. 15: 2

21. CHORUS (Andante)
And I will exalt Him.   Exod. 15: 2

22. DUET FOR TWO BASSOS (Andante allegro)
The Lord is a man of war: Lord is His name. Pharaoh's chariots and his host hath He cast into the sea; his chosen captains also are drowned in the Red Sea.   Exod. 15: 3, 4

23. DOUBLE CHORUS (Largo)
The depths have covered them: they sank into the bottom as a stone.   Exod. 15: 5

24. DOUBLE CHORUS (Andante)
Thy right hand, O Lord, is become glorious in power: Thy right hand, O Lord, hath dashed in pieces the enemy.   Exod. 15: 6

25. DOUBLE CHORUS (Adagio)
And in the greatness of Thine excellency Thou hast overthrown them that rose up against Thee.   Exod. 15: 7

26. FUGUE: DOUBLE CHORUS (Andante)
Thou sentest forth Thy wrath, which consumed them as stubble.   Exod. 15: 7

27. CHORUS (Andante)
And with the blast of Thy nostrils the waters were gathered together, the floods stood upright as an heap, and the depths were congealed in the heart of the sea.   Exod. 15: 8

28. ARIA: TENOR (Andante)
The enemy said, I will pursue, I will overtake, I will divide the spoil; my lust shall be satisfied upon them; I will draw my sword, my hand shall destroy them.   Exod. 15: 9

29. ARIA: SOPRANO (Andante larghetto)
Thou didst blow with the wind, the sea covered them; they sank as lead in the mighty waters.   Exod. 15: 10

30. DOUBLE CHORUS (Grave)
Who is like unto Thee, O Lord, among the gods? Who is like Thee, glorious in holiness, fearful in praises, doing wonders? Thou stretchedst out Thy right hand.   Exod. 15: 11, 12

31. FUGUE: DOUBLE CHORUS (Andante)
The earth swallowed them.   Exod. 15: 12

32. DUET FOR ALTO AND TENOR (Larghetto)
Thou in Thy mercy hast led forth Thy people which Thou hast redeemed; Thou hast guided them in Thy strength unto Thy holy habitation.   Exod. 15: 13

33. DOUBLE CHORUS (Largo)
The people shall hear, and be afraid: sorrow shall take hold on them; all the inhabitants of Canaan shall melt away: by the greatness of Thy arm they shall be as still as a stone; till Thy people pass over, O Lord, which Thou hast purchased.   Exod. 15: 14–16

34. ARIA: ALTO (Largo)
Thou shalt bring them in, and plant them in the mountain of Thine inheritance, in the place, O Lord, which Thou hast made for Thee

to dwell in, in the Sanctuary, O Lord, which Thy hands have established.   Exod. 15: 17

35. DOUBLE CHORUS (A tempo giusto)
The Lord shall reign for ever and ever.   Exod. 15: 18

36. RECITATIVE: TENOR
For the horse of Pharaoh went in with his chariots and with his horsemen into the sea, and the Lord brought again the waters of the sea upon them; but the children of Israel went on dry land in the midst of the sea.   Exod. 15: 19

37. DOUBLE CHORUS (A tempo giusto) [Repeat]
The Lord shall reign for ever and ever.   Exod. 15: 18

38. RECITATIVE: TENOR
And Miriam the prophetess, the sister of Aaron, took a timbrel in her hand; and all the women went out after her with timbrels and with dances. And Miriam answered them: Exod. 15: 20, 21

39. SOLO SOPRANO AND DOUBLE CHORUS
Sing ye to the Lord, for He hath triumphed gloriously; the horse and his rider hath He thrown into the sea.   Exod. 15: 21, 18

MESSIAH

2 hours, 30 minutes

Messiah unquestionably holds the position of most frequently performed choral masterpiece—a unique distinction it has maintained for nearly 260 years! Every Christmas season, particularly in America, England, and the rest of the English-speaking world, countless concert halls and churches present this magnificent work. Modern performances of *Messiah,* though, bear only minimal resemblance to the eighteenth-century performances that Handel led. One distinction is that Handel always performed this oratorio in the spring, during the Easter season—not at Christmas. Also, Handel used a small choir and a larger orchestra. The accounts of one Handel performance show that there were only twenty-one choristers and five soloists, but thirty-seven instrumentalists!

In recent years, advances in musical scholarship and the growth of the early music movement have led many to attempt "authentic" performances and recordings of *Messiah*. Unfortunately, it is virtually impossible to determine the single definitive version of *Messiah*. Leaving aside the ever present problems of trying to duplicate the tempi, performing style, and particular sound qualities of music from the distant past, there are a bewildering number of seemingly original versions of *Messiah*. Which is the most authentic version? Handel's autograph copy from 1741? The 1742 Dublin premiere copy? The music used for the Covent Garden performance of 1743, of 1745, of 1749, or of 1750? The copy from the 1759 Foundling Hospital presentation? The working score Handel used for the performances he directed? Or the published score of 1761?

To the distress of musicologists and the confusion of performers, no two of these versions are identical. Study of the various scores and of the performances makes it clear that most of the changes were made to accommodate particular performers who were available—or not available—to sing on particular dates. As an example, when the amazing and extremely popular Italian castrato Gaetano Guadagni came to London, Handel did not hesitate to transpose the bass solos up to the alto range and give them to Guadagni.

Handel himself made a few of the changes when he decided that a specific section might be improved. Believing that the original three-measure instrumental introduction to the recitative "Thus saith the Lord" lacked dramatic impact, he substituted a much more potent one-measure instrumental opening. Also, since Handel composed the music very quickly, a few of the changes were corrections of errors in the manuscript.

Handel composed *Messiah* in the incredibly short period of twenty-four days—from August 22 to September 14, 1741. During the writing he commented in a letter to his friend Dr. Allott, "I did think I did see all Heaven before me, and the great

God himself." The first performance of *Messiah* was given in Dublin on April 13, 1742, with the composer conducting.

Messiah is an oratorio—a work for soloists, choir, and orchestra created, according to Handel scholar Donald Burrows, "by the application of theatrical musical techniques to a sacred story." And Handel was indeed a master of "theatrical musical techniques." After composing two oratorios in 1708 *(La Resurrezione* and *Il trionfo del Tempo e del Disinganno),* Handel devoted all of his energies to writing and presenting Italian operas in London from 1711 until the late 1720s. By the 1730s, though, Handel's operatic ventures had fallen from favor, and it was then that the composer returned to the oratorio form, turning out close to twenty works of that type—the most famous being *Messiah.*

While Handel based his other oratorios on the Old Testament and themes from Jewish history, the *Messiah* text was largely drawn from the New Testament by Charles Jennens, Handel's friend and wealthy admirer and a part-time poet. (Although some believe the compilation was prepared by Jennens's assistant, a Mr. Pooley, there is little evidence to support that contention.)

The late, great Handel scholar Jens Peter Larsen gave perhaps the best brief description of *Messiah:*

> *Messiah* is not, as is often popularly supposed, a number of scenes from the Life of Jesus linked together to form a certain dramatic whole, but a representation of the fulfillment of Redemption through the Redeemer, Messiah. *Messiah* is divided into three Parts, the contents of which can be summarized as follows: I. The prophecy and realization of God's Plan to redeem mankind by the coming of the Messiah; II. The accomplishment of redemption by the sacrifice of Jesus, mankind's rejection of God's offer and mankind's utter defeat when trying to oppose the power of the Almighty; III. A Hymn of Thanksgiving for the final overthrow of Death.

Messiah contains about fifty individual selections, the exact number varying with the particular edition. Many modern performances, though, omit several sections either to fit in with what is appropriate for a seasonal presentation or for reasons of length.

PART I

"Sinfonia." The orchestral overture, in two connected parts— the first slow with a characteristic long/short rhythmic pattern, the second a three-part fugue in a moderately fast tempo. The mood is solemn and severe throughout.

"Comfort ye." Recitative for tenor solo, the first of the three "promise" numbers, referring to God's promise to send a Messiah. The E major tonality gives this movement a luminous glow after the darker E minor of the "Sinfonia."

"Every valley." A tenor aria of great joy and happiness, with striking expressive coloraturas on the words "exalted" and "plain."

"And the glory." The first choral number, it continues the jubilant good spirits of the two preceding movements with choral textures that range from responsorial to imitative to chordal.

"Thus saith the Lord." This bass recitative strikes an impressive note of wonder and awe as God announces the coming of the Messiah. Note especially the depiction of the trembling by the coloratura on the word "shake."

"But who may abide." An aria originally written for alto (the castrato Guadagni), which is now usually sung by a bass. Operatic in style, the aria contrasts the quiet questioning of the opening with a fast, agitated episode expressing the fear of God's intervention. Both parts are then freely repeated.

"And He shall purify." A choral reworking of an earlier vocal duet, it retains the clear, transparent sound of a duet while continuing with the text from the previous movement.

"Behold, a Virgin shall conceive." A brief recitative for alto that leads directly into:

"O thou that tellest." A joyful alto aria in which Handel uses an ascending line to illustrate the words "into the high mountain" and a leaping melody for "lift up." The aria moves, without pause, into a chorus on the same text. Although the chorus

starts with imitative counterpoint, the voices quickly coalesce into a chordal, homophonic texture.

"For, behold." In this slow, solemn recitative for bass, Handel most effectively conjures up the gloom expressed in the text.

"The people that walked in the darkness." This bass aria immediately spreads its warm, bright light, reflecting the text: "The people that walked in the darkness . . . have seen a great light."

"For unto us." A rapturous choral announcement of the birth of Jesus that starts quietly, with different imitative pairings within the choir, before whipping up to the climactic "Wonderful, Counsellor."

"Pifa." The orchestral introduction to the section dealing with the birth of Christ. In Italy it was the custom for the shepherds to play the *pifa* (an oboelike shepherd's instrument that is also known as a *pifari* or shawm) during Christmas services. Handel's *"Pifa"* is a pastoral symphony that imbues the gently rocking rhythm of a siciliano with a tender, folklike quality.

"There were shepherds." The soprano soloist first sings a group of four brief recitatives—the first and third without accompaniment, the second and fourth accompanied. The final one leads directly to:

"Glory to God." A triumphant paean of praise that starts homophonically, becomes fugal in texture, then ends quietly. This conclusion to the extremely short Christmas section confirms the interpretation of many that the focus of *Messiah* is on the coming of the Redeemer and redemption, not the birth and life of Jesus.

"Rejoice." This soprano aria opens the final group of Part I, which concerns Christ's wanderings in the period before Passion Week. Ringing out like a trumpet call, the soprano part leaps upward in exultant joy, expressing elation in brilliant coloratura. A quieter middle section, "He is the righteous Saviour," precedes a foreshortened return of the opening character.

"Then shall the eyes of the blind." A short recitative retells the story of the curing of the sick.

"He shall feed His flock." An aria in pastoral style with the

gently rocking long/short rhythmic pattern of a siciliano. The form is strange: the alto sings the aria (in F major), Handel inserts a transition, and the soprano sings a very similar aria four notes higher (in B flat). Disagreement exists as to whether Handel chose this structure to conform to the availability of a particular soloist whose presence would help sell tickets, or whether he determined to lend variety to what is essentially a repetition of the aria.

"His yoke is easy." Although this chorus is the final section of Part I, it does not convey a strong sense of closure. Handel bases the movement, a fugue, on a vocal duet that he had composed earlier. The writing throughout is rather spare and thin until the end, when the entire choir sings together.

PART II

"Behold, the Lamb of God." This section focuses on the central idea of redemption through His suffering. The chorus conveys great pain and solemnity with its descending line, but then it expresses a modicum of hope in the upward tendency of "that taketh away the sin."

"He was despised." In this section, which is structured as a classic da capo aria, the first part depicts the anguish of loneliness; the middle section, with its throbbing accompaniment, deals with the violence inflicted on Jesus; and the final part is a literal repeat of the opening.

"Surely He hath borne our griefs." The throbbing rhythm from the middle section of "He was despised" returns for this powerful chorus, which leads without pause into:

"And with His stripes." This choral fugue, based on two motifs—a slow-moving melody with some leaps, and a slightly faster descending-scale line—is restrained in emotional impact. This chorus flows directly into:

"All we like sheep." This chorus betrays its origins as a vocal duet in the two-part scoring that prevails throughout, the major exceptions being repetitions of "All we like sheep" and the ending.

"All they that see Him." The throbbing rhythm reappears for this agitated tenor aria, which is interrupted by outbursts of the crowd's anger.

"He trusted in God." A choral fugue that follows without a break, depicting the rejection of Jesus by the crowd.

"Thy rebuke has broken His heart." This sorrowful tenor recitative is the first of four tenor solos on the pain of being forsaken.

"Behold, and see." The mournful mood continues in this halting arioso.

"He was cut off." This short recitative maintains the same character.

"But Thou did'st not leave His soul in hell." An emotional aria that changes the tone to one of release from darkness and pain.

"Lift up your heads." One of the best-known choruses of *Messiah,* this movement divides the choir in various ways, especially in the early question-answer part of the movement, to achieve striking antiphonal effects.

"Unto which of the angels." A brief tenor recitative that starts the section proclaiming the gospel.

"Let all the angels of God worship Him." A fugal song of praise, in which the subject is first heard in one form and then with the note values cut in half (diminution).

"Thou art gone up." A broad, dignified aria for bass that is sometimes sung by the alto.

"The Lord gave the word." Strong and declamatory, this chorus pits the held notes of "The Lord gave the word" against the fast-moving notes of the rest of the text.

"How beautiful are the feet." Handel entrusts the soprano with this calm, quiet aria, which is pervaded by an unmistakable pastoral quality.

"Their sound is gone out." A vibrant, active chorus, fugal in texture, proclaiming the spread of the gospel to all the world.

"Why do the nations." After a fanfare-like introduction, the bass enters in this powerful, dramatic aria that perfectly expresses the "furious rage" of the text.

"Let us break their bonds." The staggered entrances of this fugal chorus contribute to the impression of an agitated, restless crowd calling out from all sides.

"He that dwelleth in heaven." A brief tenor recitative that leads to:

"Thou shalt break them." There is no rest or relaxation in the intensity of the anger in this aria.

"Hallelujah." The culminating chorus of *Messiah,* the end of Part II, and surely the best loved and most popular of all choruses. (Regarding the custom of standing during the "Hallelujah Chorus," *Messiah* scholar Donald Burrows questions whether King George II, who presumably led the audience to rise, ever attended a *Messiah* performance!)

PART III

"I know that my Redeemer liveth." A confident, self-possessed soprano aria that launches the final section, which deals with death and resurrection.

"Since by man came death." After the hushed, slow, sustained opening of this chorus, the choir bursts forth with a loud, fast-moving, detached-note section, followed by another pair of slow-fast divisions.

"Behold, I tell you a mystery." This recitative sets the stage for:

"The trumpet shall sound." The lengthy introduction, with its prominent trumpet part, proclaims the coming of the Day of Judgment and the awakening of the dead. In this movement, which is written as a da capo aria for bass, the contemplative middle section is heard before the repeat of the opening; the trumpet player usually decorates and embellishes Handel's original trumpet part in the repeat.

"Then shall be brought to pass." A very short recitative for alto.

"O death, where is thy sting?" A duet for alto and tenor in which Handel treats the voices in imitation.

"But thanks be to God." After a homophonic opening, the

texture of this chorus is mostly fugal until the last few measures, which return to homophony.

"If God be for us." Handel has made this very emotional and expressive aria a sort of dialogue between the soprano and the orchestra violins.

"Worthy is the Lamb." The beginning of the oratorio's concluding choral triptych. This homophonic chorus is alternately slow and fast, imitating human declamation.

"Blessing, and honour." A striking feature of this polyphonic chorus is the nine repetitions of the high note in the principal theme.

"Amen." Following without pause, this chorus continues the previous polyphony, starting a fugue in the basses and working up through the choir to the sopranos. Using but one word of text, the movement keeps building until the final "Amen," a glorious, ringing affirmation of faith.

Those interested in learning more details of Handel's many changes and revisions in *Messiah* may find these books useful: Jens Peter Larsen, *Handel's Messiah,* second edition (Norton, New York, 1989) and Donald Burrows, *Handel: Messiah* (Cambridge University Press, Cambridge, 1991).

1. Sinfonia

PART I

2. Arioso

Comfort ye, comfort ye my people, saith your God.

(Isaiah XL: 1)

Speak ye comfortably to Jerusalem, and cry unto her, that her warfare is accomplished, that her iniquity is pardoned: . . .

(Isaiah XL: 2)

The voice of him that crieth in the wilderness, Prepare ye the way of the Lord, make straight in the desert a highway for our God.

(Isaiah XL: 3)

3. Air

Every valley shall be exalted, and every mountain and hill . . .

made low: . . . the crooked . . . straight, and the rough places plain: (Isaiah XL: 4)

4. *Chorus*

And the glory of the Lord shall be revealed, and all flesh shall see it together: for the mouth of the Lord hath spoken it.

(Isaiah XL: 5)

5. *Accompanied Recitative*

. . . thus saith the Lord of hosts; Yet once, . . . a little while, and I will shake the heavens, and the earth, . . . the sea, and the dry land; (Haggai II: 6)

And I will shake all nations, and the desire of all nations shall come: . . . (Haggai II: 7)

. . . the Lord, whom ye seek, shall suddenly come to His temple, even the messenger of the covenant, whom ye delight in: behold, He shall come, saith the Lord of hosts. (Malachi III: 1)

6. *Air*

But who may abide the day of His coming? And who shall stand when He appeareth? For He is like a refiner's fire, . . .

(Malachi III: 2)

7. *Chorus*

. . . and He shall purify the sons of Levi, . . . that they may offer unto the Lord an offering in righteousness. (Malachi III: 3)

8. *Recitative*

. . . Behold, a virgin shall conceive, and bear a son, and shall call His name Immanuel, "God-with-us." (Isaiah VII: 14)

9. *Air and Chorus*

O thou that tellest good tidings to Zion, get thee up into the high mountain; O thou that tellest good tidings to Jerusalem, lift up thy voice with strength; lift it up, be not afraid; say unto the cities of Judah, Behold your God! (Isaiah XL: 9)

Arise, shine; for thy light is come, and the glory of the Lord is risen upon thee. (Isaiah LX: 1)

10. *Arioso*

For, behold, . . . darkness shall cover the earth, and gross darkness the people: but the Lord shall arise upon thee, and His glory shall be seen upon thee. (Isaiah LX: 2)

And the Gentiles shall come to thy light, and kings to the bright-
ness of thy rising.   (Isaiah LX: 3)

11. *Air*
   The people that walked in the darkness have seen a great light:
and they that dwell in the land of the shadow of death, upon them
hath the light shined.   (Isaiah IX: 2)

12. *Chorus*
   For unto us a child is born, unto us a son is given: and the
government shall be upon His shoulder: and His name shall be
called Wonderful, Counsellor, The Mighty God, The Everlasting
Father, The Prince of Peace.   (Isaiah IX: 6)

13. *Pifa (Pastoral Symphony)*

14. *Recitative*
   . . . there were . . . shepherds abiding in the field, keeping
watch over their flock by night.   (Luke II: 8)

15. *Arioso*
   And, lo, the angel of the Lord came upon them, and the glory of
the Lord shone round about them: and they were sore afraid.
                                                       (Luke II: 9)

16. *Recitative*
   And the angel said unto them, Fear not: for, behold, I bring you
good tidings of great joy, which shall be to all people.
                                                      (Luke II: 10)
   For unto you is born this day in the city of David a Saviour,
which is Christ the Lord.   (Luke II: 11)

17. *Arioso*
   And suddenly there was with the angel a multitude of the heavenly host praising God, and saying,   (Luke II: 13)

18. *Chorus*
   Glory to God in the highest, and peace on earth, good will to-
wards men.   (Luke II: 14)

19. *Air*
   Rejoice greatly, O daughter of Zion; shout, O daughter of Jeru-
salem: behold, thy King cometh unto thee: He is the righteous
Saviour, . . .   (Zechariah IX: 9)

. . . and He shall speak peace unto the heathen: . . .

(Zechariah IX: 10)

20. *Recitative*

Then shall the eyes of the blind be opened, and the ears of the deaf . . . unstopped. (Isaiah XXXV: 5)

Then shall the lame man leap as a hart, and the tongue of the dumb shall sing: . . . (Isaiah XXXV: 6)

21. *Air*

He shall feed His flock like a shepherd: and He shall gather the lambs with His arm, and carry them in His bosom, and . . . gently lead those that are with young. (Isaiah XL: 11)

Come unto Him, all ye that labour and are heavy laden, and He will give you rest. (Matthew XI: 28)

Take His yoke upon you, and learn of Him, for He is meek and lowly of heart: and ye shall find rest unto your souls.

(Matthew XI: 29)

22. *Chorus*

. . . His yoke is easy, and His burthen is light.

(Matthew XI: 30)

PART II

23. *Chorus*

. . . Behold, the Lamb of God, that taketh away the sin of the world! . . . (John I: 29)

24. *Air*

He was despised and rejected of men; a man of sorrows, and acquainted with grief: . . . (Isaiah LIII: 3)

He gave His back to the smiters, and His cheeks to them that plucked off the hair: He hid not His face from shame and spitting. (Isaiah L: 6)

25. *Chorus*

Surely He hath borne our griefs, and carried our sorrows: . . . (Isaiah LIII: 4)

. . . He was wounded for our transgressions, He was bruised for our iniquities: the chastisement of our peace was upon Him; and with His stripes we are healed. (Isaiah LIII: 5)

All we like sheep have gone astray; we have turned every one to his own way; and the Lord hath laid on Him the iniquity of us all.   (Isaiah LIII: 6)

26. *Arioso*

All they that see Him laugh Him to scorn: they shoot out their lips, and shake their heads, saying,   (Psalm XXII: 7)

27. *Chorus*

He trusted in God that He would deliver Him: let Him deliver Him, if He delight in Him.   (Psalm XXII: 8)

28. *Accompanied Recitative*

Thy rebuke hath broken His heart; He is full of heaviness: He looked for some to have pity on Him, but there was no man; neither found He any to comfort Him.   (Psalm LXIX: 20)

29. *Arioso*

. . . Behold, and see if there be any sorrow like unto His sorrow, . . .   (Lamentations I: 12)

30. *Accompanied Recitative*

. . . He was cut off out of the land of the living: for the transgression of thy people was He stricken.   (Isaiah LIII: 8)

31. *Air*

But thou didst not leave His soul in hell; nor didst thou suffer thy Holy One to see corruption.   (Psalm XVI: 10)

32. *Chorus*

Lift up your heads, O ye gates; and be ye lift up, ye everlasting doors; and the King of glory shall come in.   (Psalm XXIV: 7)

Who is this King of glory? The Lord strong and mighty, the Lord mighty in battle.   (Psalm XXIV: 8)

Lift up your heads, O ye gates; and be ye lift up, ye everlasting doors; and the King of glory shall come in.   (Psalm XXIV: 9)

Who is this King of glory? The Lord of hosts, He is the King of glory.   (Psalm XXIV: 10)

33. *Recitative*

. . . unto which of the angels said He at any time, Thou art my Son, this day have I begotten thee? . . .   (Hebrews I: 5)

34. *Chorus*

. . . let all the angels of God worship Him.   (Hebrews I: 6)

35. *Air*

Thou art gone up on high, thou hast led captivity captive: and received gifts for men; yea, even for thine enemies, that the Lord God might dwell among them.   (Psalm LXVIII: 18)

36. *Chorus*

The Lord gave the word: great was the company of the preachers.   (Psalm LXVIII: 11)

37. *Air and Chorus*

. . . How beautiful are the feet of them that preach the gospel of peace, and bring glad tidings of good things! (Romans X: 15)

. . . their sound is gone out unto all lands, and their words unto the ends of the world.   (Romans X: 18)

38. *Air—Accompanied Recitative*

Why do the nations so furiously rage together, . . . why do the people imagine a vain thing?   (Psalm II: 1)

The kings of the earth rise up, and the rulers take counsel together, against the Lord, and against His anointed, . . .

(Psalm II: 2)

39. *Chorus*

Let us break their bonds asunder, and cast away their yokes from us.   (Psalm II: 3)

40. *Recitative*

He that dwelleth in heaven shall laugh them to scorn: the Lord shall have them in derision.   (Psalm II: 4)

41. *Air*

Thou shalt break them with a rod of iron; thou shalt dash them in pieces like a potter's vessel.   (Psalm II: 9)

42. *Chorus*

Hallelujah: for the Lord God omnipotent reigneth.

(Revelation XIX: 6)

. . . The kingdom of this world is become the kingdom of our Lord, and of His Christ; and He shall reign for ever and ever.   (Revelation XI: 15)

. . . King of Kings, and Lord of Lords. (Revelation XIX: 16)

Part III

43. *Air*

. . . I know that my redeemer liveth, and that He shall stand at the latter day upon the earth: (Job XIX: 25)

And though . . . worms destroy this body, yet in my flesh shall I see God.   (Job XIX: 26)

For now is Christ risen from the dead, . . . the first fruits of them that sleep.   (I Corinthians XV: 20)

44. *Chorus*

. . . since by man came death, by man came also the resurrection of the dead.   (I Corinthians XV: 21)

For as in Adam all die, even so in Christ shall all be made alive.(I Corinthians XV: 22)

45. *Accompanied Recitative*

Behold, I tell you a mystery; We shall not all sleep, but we shall all be changed,   (I Corinthians XV: 51)

In a moment, in the twinkling of an eye at the last trumpet:
(I Corinthians XV: 52)

46. *Air*

. . . the trumpet shall sound, and the dead shall be raised incorruptible, and we shall be changed.   (I Corinthians XV: 52)

For this corruptible must put on incorruption, and this mortal must put on immortality.   (I Corinthians XV: 53)

47. *Recitative*

. . . then shall be brought to pass the saying that is written, Death is swallowed up in victory.   (I Corinthians XV: 54)

48a. *Duet*

O death, where is thy sting? O grave, where is thy victory?
(I Corinthians XV: 55)

The sting of death is sin; and the strength of sin is the law.
(I Corinthians XV: 56)

48b. *Chorus*

But thanks be to God, who giveth us the victory through our Lord Jesus Christ.   (I Corinthians XV: 57)

49. *Air*

. . . If God be for us who can be against us?
(Romans VIII: 31)

Who shall lay any thing to the charge of God's elect? It is God that justifieth.   (Romans VIII: 33)

Who is he that condemneth? It is Christ that died, yea rather, that is risen again, who is . . . at the right hand of God, who . . . maketh intercession for us.   (Romans VIII: 34)

50. *Chorus*

. . . Worthy is the Lamb that was slain and hath redeemed us to God by His blood to receive power, and riches, and wisdom, and strength, and honour, and glory, and blessing. (Revelation V: 12)

. . . Blessing, and honour, . . . glory, and power, be unto Him that sitteth upon the throne, and unto the Lamb for ever and ever.   (Revelation V: 13)

AMEN

SAMSON

2 hours, 5 minutes

Newburgh Hamilton, librettist of *Samson,* probably approached Handel sometime in 1741 to suggest an oratorio on the subject of the ancient Jewish hero. Hamilton proposed to draw the text from John Milton's 1671 poetic drama *"Samson Agonistes"* ("Samson, the Wrestler"), to shorten the poem by about half, and to select additional material from the Bible and other Milton poems.

In his preface to the word book of *Samson,* Hamilton clearly states his view of the work: "A musical Drama, whose subject must be Scriptural, and in which the Solemnity of Church Musick is agreeably united with the most pleasing Airs of the Stage." Evidence that Hamilton was concerned with the theatrical is found in his division of the oratorio into three "acts," instead of the more usual "parts." All this despite the fact that Milton was a Puritan and wanted the drama to be read, not presented as theatrical entertainment.

Some fault Hamilton for tampering with Milton's words and with the poet's vision of his own work. On the other hand, many agree with Winton Dean, who, in his book on the Handel oratorios, praises Hamilton for his skill in reworking Milton's poem to create a very successful libretto that fulfills the musical needs of the oratorio without unnecessarily violating Milton's original concept.

Handel composed *Samson* very quickly, in about five weeks sometime late in 1741, after finishing *Messiah* in September of that year. He revised and expanded the work during the following year and led the first performance in London's Covent Garden on February 18, 1743. *Samson* proved to be a huge success, greater than the initial success of *Messiah*. *Samson* was repeated eight more times that season, had several performances every year for the following nine seasons, and was the first of Handel's oratorios to be published.

Handel gave solo parts in *Samson* to five major characters: Samson (tenor), a hero of ancient Israel famed for his amazing strength; Delilah (soprano), a beautiful Philistine who betrayed Samson; Micah (alto), a friend of Samson's, who was created by Hamilton; Manoah (bass), Samson's father; Harapha (bass), a Philistine giant, who was created by Milton.

The oratorio opens with a lengthy, solemn orchestral sinfonia. Handel devotes most of Act I to Samson, blinded and a prisoner of the Philistines, singing of his despair and misery and trying to understand the philosophical meaning of his hopeless situation. The composer then presents, in stark contrast, the wild abandon of the Philistine festival dedicated to the pagan god Dagon, an event of Hamilton's invention. Handel sounds the only note of hope in the chorus of Israelites, who sing "Oh first created beam."

Samson's beloved, Delilah, appears in Act II. By having his hair cut while he slept, she robbed him of his strength. Now she tries to rekindle Samson's love for her, but he angrily rejects her advances. Near the end of the act, Samson battles and vanquishes the Philistine giant, Harapha.

Act III builds up to the climactic scene of the oratorio, in which Samson is brought to the temple of Dagon to be mocked by the Philistines. His hair, and strength, now back, the once again mighty Samson pushes apart the pillars of the temple, bringing down the monumental structure and killing himself along with the Philistines. Handel vividly describes the scene in another sinfonia.

Some of the most inspired music of the oratorio follows: the chorus of Philistines bewailing the destruction of the temple; a recitative for Micah, Manoah, and a Messenger describing the scene; Micah's mourning aria, "Ye sons of Israel"; the lamenting chorus of Israelites singing "Weep, Israel"; the funeral march; and the Requiem for Samson sung by the Israelites.

In his original version of 1741, Handel ended the oratorio at this point. The following year he expanded the work and added a soprano aria, "Let the bright Seraphim"—which has become one of the best-known selections of the work—and a concluding chorus. Dramatically, the additions do not contribute to *Samson,* but the music is so glorious that we would all be the poorer without them.

JUDAS MACCABAEUS

2 hours, 50 minutes

On August 12, 1745, Prince Charles Edward, the "Young Pretender," landed in Scotland and rallied his supporters in a final attempt by the house of Stuart to overthrow the Hanoverian King George II. The prince's forces gained some victories, but on April 16, 1746, they were soundly defeated at Culloden Muir (near Inverness) by the English troops led by King George II's younger son, William, Duke of Cumberland.

Shortly after the victory, the duke's older brother, Frederick, Prince of Wales, asked Handel to compose an oratorio celebrating the event—a work which might be performed to honor the Duke of Cumberland on his return to London. Being a loyal supporter of King George, the composer was only too happy to oblige. Scholars believe that it was Frederick who proposed that

Handel use the story of Judas Maccabaeus as metaphor for the recent battle and triumph.

The ancient hero, Judas Maccabaeus, freed the Jewish people from the bondage imposed on them by King Antiochus IV (called Epiphanes) of the Seleucid Empire. Antiochus, in order to impose a belief in the pagan Greek gods on the Jewish people, forbade them to practice their religion and erected an altar to Zeus in the Temple in Jerusalem.

Judas brought together a Jewish army that, although vastly outnumbered, defeated Antiochus. Around the year 165 B.C., Judas entered Jerusalem and rededicated the Temple—an event that is commemorated by the eight-day Jewish festival of Hanukkah.

For the libretto, Handel called on the Reverend Thomas Morell, who used as his source Book I of the Maccabees. According to the manuscript, the composer started on the music either July 8 or 9, 1746, and completed the task in just over a month, on August 11.

As was the custom of the day, Handel borrowed and adapted several sections of *Judas Maccabaeus* from portions of works by other composers. Scholars have traced parts of *Judas Maccabaeus* to compositions by Georg Philipp Telemann, Giacomo Carissimi, Giovanni Bononcini, and Gottlieb Muffat. In addition, Handel included music from his own earlier compositions, among them the *Occasional Oratorio* of 1746 and the 1709 opera *Agrippina*.

The premiere—on April 1, 1747, led by the composer at Covent Garden in London—was an immense success. The work was repeated five more times that season and was frequently performed thereafter; Handel is reputed to have conducted it well over thirty times!

One reason for the appeal of *Judas Maccabaeus* had to do with the Jews of London. Never big supporters of Handel's previous oratorios (as he said about another oratorio, "The Jews will not come because it is a Christian story"), they flocked to hear *Judas Maccabaeus*. Also, the Duke of Cumberland was a popular figure, even though he was nicknamed "Billy the

Butcher" because of his cruelty in battle, and many wanted to participate in ceremonies honoring his victory. Finally, the lively, tuneful choral writing captivates with its appealing songs of courage and patriotism.

After the rather stern overture of Part I (the part's title reads *Chorus of Israelites, Men and Women, Lamenting the Death of Mattathias, Father of Judas Maccabaeus)*, the chorus bewails the death of Mattathias, the High Priest. Various figures emerge as the mourning continues, but curiously enough, the libretto names only two characters: Judas (tenor) and his brother, Simon (bass). The focus gradually turns to the future of Israel and the need for a new leader. Simon announces in a recitative and following aria ("Arm, arm, ye brave!") that Judas is the one to help the Jewish people. Judas accepts the challenge, and Part I ends with a chorus of prayer, "Hear us, O Lord."

Part II, *The Israelites Celebrating the Return of Judas from the Victories over Apollonius and Seron,* is happy and joyful until a messenger brings the news that Antiochus (read Prince Charles Edward) is advancing on Israel. In a famous aria, "Sound an alarm," that glistens with brilliant trumpet writing, Judas calls his men to battle. The choir sings of the Israelite's resolve, "We never will bow down," to end Part II.

The victorious return of Judas (read Duke of Cumberland) becomes the central theme of Part III, *Israelitish Priests, Etc., Having Recovered the Sanctuary.* Word comes of the distant success in battle, and the chorus of Israelites sings the stirring "See, the conqu'ring hero comes!" for mixed choir and boys' choir. Handel actually added this chorus after the first performance, appropriating it from his 1747 oratorio *Joshua.* Several numbers in praise of peace follow, capped off by the resplendent choral "Amen!" that brings the entire oratorio to a thrilling conclusion.

SOLOMON

2 hours, 35 minutes

Letters and other papers from the time show that Handel wrote his oratorio *Judas Maccabaeus* as metaphor for the victory of the Duke of Cumberland over the rebel forces of Prince Charles Edward. Although lacking such specific evidence, many scholars believe that *Solomon* is Handel's portrayal of an ideal society as metaphor for England under King George II, who was Handel's patron and object of great admiration.

Information is also lacking on the librettist for *Solomon*. Some commentators suggest that the Reverend Thomas Morell is the writer, but the text is so unlike Morell's other efforts that this claim is most suspect; although based on biblical sources— mostly II Chronicles and I Kings—the story does not stress the religious aspects.

Solomon, son of David, ruled Israel in its greatest days of power and prosperity. Perhaps his most signal accomplishment was the construction of the magnificent Temple in Jerusalem. According to the biblical account, the Lord appeared to Solomon in a dream, and the great ruler asked for the gift of wisdom so he might govern his people well. God granted his wish, allowing Solomon to bring ever greater glories to the land of Israel. In time, though, Solomon's unlimited success and power led to abuses, and his fortunes, like those of Israel, faded away.

Handel composed *Solomon* in the few weeks from May 5 to June 13, 1748, and led the first performance at Covent Garden, London, on March 17, 1749. The reception did not live up to expectations, and after repeat performances on March 20 and 22, the work was not heard again until March 1759, a few weeks before the composer's death.

In addition to the mixed choir—which is often divided into either five or eight parts—Handel's score calls for a number of vocal soloists: Solomon, King of Israel, originally written for alto, now usually sung by a baritone; Zadok, High Priest, tenor; the Queen, Pharaoh's daughter and wife of Solomon, soprano; Queen of Sheba, soprano; the two harlots, sopranos; and a Levite, bass.

Solomon opens with a substantial overture. The ensuing first act shows us Solomon's piety, first as builder of the Temple and then as devoted husband to his queen. Interestingly enough, the text makes no mention of his seven hundred wives and three hundred concubines! The opening chorus, "Your harps and cymbals sound," issues a bold call for music to sanctify the new Temple; this chorus is followed by the movements devoted to the Temple's consecration. The scene and mood then change for the conversation between Solomon and his queen, with a brief interpolation by Zadok, the High Priest, and a final chorus.

A glorious eight-part chorus of praise for Solomon, "From the censer curling rise," and his response, the recitative "Praised be the Lord," open the second act. Handel devotes the rest of this section to the famous story of the two harlots, each claiming to be the mother of an infant, who ask Solomon to decide between them. When Solomon suggests that he will split the child in two so each can have a share, the first harlot immediately offers to relinquish her share to spare the baby, convincing Solomon that she is indeed the true mother.

Act III, which Handel precedes with a sinfonia, recounts the visit of the Queen of Sheba to Solomon's court and her admiration of its wealth and splendor. (Handel approved of having both queens sung by the same soprano, probably since their appearances are separated by Act II.) Handel projects a wide variety of emotions in the music that follows: tender beauty in the five-part chorus of greeting, "Music, spread thy voice around"; harsh war sounds in the eight-part chorus "Shake the dome and pierce the sky"; mourning for those slain in battle in "Draw the tear from hopeless love"; and the return of serenity in "Thus rolling surges rise." The Queen of Sheba next delivers the gifts she has brought for Solomon, and after they sing their warm farewells, the chorus brings the work to a close with a song of praise to God.

JEPHTHA

2 hours, 45 minutes

Jephtha was Handel's last oratorio and, in fact, his last major work of any kind. Although there was no flagging of his creative imagination or compositional skill, Handel's failing health and worsening eyesight made it very difficult for him to complete this monumental work.

Handel began the composition on January 21, 1751, and stopped on February 13, having only completed the first two parts. On the manuscript he wrote, in German, "Reached here on February 13, 1751; had to quit because of weakening of sight in my left eye." On returning to his desk ten days later, he wrote, "On the 23rd it is a little better, I will resume." He composed for only a few days before quitting once again, and he did not return until the middle of June, when he resumed work, completing the score on August 30, 1751.

By the end of 1751, Handel was completely blind, a condition probably caused by cataracts and three torturous operations that included using a needle to pierce the eyeball—without anesthetic. Nonetheless, he conducted the premiere at Covent Garden, London, on February 26, 1752. In response to the warm reception, Handel repeated the oratorio twice that season and revived it for performances the following year, in 1756, and in 1758.

The Book of Judges, chapter 11, recounts the story of Jephtha. As detailed in the oratorio, the events take place in the land of Israel, which was then under the control of the Ammonites, who force the Israelites to worship their god, Moloch. The Israelites call on Jephtha, an Israelite military leader in exile, to lead them into battle against the oppression of the Ammonites. Before going off to the war, Jephtha vows that, if victorious, he will offer as a sacrifice whoever comes out of his house to greet him on return from battle. Ultimately it is his beloved daughter, his only child, who rushes out to meet him, but both she and Jephtha accept that the vow must be honored and she is sacrificed for the Israelite victory.

The Reverend Thomas Morell, librettist for *Jephtha*, made a few basic revisions in the biblical account. For example, he completely recast the ending, which in the Bible culminates with the sacrifice of the daughter. In the oratorio, a last-minute intercession by an angel spares her life and leads to a happy ending. Further, he either added or named all the characters that join Jephtha (sung by a tenor) in the oratorio: Zebul, Jephtha's half brother (bass); Storgè, Jephtha's wife (alto); Iphis, Jephtha's daughter (soprano); Hamor, an Israelite soldier in love with Iphis (alto); and Angel (boy soprano).

Handel quarreled with a few parts of Morell's text, including the five different places where the composer substituted other expressions for Morell's use of the word "God"—difficult changes to explain since Handel was so firm a believer. Then, in the terribly important chorus that ends Part II—"How dark, O Lord, are Thy decrees!"—Handel altered Morell's last line from "What God ordains is right" to "Whatever is, is right."

Undoubtedly, Handel made *Jephtha* a most profound and personal manifesto. The composer identifies with Jephtha in exploring the theme of humankind's battle with fate and the necessity of submitting to destiny. He states the theme in the words of the solemn recitative that opens *Jephtha*—"It must be so"—and the theme reaches its culmination in the amazing chorus that ends the second part, "How dark, O Lord, are Thy decrees!" Of particular interest are the last two lines of this chorus: "Yet on this maxim still obey./Whatever is, is right." Handel found these words in Alexander Pope's *Essay on Man*. With good reason, Winton Dean, author of *Handel's Dramatic Oratorios and Masques,* calls this chorus "perhaps the profoundest music he [Handel] ever wrote."

In addition to exploring serious philosophical questions in *Jephtha,* Handel creates some of the most remarkably insightful characterizations found in any of his oratorios. He introduces Jephtha as a confident, forthright soldier, soon to be faced with the terrible choice of renouncing his vow or losing his only child. Handel masterfully conveys Jephtha's torment ("Open thy marble jaws, O tomb"), his despair ("Hide thou thy hated beams"), and his final acceptance ("Waft her, angels").

Equally brilliant is Handel's depiction of the personality of the other major figure, Iphis. He perfectly captures her joyful nature by infusing all of her music in the first part of the oratorio with dancelike rhythms. Only after she learns of her father's vow do we become aware of her nobility of character ("For joys so vast") and her self-assured willingness to depart this world ("Ye sacred priests").

The oratorio opens with an impressive overture, after which Zebul describes the situation of the Israelites; then the chorus, representing the Israelites, conjures up the fierce abandon of a wild pagan festival. The subsequent numbers, mostly for solo voices, present Jephtha agreeing to lead the army and making his vow, Hamor and Iphis expressing their love for each other, and Storgè telling of her presentiment of disaster in the recitative and aria "Some dire event hangs o'er our heads."

Part II starts with Hamor's return from the battlefield to report the Israelites' victory. This is followed by a chorus of thanksgiving, "Cherub and Seraphim." The scene shifts to the battlefield and more songs of triumph. Handel then interpolates a sinfonia just before the tragic climactic moment, when Iphis runs out to greet her returning father with the guileless, joyful aria "Welcome as the cheerful light." In the following highly emotional and deeply moving section, all the characters react in their own ways to the impending disaster. The part reaches its climax with the chorus "How dark, O Lord, are Thy decrees!"

Jephtha, Iphis, and the priests prepare for the sacrifice at the beginning of the third part. Again, Handel stops the action for an orchestral sinfonia, after which the Angel appears to announce that it is God's will that Iphis live and serve Him as a virgin priestess. Everyone—even Hamor—expresses satisfaction at this joyful outcome, with all five voices joining in a quintet that leads directly to the concluding choral "Hallelujah, Amen."

FRANZ JOSEPH
HAYDN

Born March 31, 1732, in Rohrau, Austria
Died May 31, 1809, in Vienna

Franz Joseph Haydn was born into a poor wheelwright's family in rural Austria. By age five, though, his very considerable musical talent was noted by his cousin Johann Mathias Franck, a choral director at Hainburg, who took the youngster into his home and gave him his first instruction in music. By age eight, young Haydn was recruited to become a choirboy at Vienna's famed St. Stephen's Cathedral in a group now known as the Vienna Choirboys.

When Haydn reached age seventeen, though, his voice changed, and he was thrown out of St. Stephen's with little more than the clothes on his back and no idea how he could survive. Survive he did, though, by joining a group of itinerant street musicians and finding a few students seeking music lessons. All the while, though, he continued teaching himself more and more about composition by studying the works of the masters and by reading the few textbooks on composition and theory that were available.

Since public concerts were still a rarity, the only way Haydn could manage as a composer was to find employment in the court of a wealthy aristocrat or member of the church hierarchy. In 1755, Haydn became composer at the court of Count Ferdinand Maximilian Morzin, and in 1761 he moved to the renowned court of Prince Paul Anton Esterházy in Eisenstadt, where he remained until 1790.

During his years with Esterházy, Haydn's abilities as a composer continued to develop and grow. All of his great choral masterpieces—*The Seven Last Words of Christ, The Creation, The Seasons,* and the remarkable six last Masses—date from his final years at Esterházy and the years immediately after he left that position, the period when he was at the very peak of his creative powers.

The Haydn choral works discussed here are identified by the numbers assigned in Anthony van Hoboken's 1957 thematic catalog of Haydn's music.

THE SEVEN LAST WORDS OF CHRIST, Hob. XX:2
(The Seven Words of Our Savior on the Cross)

1 hour

Although originally composed as an orchestral work, without voices, *The Seven Last Words of Christ* is best known as a choral work and in a string-quartet transcription. In March 1801, Haydn explained the genesis of the orchestral version:

About fifteen years ago I was asked by the Cathedral Chapter of Cadiz to compose instrumental music on the Seven Words of Jesus on the Cross. In those days they used to give an oratorio every year during Lent at the principal church of Cadiz, and the following circumstances contributed not a little to increasing the general mood: The walls, windows and pillars of the church were clothed in black material, and only one light, hanging in the middle of the church, increased the holy gloom. At noon all the doors to the church were shut; then the music began. Following an appropriate prelude, the bishop ascended the pulpit, said one of the words and then added his own sermon on it. When he had finished, he descended and knelt before the altar. This interval was filled with music. The bishop ascended and descended the pulpit for the second time, third time, and so forth, and each time the orchestra filled in the intervening period with music. This description served me in composing my music. The task of writing seven adagios, of which each should last some ten minutes, to follow one another without tiring the listeners, was not one of the easiest; and I soon found that

I could not adhere to the given time. The music was originally without text, and as such it was printed.

Over the years, scholars have added some details to Haydn's account. Haydn, at the time the best-known composer in Europe, received the commission in 1785 from the Cathedral of Santa Cueva in Cádiz, Spain. The work received its premiere performance there on March 26, 1796, as an orchestral composition that was part of the three-hour Good Friday services. The so-called seven last "words" were actually the seven last sentences uttered by Jesus before his death on the cross. Haydn actually composed nine selections, starting with an introduction and concluding with a section entitled *"Terremoto"* ("Earthquake"), a reference to the biblical account of what happened on the death of Jesus: "Break open, earth upon which the murderers stand!"

On receiving the score, the canon of Cádiz sent Haydn a gift box, which at first disappointed the composer. Haydn's gratitude greatly increased when he opened the box and discovered it was filled with gold pieces.

To widen the audience for *The Seven Last Words,* Haydn, in 1787, arranged the music for string quartet—which is probably its most popular form today—and for solo piano. Then, in 1794, Haydn heard a version of his music for choir and orchestra that Joseph Friebert, *Kapellmeister* to the bishop of Passau, Germany, had based on Haydn's original score. While he approved of the idea, Haydn felt he could do a better job with the choral writing.

To prepare his version, Haydn asked an assistant to write out the orchestral score on manuscript paper, leaving extra lines for the choral parts. He engaged Baron Gottfried van Swieten, director of the court library in Vienna, to prepare the text, which he based largely on Friebert's words. Haydn also made some changes in the orchestration, dropping the flutes from the original orchestra and adding pairs of clarinets and trombones. Further, he inserted one movement, a chilling slow interlude for wind band, before the fifth word.

Haydn set the individual sections with stately, dignified melodies. He opened the work with a somber introduction and concluded it with the fiery earthquake, which he directed be performed *Presto e con tutta la forza* ("Very fast and with full force"). Perhaps Haydn best described the composition in a letter to an English publisher in 1787: "Each word is expressed by purely instrumental means in such a way as to make the most profound impression on even an inexperienced listener's soul."

Composed for four soloists, mixed choir, and orchestra, *The Seven Last Words of Christ* does not currently enjoy the popularity of some of Haydn's other choral works. One can only hope, however, that more choral directors will introduce this profound and stirring work to their audiences.

1. "Father, forgive them, for they know not what they do." (St. Luke 23:34)
2. "Truly I say unto thee, this day shalt thou be with Me in paradise." (St. Luke 23:43)
3. "Woman, behold thy son, and thou, behold thy mother." (St. John 19:26, 27)
4. "My God, my God, why hast Thou forsaken Me?" (St. Matthew 27:46)
5. "Jesus called: I thirst." (St. John 19:28)
6. "It is finished." (St. John 19:31)
7. "Father, into Thy hands I commend My spirit." (St. Luke 23:46)

THE CREATION, Hob. XXI:2
(Die Schöpfung)

2 hours

Haydn spent a major part of his creative life, from 1761 to 1790, as *Kapellmeister* in the court of the Esterházys. The year after leaving this position, the composer went on an extended visit to England, and he enjoyed another lengthy stay there in 1794–95. While in London he heard—and was much impressed by—the Handel Commemorative Festival in May 1791. And thus, when impresario Johann Peter Salomon approached him with the idea of composing an oratorio, Haydn was extremely receptive.

It was during Haydn's second trip to London that Salomon gave the composer a text, one prepared by Thomas Linley, on the creation of the world as described in Milton's *Paradise Lost* and the Book of Genesis from the Bible—taking much more from the latter than the former. Haydn's enthusiasm was so great that he immediately began to write out some preliminary sketches for the music—"so I can remember it," as he wrote on the first page.

On Haydn's return to Vienna in August 1795, he turned the text over to Baron Gottfried van Swieten, an amazing individual who was director of the imperial library as well as an esteemed poet, composer, and patron of the arts. Haydn set out three goals for van Swieten: cut the four-hour-long libretto down to manageable length; translate the English text, with which Haydn felt uncomfortable, into German; and offer suggestions about the musical setting—all conditions the baron met.

Haydn began the actual composition toward the end of 1796 at age sixty-four, and he provided much evidence that he considered this a most important and meaningful project. As he worked on the composition, he prepared many sketches and drafts, a practice he did not usually follow. Twenty-three pages of such material are now held in the National Library in Vienna, including a full seven versions of the opening "Chaos" section! In general, the changes were mostly in the direction of simplification.

The composition went very slowly; Haydn explained the sluggish pace by saying, "I spend much time over it because I intend it to last a long time." And when it was done, Haydn wrote, "When I was half-way through my composition, I could see it was going to come out well. I have never felt so devout as when I was working on *The Creation*. Every day I fell on my knees and prayed to God to give me strength to finish the work successfully."

Haydn entered the last notes on April 6, 1798, a scant three weeks before he conducted the first private performance at the palace of Prince Schwarzenberg in Vienna on April 29, 1798. We know that he had a deep personal involvement in the music from the description he left of his feelings at the premiere: "Now I was ice-cold all over, now a hot glow came over me, and more than once I feared I should have a stroke!" This from a man noted for his calm, self-possessed demeanor!

A huge success at its premiere, *The Creation* was quickly taken up for public performances all over Europe. One interesting incident occurred in connection with the Paris premiere on Christmas Eve 1800. Napoléon Bonaparte, who was then first consul, was on his way to the performance when an assassin threw a bomb at his carriage. Napoléon was not injured—but it is reported that he did not arrive at the Théatre des Arts until after the performance had ended!

At a public performance in Vienna in 1808, which Haydn attended, there was a loud ovation after "Let there be light." The composer, already ill and feeble, weakly pointed upward, indicating, "Not from me, from thence comes everything." After the concert, Beethoven, whose relations with the older master were strained, approached Haydn, knelt, and humbly kissed his hands.

Audiences throughout Europe and North America responded

enthusiastically to the music's honest piety. Some clerics, though, suspected that the God that Haydn portrayed in *The Creation* bore too close a resemblance to the God of the Freemasons, a group of which Haydn was a member. As a result, a number of churches banned performances of the work.

Haydn composed *The Creation* for three soloists—soprano, tenor, and bass—who replace the more traditional single Evangelist or narrator and sing the parts of the three archangels Gabriel, Uriel, and Raphael respectively. In addition, there are parts for Adam (bass) and Eve (soprano). For the performances he conducted, Haydn asked the soprano and bass to sing the parts of angels *and* of Adam and Eve. Modern performances, though, often have additional performers for the Adam and Eve roles. Curiously enough, while Haydn set both the German and English texts—providing an alternate melodic line to fit the syllabification of each language—*The Creation* is almost always sung in German.

The opening, "The Representation of Chaos," is one of the most miraculous moments in the entire body of music. From the movement's opening note, a loud, unison orchestral C—a musical analog, some commentators feel, to the big bang of cosmology—there emerges an amazing musical depiction of chaos. It is replete with amorphous rhythms and ill-defined melodic snatches, sudden outbursts of fury that quickly fade away, eerie ascending figures and mysterious upsweeps, strange harmonies and unsettling dissonances, a sinister pulsing under much of the music, all of which Haydn combines to paint a vivid tonal picture of the frightening, foreboding void before the glorious moment of creation.

Then comes the climax. At the last word of "And there was light," there is a sudden blaze of wondrous sound as the chorus and entire orchestra join in an overwhelming C major chord, fully and richly harmonized.

Haydn follows this magnificent high point with a succession of choruses, arias, duets, trios, and recitatives (some accompanied by orchestra, some just by a continuo of cello and harpsichord) that tell the story of the creation in joyful, though reverential, musical terms, ending with the appearance of Adam and Eve.

Urged on by Baron van Swieten, Haydn makes frequent use of tone painting—imitating natural sounds in his music. Some examples are the precreation chaos of number one; the storm, thunder, and lightning in number three; the "foaming billows" in number six; the birds in number twenty-one; and the animals in number twenty-two.

Although Haydn employs a good deal of tone painting in *The Creation,* he apparently realized its limitations as a musical device. One example: when he played and sang the aria "Rolling in foaming billows" for a friend, he exclaimed, "You see, you see how the notes run up and down like the waves? One has to have some amusement after one has been serious for so long."

The composer organizes *The Creation* into three parts. Part I covers the first four days of creation; Part II is concerned with the appearance of life; and Part III, starting with a magical evocation of dawn, introduces Adam and Eve.

Perhaps Haydn biographer Karl Geiringer described this magnificent composition best when he wrote, "In this work, childlike naiveté, joy in the world of the senses, and gentle humor are combined with profound faith, nobility of expression and hymnlike fervor."

THE SEASONS, Hob. XXI:3
(Die Jahreszeiten)

2 hours, 20 minutes

The success of Haydn's first major oratorio, *The Creation,* extended his reputation as a great composer of instrumental music into the realm of vocal music. Therefore, according to reports from the time, it took little urging on the part of Baron Gottfried van Swieten, librettist for *The Creation,* to convince Haydn to write another work in that form. Haydn's only concerns were his advanced age (he was approaching seventy) and his deteriorating health (modern scholars believe he was suffering from arteriosclerosis).

In any case, Haydn agreed to go ahead. Van Swieten produced a libretto based on a 1726 poem by the English poet James Thomson entitled "The Seasons." The original poem consists of cheerful, lyrical images and descriptions of the changing scenes of nature through the year and the influence of these changes on life in the country.

Van Swieten, however, made several significant changes in the Thomson poem. In addition to translating it into German, he introduced three characters—Simon (bass), a farmer; Jane (soprano), his daughter; and Lucas (tenor), a young peasant—along with a chorus of country people and hunters.

The librettist also tampered with Thomson's original ending, in which the wanderer dies in the winter cold. Van Swieten added outside texts—poems by Gottfried August Bürger and Christian Felix Weisse—in order to set the famous "Spinning Song" (No. 38) in a warm, inviting peasant cottage. And at the end, he compared the seasons of nature to stages of life, postulating that virtue and industry are the means to achieve true happiness.

While Haydn had welcomed van Swieten's suggestions on setting the text of *The Creation,* the composer was much less accepting of van Swieten's ideas for *The Seasons.* In particular, Haydn railed against the imitations of country sounds that van Swieten called for, which he referred to as "Frenchified trash."

Nevertheless, Haydn began composing in 1799 and took until February 1801 to complete the score for *The Seasons.* Haydn called the hard, laborious work "terrible worry and torture." At the end he stated, *"The Seasons* has finished me off. I should never have written it." Indeed, *The Seasons* remains close to his last major work, followed only by the *"Harmoniemesse"* of 1802.

Of the forty-four numbers in *The Seasons,* the one that gave Haydn the greatest difficulty was the Terzetto, No. 23, "So nature ever kind." About this section Haydn complained, "For days on end I have had to toil away at one passage." He also commented, "I have always been a diligent, hardworking person, but I have never been able to set this quality to music." The music for "So nature ever kind" does in fact betray Haydn's problems in setting words in praise of industry; it is noticeably on a lower level of inspiration than most of the other music in the work, which is characterized for the most part by great freshness, spontaneity, and easy lyrical charm. In this completely secular work, Haydn did not hesitate to adapt folklike melodies to the needs of the composition.

Haydn structured *The Seasons* into the four obvious parts, starting with spring. Each section opens with an orchestral introduction that sets the mood and character of the music that will follow. Haydn wrote a few words of description above each of these selections: for spring, "The passage of Winter to Spring"; for summer, "The dawn of day"; for autumn, "The husbandman's satisfaction at the abundant harvest"; and for winter, "The thick fog at the beginning of winter."

Each vocal selection offers its own special pleasures and beauties. A few can, however, be separated out for individual comment:

No. 2. After greeting the arriving spring with a charming folklike melody, the choir splits up—the women savoring the life-giving warmth of spring, the men warning that winter may not yet be gone for good.

No. 4. Plowing his fields, Simon whistles a tune (piccolo) that proves to be the famous second-movement theme from Haydn's "Surprise" Symphony—a theme that was, and is, easily recognized by all music lovers.

No. 9. A powerful fugal movement that brings spring to a close.

No. 19. One of the most rampageous and impressive musical depictions of a thunderstorm in the entire literature.

No. 20. The storm clears, and through tone painting Haydn evokes images of lowing cows, birds in song, chirping crickets, and croaking frogs.

No. 23. The paean to industry that proved so difficult for Haydn.

No. 25. A duet for the two lovers in the style of Italian opera.

Nos. 27–29. An evocation of the hunt, including much tone painting; all four French horns are heard in the chorus "Hear, hear the clank and noise."

No. 31. Haydn adds a triangle and tambourine to the joyful peasant merrymaking at the grape harvest.

No. 38. The "Spinning Song," a delightful movement, which predates other well-known spinning songs by Schubert, Saint-Saëns, and Wagner.

No. 44. The finale, and climax of the entire composition, in which the choir (now divided into a double chorus) and the three soloists sing solemnly on the true meaning of life and how one must perform noble deeds to achieve eternal life. So strong is the religious fervor of this number that it seems perfectly natural to end this secular oratorio with two mighty "Amens!"

SIX LAST MASSES, Hob. XXII:9–14

No. 9. Missa in tempore belli
("Mass in Time of War")
(Paukenmesse or Kettledrum Mass)

No. 10. Missa Sancti Bernardi von Offida
("St. Bernard of Offida Mass")
(Heiligmesse or Holy Mass)

No. 11. Missa in angustiis
("Mass in Time of Need")
(Nelson Mass or Imperial Mass)

No. 12. Missa
(Theresienmesse or Theresa Mass)

No. 13. Missa solemnis
("Solemn Mass")
(Schöpfungmesse or Creation Mass)

No. 14. Missa
(Harmoniemesse or Wind-Band Mass)

Each circa 45 minutes

Haydn wrote a total of fourteen Masses, including two juvenile works that have been lost. He composed the first six of the extant Masses between the years 1749 and 1782; then, after a fourteen-year hiatus, he wrote the last six Masses from 1796 to 1802.

The long silence before Mass No. 9 was due, in part, to the 1780 ascent to the Austrian throne of Emperor Joseph II, who issued a number of decrees simplifying the liturgy and banning the use of orchestras in church. It was only during the 1790s, after Leopold II succeeded Joseph, that music was fully restored to the church. Further, it took that long to blur the distinction between secular and sacred music, allowing composers to bring all the expressive devices they had developed for the concert hall to their church music.

The last six Masses find Haydn at the very peak of his creative powers. His astonishing ability soars forward from the exceedingly high level of his last symphonies, the second and final set of "London" Symphonies, which he composed between 1793 and 1795. In each of the Masses, he added soprano, alto, tenor, and bass soloists and mixed choir to the orchestra. And whereas, in the earlier Masses, Haydn had the instruments doubling the voices, he now kept the orchestra much more independent of the singers.

Haydn composed *Missa in tempore belli* in 1796. The subtitle, *"Paukenmesse,"* comes from the prominent timpani and brass instruments in the last section of the Mass, the *"Agnus Dei"*—particularly in the very last part, *"Dona nobis pacem."* The dramatic military sounds are made all the more striking as Haydn transforms the music into a fervent prayer for peace. Haydn added the subtitle as Napoléon was threatening Vienna, a short distance from Eisenstadt, where Haydn composed the music and where the work received its premiere performance on September 13, 1796.

Also composed in 1796, *Missa Sancti Bernardi von Offida* honors a Capuchin monk from the seventeenth century who was beatified by Pope Pius VI in 1795. The work is known as the *"Heiligmesse"* because in the *"Sanctus"* the altos and tenors sing a phrase from the old hymn *"Heilig, Heilig, Heilig"* ("Holy, holy, holy"). An exquisite merging of the sacred and secular appears in the *"Et incarnatus est,"* perhaps the most solemn moment in the entire Mass, when Haydn uses a melody he had previously used for a canon that had the following words:

> God in your heart,
> A good woman in your arms,
> The one beatifies,
> The other warms.

Yet despite its racy origins, this melody, in a different key, becomes a very fitting setting of the holy words of the Mass.

Napoléon also lurks in the background of Haydn's next Mass, *Missa in angustiis,* which he composed in the fifty-three days from July 10 to August 31, 1798. The piece received its first performance on September 23 of that year at St. Martin's Church, Eisenstadt.

The "time of need" of the title was probably Haydn's reference to the dire straits of the European countries as Napoléon's armies continued their conquests. This despair can be heard most clearly in the *"Kyrie eleison,"* as well as in the *"Credo"* and the *"Sanctus."*

The military situation, however, changed on August 1. While Haydn was composing the music, Admiral Horatio Nelson soundly defeated Napoléon's fleet in the so-called battle of the Nile. Scholars associate the brilliant, ringing trumpet calls in the triumphant *"Benedictus"* of the Mass with Haydn's reaction to Nelson's victory. Proof of Haydn's interest in this famous sea battle came to light after his death, when a chart following the strategies of both the English and French fleets was found among his effects.

This Mass also became connected with Nelson in 1800 when the admiral and his lover, Lady Emma Hamilton, called on Haydn to pay their respects. Lady Hamilton, an excellent amateur singer and a great admirer of Haydn, charmed the composer by singing some of his songs on that occasion. At the same time, the admiral asked if he might have the pen Haydn had used to write the Mass, in return for which he gave the flattered composer his valuable gold watch. The "Nelson" Mass is probably the most popular and best loved of all the Haydn Masses.

The Mass that Haydn composed in 1799 was nicknamed "Theresa" Mass, though the reason is somewhat confused. People assume that Haydn dedicated the work to Empress Maria Theresa, as he did his Forty-eighth Symphony. The Mass, however, was probably composed to honor Maria Theresa, consort of Francis II, who was emperor at the time. This Maria Theresa was an outstanding soprano who went on to sing the solo part in the premiere of Haydn's oratorio *The Seasons*.

Haydn composed the thirteenth of his Masses, subtitled "The Creation," in even less time than the "Nelson" Mass—from July 28 to September 11, 1801—and he gave the premiere in Eisenstadt two days later. At a subsequent Vienna performance, Maria Theresa objected to Haydn's quotation of a melody from his non-liturgical oratorio *The Creation* in a sacred Mass. He used the melody of the duet *"Der tauende Morgen"* from *The Creation* oratorio in the *"Qui tollis"* section of the Mass—hence the nickname "Creation" Mass. Haydn acceded to Maria Theresa's objection and did change the melody.

Haydn composed his last major work of any kind, the *"Harmoniemesse,"* in 1802, and he led the premiere in Eisenstadt on September 8 of that year. Its nickname, translated as "Wind-Band Mass," comes from the large component of wind instruments in the orchestra it requires (flute, two oboes, two clarinets, two bassoons, two French horns, two trumpets, timpani, organ, and the usual strings) and the especially prominent role Haydn gives to the orchestra winds. A majestic work—all encompassing in its conception, with an air of serene dignity and acceptance—the *"Harmoniemesse"* was a fitting way for this astounding composer to bid farewell to the world of music.

Standard Text (see Appendix)

ARTHUR
HONEGGER

Born March 10, 1892, in Le Havre, France
Died November 27, 1955, in Paris

Music history books cite Arthur Honegger as a member of *Les Six*—that saucy, iconoclastic group of young French composers, formed right after World War I, which wanted to move French music in a more popular and jazzy direction, away from the style of Debussy and Ravel. Honegger found himself in *Les Six* more because of personal friendship for the other members than because of any strong musical affinity. He soon went his own way, composing highly expressive music that tends to be lyrical in sound and dramatic in impact.

Born in France of Swiss parents, Honegger received his training at the Zurich and Paris conservatories. His first fame came in the early 1920s with his short orchestral piece *Pacific 231,* a portrayal in sound of a powerful locomotive starting up, reaching full speed, and then slowing down and coming to a stop. (Honegger later insisted that he looked on *Pacific 231* as an abstract study in acceleration and deceleration, and that he only added the title after the work was done.) *Pacific 231* won the composer much notoriety as the writer of "machine age" music, the music of the future.

Honegger did not long pursue this line of composition; instead he began to draw more on musical styles of the past. His favored models were Richard Wagner, Richard Strauss, and, perhaps more than either, Johann Sebastian Bach. Although he found inspiration in the music of previous centuries, Honegger's own style relied heavily on some of the most advanced techniques of twentieth-century composition—producing music that audiences find both appealing and challenging.

The first of Honegger's truly mature works was the dramatic

oratorio *Le roi David* of 1921. Two other choral works have also won enduring places in the repertoire—*Jeanne d'Arc au bûcher* (1935) and *Une cantate de Noël* (1953).

LE ROI DAVID
(King David)

1 hour, 15 minutes

In 1921, Honegger was asked to supply the music for *Le roi David*, a so-called "dramatic psalm" by René Morax, which was being produced by a semiprofessional theater group in Mézières, France. The great success of the premiere, on June 11, 1921, led Honegger to revise the work for concert presentation by having a narrator speak the biblical text, by giving vocal parts to soprano, alto, and tenor soloists and mixed choir, by expanding the few instruments accompanying the original to a full symphony orchestra, and by inserting a few additional musical passages. In this form, *Le roi David* received its first performance in Winterthur, Switzerland, on February 2, 1923, to a most enthusiastic reception. Over the following three years the work was heard in virtually every music center around the world, establishing its reputation as one of the outstanding choral works of this century and winning international recognition for the composer.

Through the three large parts of *Le roi David*, Honegger follows the major events in the biblical story of David—his youth as a shepherd, his battle with Goliath, the enmity of Saul, David's being crowned king, his love for Bathsheba, the rebellion of Absalom, David's death, and finally the crowning of his son Solomon as the new king.

In *Le roi David*, Honegger successfully weds a number of different stylistic influences to create the work's powerful impact. From time to time (the overture is an example), the composer employs Hebraic melodic forms, including the striking interval of the augmented second. In places he uses choral writing that is polyphonic in texture, recalling Handel's treatment of the choir. Many of Honegger's melodies are clear, simple, and very appealing, much like popular folk tunes, and they show the human voice off to its very best advantage. With his secure technical command, Honegger is able to introduce many pictorial and programmatic effects that bring the text vividly to life. In addition, Honegger employs some of the most advanced compositional techniques of the time—irregular rhythms, sharp dissonances, and polytonality (two keys at the same time). Honegger is able to integrate these varied elements to make *Le roi David* a true twentieth-century masterpiece.

JEANNE D'ARC AU BÛCHER
(Joan of Arc at the Stake)

1 hour, 20 minutes

Ida Rubinstein (1885–1960), the breathtakingly beautiful, highly intelligent, and extremely wealthy Russian-born actress and mime, approached composer Arthur Honegger and poet Paul Claudel with the idea of creating a popular sort of mystery play for her on the subject of Joan of Arc. Knowing that she could neither sing nor dance, and was a rather poor actress, posed a problem for the composer and poet, until they hit on the idea of having her bound to the stake for the entire work!

Honegger and Claudel worked on *Jeanne d'Arc* in 1935, entitling the work a "dramatic oratorio." Even though Claudel was only engaged to write the text, he conveyed his very clear ideas about the music to Honegger, which the composer found extremely helpful. "Claudel's contribution was so great," Honegger wrote, "that I hardly see myself as the real author, but as a humble collaborator."

The men completed the work on August 30, 1935, and Ida Rubinstein—along with three actors with speaking roles, six vocal soloists (two sopranos, alto, tenor, bass, and child soprano), a mixed choir and a children's choir, and a large orchestra—gave the fully-staged premiere in Basel on May 12, 1938. Most subsequent performances have been concert presentations with, at most, minimal costuming and lighting.

The oratorio tells the story of Joan (1412–1431), a simple French peasant girl, who heard voices that made her believe that she had been chosen to drive the conquering English armies out of France. Given command of the French army, she was able to break the English siege of Orléans, defeat the English in other battles, and stand at the side of Charles as he was crowned Charles VII, King of France. By then, Joan no longer heard the voices and wanted to return to her home, but the king insisted she continue to lead his army. Eventually she failed in her attempt to liberate Paris and soon thereafter was captured by the English and burned at the stake as a witch and heretic. She was later canonized as Saint Joan.

Honegger creates a stunning and varied array of tonal effects in *Jeanne d'Arc*. One particularly effective device is to have the soloists and the choir speak the words, often over an orchestral accompaniment. This technique, called melodrama, heightens and intensifies the expression by the symbiosis of the spoken words and the emotional tone the orchestra imparts.

UNE CANTATE DE NOËL
(Christmas Cantata)

27 minutes

Most cantatas are divided into separate movements in their presentation of a single text. Honegger's *Une cantate de Noël* is the opposite. He wrote it as a single movement and drew his words from several disparate sources: Old Latin hymns *("De profundis," "Gloria in excelsis," "Laudate Dominum")*; traditional French Christmas carols *("Joie et paix" and "Il est né")*;

and German Christmas carols *("Est ist ein Ros'," "Von himmel hoch," "O du fröliche,"* and *"Stille Nacht, heilige Nacht").*

Honegger undertook work on *Une cantate de Noël* late in 1940, setting to music the first part of "La Passion de Selzach" by poet Caesar von Arx. The opening episode on the Nativity of Christ served as the basis for *Une cantate de Noël,* although with a number of changes.

The first chorus is an anguished appeal to the Savior, which is answered by the archangel announcing the coming of the Messiah. Following this, joyous songs from all over the world are intermingled, reaching a climax in the hymn *Laudate Dominum.* An orchestral postlude concludes the selection of Christmas songs.

Honegger summed up the composition: "The score is written in a style both simple and tonal, in a way that is compatible with the character of these songs, whose artless poetry exerted such a charm in our childhood."

Honegger abandoned his early work on the cantata upon the death of the poet von Arx. He did not pick it up again until the fall of 1953, when he received a commission from Paul Sacher, conductor of the Basel Chamber Orchestra, to celebrate the twenty-fifth anniversary of that orchestra. Completed that winter, *Une cantate de Noël*—which is written for baritone soloist, children's choir, mixed choir, organ, and orchestra—received its first performance in Basel, under the direction of Sacher, on December 18, 1953.

After a few measures of somber orchestral introduction, the choir enters singing wordlessly. The Latin hymn *"De profundis,"* from Psalm 130, segues as the music becomes faster and more agitated, leading to the first French carol, which is sung by the children's choir. Over the next section the two choirs and the baritone bring together Latin phrases and French and German carols. (The composer asked that the cantata be sung in the original languages, "the general idea being that Christmas is a universal holiday and that the three most important languages are represented.") Probably the musical high point comes when Honegger weaves three well-known German songs together. The final choral portion is in Latin, followed by the lengthy orchestral postlude.

LEOŠ JANÁČEK

Born July 3, 1854, in Hukvaldy, Moravia (now Slovakia)
Died August 12, 1928, in Ostrava, Moravia

Along with the classical training that Janáček received at the Organ School in Prague and at the conservatories in Leipzig and Vienna, a major influence on his compositions was the folk music of his native Moravia. "The whole life of man," he once said, "is in folk music—body, soul, environment, everything." In addition, Janáček was an avid student of human speech patterns, stating, "I am certain that all melodic and rhythmic mysteries in general are to be explained solely from the rhythmical and melodic points of view on the basis of melodic curves of speech."

From about 1875 until 1920, Janáček played a prominent role in the musical circles of Brno—conducting the Brno Philharmonic and directing the Brno Organ School. Elsewhere, however, he was largely unknown and his compositions were seldom performed.

It was not until Janáček was in his midsixties that he composed the several works that earned him an international reputation and his music a place in the modern repertoire. Prominent among these are the operas *The Cunning Little Vixen, The Makropoulos Affair,* and *From the House of the Dead,* the two string quartets, the Sinfonietta for Orchestra, and the *Glagolitic* (or "Slavonic") *Mass.*

GLAGOLITIC MASS
(Msa glagolskaja)

39 minutes

The *Glagolitic Mass* ("Glagolitic" is a reference to the tenth-century form of the Slavic language) originated in a conversation between Janáček and Archbishop Prečan of Olomouc around 1921 or 1922. Janáček complained of the poor quality of church music, to which the archbishop responded, "Well, Maestro, why don't you write something worthwhile?"

Janáček's initial response is unknown, but later, when he recounted the incident to a friend, Father Josef Martínek, the composer added, "If only I could get hold of an Old Slavonic text!" Whereupon Father Martínek presented Janáček with a copy of a ninth-century vernacular version of the Latin words.

Evidence indicates that Janáček started work on the score on August 2, 1926, finishing it on October 15—even though he later claimed that he composed the entire work in three weeks! The premiere was given on December 5, 1927, in Brno, with Jaroslav Kvapil conducting.

While Janáček composed the *Glagolitic Mass*, in part, as a response to Archbishop Prečan's challenge, he also used the work to express his unique relationship to Catholicism. In 1940, Janáček's niece, Vera Janácková, wrote, " 'A church,' he told me, 'is concentrated death. Tombs under the floor, bones on the altar, pictures that show nothing but torture and dying. I don't want to have anything to do with it.' "

Janáček's comments on what he hoped to achieve with the *Glagolitic Mass* reveal a rather pantheistic vision: "I want to show my people how to talk to God. The cathedral stretches to the vaults of Heaven; its candles are tall pine trees with stars at their tops; the fragrance of the moist woods of Luhačovice is its incense; its bells are sheep bells. My work deals with this cathedral. I depict in it, to a certain extent, the legend that says that Christ was hanged on the Cross, and that Heaven was torn asunder. Well, I am making thunder and lightning; and nightingales, thrushes, ducklings and geese make music with me."

Because of the *Glagolitic Mass*'s special nature, its church use is mostly confined to July 5; this is the day dedicated to SS. Cyril and Methodius, two saints who lived in the ninth century, when the vernacular Slavonic language was spoken and understood. On every day of the year, though, the *Mass* may be heard in concert halls throughout the world.

Glagolitic Mass starts with a fanfare-like orchestral introduction *("Úvod")*, from the tradition of having festive music mark the entry of the clergy. Janáček lowers the pitch of the introductory motif and compresses the rhythm to furnish the theme for the *"Gospodi pomiluj"* (corresponding to the *"Kyrie"* of the Latin Mass) for solo soprano and choir.

The soprano introduces the joyful *"Slava" ("Gloria")*, which she builds up to an exultant conclusion. *"Věruju" ("Credo")*, the most elaborate movement of the *Mass,* is heard by some as a longing for faith, rather than an affirmation of faith. Dr. Ludvík Kundera, a musicologist contemporary of Janáček, once suggested that the extended orchestral interlude in this movement represents three scenes: Jesus praying in the desert; Christ, the sower of bliss; and Christ's agony. As far as is known, Janáček never contradicted this interpretation.

For *"Svet" ("Sanctus")*, Dr. Kundera conjures up this image: "Christ the King is walking in the streets, His path strewn with flowers and the crowds chanting, 'Blessed is He. . . .' " The *"Agneče Božij" ("Agnus Dei")* is in three sections: three devout a cappella prayers by the choir with orchestral interludes; more impassioned pleas by the soloists; and a foreshortened repeat of the first section.

The last two movements are instrumental. First comes an overwhelming sonic onslaught in the form of an organ solo that, in effect, releases the tensions that have been building up throughout the *Mass.* And the *Mass* concludes with *"Intrada,"* which is Italian for "entrance." Janáček probably used this music originally for both the introduction and conclusion, and when he substituted the present introduction, he kept the name for the final section. *"Intrada"* provides a jubilant, highly burnished ending to a most exciting, dramatic, and colorful twentieth-century choral masterpiece.

JOSQUIN DES PREZ

Born c. 1440
Died August 27, 1521, in Condé-sur-l'Escaut, northern France

With the possible exception of Guillaume de Machaut from the fourteenth century, Josquin des Prez, who straddled the fifteenth and sixteenth centuries, is the earliest composer whose choral music is still regularly performed and recorded.

Very few biographical facts are available on the life of Josquin. We know, however, that he was born in what is today Belgium and died not far from there some eighty years later. While still a young man, he made his way to Italy, where he spent close to forty years working in various courts and cathedrals, including a stint in the Papal Chapel in Rome.

A gap exists concerning Josquin's whereabouts immediately after his stay in Italy. Then, apparently, he spent the final years of his life as provost at the Church of Notre Dame in Condé-sur-l'Escaut, where he died in 1521.

Josquin was widely considered the greatest composer of his age—during his lifetime as well as now. Martin Luther said of Josquin, "He is the supreme master of the notes. They must express whatever he wants them to, whereas other musicians can only do what the notes demand."

Historically, Josquin lived in the period of musical development when the old music of the Middle Ages was giving way to the new music of the Renaissance. Josquin was in the forefront of the early Renaissance composers. His music displays the essential characteristics of the developing style: a focus on vocal music over instrumental; a polyphonic texture, with a great deal of imitation, in which the voices are treated as equals; melody that moves mostly by step with few large leaps; and a gently flowing rhythm with few strong beats or accents.

But Josquin went far beyond the quality of most of his contemporaries. He was able to achieve classical perfection in his melodic line, to display absolute control of the polyphonic texture no matter how complex, and to infuse all of his music with warmth, clarity, balance, and great expressive value. It was with good reason that he was widely known as the "Prince of Music" during his lifetime.

MISSA PANGE LINGUA

33 minutes

Although musicologists cannot set a date for the composition of Josquin's glorious and moving *Missa Pange Lingua,* most agree that it was near the end of his life, in the early sixteenth century, when he was at the very apex of his powers. Some even believe the work may be the last of his approximately eighteen Masses, so extraordinary is his technical mastery and the skill with which he captures the emotional meaning of the text.

Josquin based the Mass on a Gregorian chant for the Feast of Corpus Christi, which is celebrated every year on the seventh Thursday after Easter. He does not, however, state the melody as a cantus firmus, a "fixed melody," that could serve as the basis for an entire Mass. Instead, he gives all the voices a go at the chant melody at different times, often presenting no more than a brief fragment before allowing it to disappear in the flowing polyphony.

Such a Mass is known as a paraphrase Mass; in this case, Josquin paraphrases, or ornaments, the Gregorian chant as it passes from voice to voice, sometimes directly quoting the chant, sometimes just alluding to the notes of the melody. Musicologist Gustave Reese called *Missa Pange Lingua* "a fantasy on a plainsong."

Missa Pange Lingua projects a sense of calm and poise and a feeling of melodic and rhythmic perfection that contrast sharply with the world in which we live. The gentle forward movement of the notes lends a strange and wonderful enchantment to this remarkable piece of music that is nearly five hundred years old.

Standard Text (see Appendix)

ZOLTÁN KODÁLY

Born December 16, 1882, in Kecskemet, Hungary
Died March 6, 1967, in Budapest

Few composers were as deeply involved with choral music as
Zoltán Kodály. While still in school, he sang in a cathedral choir
and spent many hours in the music library there, familiarizing
himself with the major works of the sacred choral repertoire.
Beethoven's Mass in C especially affected the young Kodály and
inspired him to make his very first composition a Mass, written
when he was but sixteen years old.

During his student days at university, Kodály started what
became a lifelong fascination with the folk music of his native
Hungary. In addition to collecting, studying, codifying, and arranging huge quantities of folk songs and dances, he wrote the
dissertation for his doctorate on the strophic structure of Hungarian folk song.

In his mature years, he composed a number of important choral works. Three have gained significant places in today's choral
repertoire—*Psalmus hungaricus, Te Deum,* and *Missa brevis.*
Critics consider *Psalmus hungaricus,* in particular, as an outstanding choral creation of this century.

While Kodály primarily regarded himself as a composer, he
also taught composition at the Budapest Academy of Music and
concerned himself with the musical education of the young. According to his thesis, group singing was the key to unlocking
children's musicality. To this end he developed an entire course
of musical study based largely on Hungarian folk songs.
Kodály's deep affection for the sound of the human voice—
especially when joined with others—distinguishes each of his
choral works.

PSALMUS HUNGARICUS, Op. 13

23 minutes

In 1923, to celebrate the fiftieth anniversary of the creation of the unified city of Budapest, which joined together Buda and Pest on the two sides of the Danube River, government authorities asked Hungary's three greatest composers to compose major works. Béla Bartók wrote his *Dance Suite,* Ernö Dohnányi penned his *Festival Overture*—both orchestral works—and Zoltán Kodály submitted his *Psalmus hungaricus* for tenor soloist, mixed choir, optional children's chorus (to reinforce the sopranos and altos of the choir), and orchestra. Composed in just over two months during the summer of 1923, *Psalmus hungaricus* received its premiere on November 19 in Budapest.

Kodály based his text on a version of Psalm 55 by the sixteenth-century Hungarian poet Mihály Vég. Written during the Turkish occupation of Budapest, the psalm had interpolations by Vég that made the sacred song a very personal plea for divine help in ridding his beloved Hungary of the foreign conquerors.

After an impassioned orchestral introduction, the altos and basses enter in a quiet chant that relates David's prayers to God. This all-important passage comes back some four times, lending the work an overall formal structure. Between its appearances, David, represented by the tenor soloist, asks God to intervene in his struggle against the "wicked men" who oppress him. Sometimes he plaintively begs for help; at other times he loudly demands such intercession. In addition to the repetitive chantlike section, the choir performs other material that symbolizes the unity of the Hungarian people.

In this powerful, eloquent work, a few sections are especially striking: the interchanges between the wordless choir and solo tenor when he sings, "They take their evil counsel in secret" and when they recall the melody of the orchestral introduction; the ethereal orchestral intermezzo that follows the singing of "Thou art my helper/When those that hate Thee, sorely do oppress me"; the touching tenor aria "So in Jehovah I will put my trust"; and the full and utter confidence in God's omnipotence expressed in the final chorus, "Thou art our one God."

TE DEUM
(Budavári Te Deum)

21 minutes

Kodály wrote *Te Deum* (for four soloists, mixed choir, and orchestra) in response to a commission from the city of Budapest as part of the 250th anniversary celebration of the city's liberation from the Turks; the first performance was in Budapest on September 2, 1936. The Turks had ruled most of southeastern Europe, starting in 1541, with Buda (then called Ofen) as their capital. Their defeat in a decisive battle in 1683 led to an end of their domination three years later.

The composer organized this compelling work in ternary (three-part) form and cast it as one extended movement—opening with a fast (Allegro) tempo in four-beat time, following with a slow (Adagio) middle section in three-beat time, and finally returning to the fast tempo and four-beat time of the opening, albeit with much new melodic material.

A number of discrete sections make up the overall structure; each has its own distinctive motif, rhythm, or texture. Due largely to Kodály's keen discernment of the meaning and inflection of the Latin text, each section achieves a perfect union of words and music.

One can easily go through the work, section by section, and see how skillfully Kodály conveys, and intensifies, the meaning of the text. The *Te Deum* opens with a brief, brilliant trumpet fanfare, which is immediately followed by a forceful unison outburst by the choir singing in fanfare-like rhythm the words *"Te Deum laudamus, Te Dominum confitemur"* ("We praise Thee,

O God, we acknowledge Thee to be the Lord"), conveying in music all the joy and exultancy of the words.

At the first climax, to the words *"Pleni sunt coeli et terra majestatis gloriae tuae"* ("Heaven and earth are full of the majesty of Thy glory"), the choir embarks on a powerful fugue. At the fugue's conclusion, the heretofore independent voices come together for a chorale, *"Te gloriosus Apostolorum chorus"* ("The glorious company of the Apostles praise Thee"). Kodály perfectly expresses the supplication of *"Te ergo quaesumus"* ("We therefore pray Thee") with the whispering tenors and basses accompanied by strange off-beat accents in the brass. The *"Miserere nostri Domine"* ("O Lord, have mercy upon us") alternates shouted cries and quiet plaints. At the end, in a mood of peace and contentment, the orchestra and voices fade away with the words *"Non confundar in aeternum"* ("Let me never be confounded").

Standard Text (see Appendix)

MISSA BREVIS

32 minutes

Kodály composed *Missa brevis* ("Short Mass") for mixed choir and organ in 1944, during the time the Russian army held the city of Budapest under siege to drive out the occupying Germans. The composer dedicated the work to his wife. A shelling of the city that followed the siege destroyed Kodály's house but fortunately left his music manuscripts and papers undamaged.

While the battle still raged in and around the city the following year, *Missa brevis* received its premiere in the cloakroom of the Budapest Opera House, which had been converted into a miniature concert hall for the occasion. In 1951, the composer further expanded the work by orchestrating the original organ part, and he published the new arrangement.

Kodály grounds *Missa brevis* in the spirit of sixteenth-century vocal polyphony. Overall, the composer superimposes the particular turns of melody and rhythmic figures of authentic Hungarian (Magyar) folk music that are an integral part of Kodály's musical vocabulary. He flavors this outstanding mix with the "modern" sounds of twentieth-century compositional technique.

"Introitus," a solemn, majestic movement for orchestra alone, precedes the traditional parts of the Mass and previews the principal theme of the following *"Kyrie."* The lower voices (altos and basses), singing in imitation, present the *"Kyrie."* Three soprano soloists from within the choir bear the burden of the *"Christe eleison,"* and the entire choir joins in for the return of the *"Kyrie."*

In some performances, a solo tenor sings the plainsong melody of the *"Gloria"* before the choir and orchestra unite in this strong, forthright movement. The *"Credo"* opens quietly with the archaic flavor of modal plainsong, but it ends in a joyous song of triumph. The *"Sanctus"* exhibits the sixteenth-century polyphonic tradition most clearly. The "Hosannas," which most composers make loud and forceful throughout, start powerfully here before quickly fading away and disappearing into silence; they reappear at the end of the *"Benedictus"*—expanded in length, but again mostly quiet and subdued.

Kodály brings back melodies from the *"Kyrie"* and *"Gloria"* in the *"Agnus Dei,"* including the special sound of the three soprano soloists. Finally, he ends the heavenly Mass by adding *"Ite, Missa Est,"* which is based on melodies from *"Credo"* and *"Sanctus."*

Standard Text (see Appendix)

GUSTAV MAHLER

Born July 7, 1860, in Kalischt, Bohemia
Died May 18, 1911, in Vienna

Like many great composers, Gustav Mahler showed an interest in music from a very early age. By the time he was three his parents had given him a tiny accordion, which was followed a few years later by a piano and music lessons with the leading musicians in their small hometown. Right from the start of his musical experiences, Mahler found himself drawn to composing, giving his first piece the intriguing title *Funeral March and Scherzo*.

When he was fifteen, Gustav entered the Vienna Conservatory. Despite his deep and growing interest in composing, he enrolled as a piano major. His composing did, however, gain him special recognition; his Piano Quartet from 1878 won a prize and gained him some measure of local fame.

In the summer of 1880, Mahler accepted a post as conductor at a tiny operetta theater in a resort area. That experience turned him away from the piano and helped him envision a life divided between composing and conducting. Indeed, for the remainder of his life, Mahler spent most of his time building a career as a conductor, going from the opera houses of Prague, Budapest, and Hamburg to some of the most prestigious conducting posts in the entire world—the Vienna Opera, the Metropolitan Opera, and the New York Philharmonic. Since he remained deeply committed to composing, though, he was forced to work on his own scores during summers and in breaks between conducting assignments.

During his lifetime, Mahler's music received frequent performances, often under his baton. After his death in 1911, though, interest in his music dropped off considerably. Not until the 1950s and 1960s, with the advocacy of conductors like Bruno Walter (a protégé and disciple of Mahler) and Leonard Bernstein (who was then music director of the New York Philharmonic), did Mahler become accepted as a leading composer and his music take its rightful place in the international concert repertoire.

Mahler, a most thoughtful and philosophical composer, wrote music that reflected his never-ending search for answers to the most basic human questions. He once posed to Bruno Walter a list of the subjects he was exploring in his compositions: "Whence do we come? Whither does our road take us? Have I really willed this life, as [Arthur] Schopenhauer thinks, before I was even conceived? Why am I made to feel that I am free while yet I am constrained within my character, as in a prison? What is the object of toil and sorrow? How am I to understand the cruelty and malice in the creations of a kind God? Will the meaning of life be finally revealed by death?"

To lend expression to the thoughts with which he was wrestling, Mahler, in such compositions as his Second, Third, and Fourth Symphonies, added the human voice to works that were traditionally for orchestra alone. But it was only in his Symphony No. 8, "Symphony of a Thousand," that he truly created a choral symphony.

SYMPHONY NO. 8 IN E FLAT MAJOR, "SYMPHONY OF A THOUSAND"

1 hour, 25 minutes

As with many creative artists, Gustav Mahler was always fearful that his inspiration and creative impulse would leave him. Starting around 1900, when he was working on his Fifth, Sixth, and Seventh Symphonies, he was filled with great self-doubt. "From the Fifth onwards," wrote his wife, Alma Maria Mahler, "he found it impossible to satisfy himself."

More than any other work, the Eighth Symphony makes us feel that Mahler engaged in mortal combat with the spirit of creativity—and emerged triumphant. As Alma put it, "His self-assurance returned with the Eighth." That he was able to complete the symphony in just eight weeks in the summer of 1906 (he completed the orchestration the following year), and that the manuscript shows no sign of the changes and revisions that permeate his earlier symphonies, support the view that he had successfully overcome his fear of failing creativity.

Mahler initially planned a four-movement symphony, with two orchestral and two choral movements, but he finally decided on a two-movement, entirely choral composition. For the text he chose two widely different approaches to the subject of inspiration and the human spirit. The first was the Latin hymn *"Veni, Creator Spiritus"* ("Come, Creative Spirit"), which Mahler described as "a song of yearning, of rapturous devotion in invocation of the creative spirit, the love that moves the worlds." Written in the ninth century by Hrabamus Magnentius Maurus, bishop of Mainz, *"Veni, Creator Spiritus"* traditionally belongs to the Pentecost or Whitsun liturgy, which marks the descent of the Holy Spirit to the Apostles.

The composer found the second text in the final scene of the second part of Goethe's *Faust*. Here, instead of looking to God or the Holy Ghost as a source of inspiration (as in *"Veni, Creator Spiritus"*), Mahler found the creative spark in love as symbolized by woman. In a letter to Alma, Mahler wrote, "The essence of it is really Goethe's idea that all love is generative, creative, and that there is a physical and spiritual generation that is the emanation of this 'Eros.' You have it in the last scene of *Faust*, presented symbolically."

Mahler realized that in order to achieve his vision for the Eighth Symphony, he required tremendous performing forces. For the premiere in Munich on September 12, 1910, which he conducted, Mahler used an enlarged orchestra of 171, plus 4 trumpets and 3 trombones performing offstage, 850 choristers in 2 mixed choruses and a boys' chorus, and 8 vocal soloists.

Taking advantage of the publicity value of the huge number of musicians involved, impresario Emil Gutmann advertised the work as the "Symphony of a Thousand"—a subtitle that has stuck to the work, despite Mahler's objection to the "Barnum and Bailey" atmosphere that the press-agentry engendered.

The first performance was an immense success, and the composer-conductor was afforded a thirty-minute ovation at its conclusion. Mahler was aware that his Eighth Symphony was not only monumental in size, but also a most outstanding artistic creation. A month before the premiere he wrote to conductor Willem Mengelberg, "I have just finished my Eighth! It will be something the world has never heard the likes of before. All nature is endowed with a voice in it. It is the biggest thing I have done so far. Imagine the universe beginning to ring and resound. It is no longer human voices. It is planets and suns revolving in their orbits. All my other symphonies are but preludes to this one."

Although Mahler carried the symphonic form to its ultimate dimension in his Eighth Symphony, he maintained a thread of connection to Haydn's first efforts in the form. Thus he cast the first part, *"Veni, Creator Spiritus,"* in traditional symphonic first-movement form of theme, contrasting theme, development of the two themes, and restatement of the two themes.

The two mixed choruses join together to open the symphony with a powerful statement of the principal theme. After briefly expanding the melody, Mahler has a soprano solo introduce the quiet, lyrical second subject to the words *"Imple superna gratia."* He follows the exposition of the two themes with an extended, far-ranging development section that reaches its climax with an impressive double fugue, followed by a brief recapitulation of the two melodies.

The much longer second part falls into three sections, corresponding to the slow movement, scherzo, and finale of a traditional symphony. The second-part opening puts forth the longest orchestral interlude in the symphony; it is largely based on themes that have been introduced in the first part. Mahler then introduces the voices of anchorites echoing in the mountain gorges, followed by the solo voices of Pater Ecstaticus (baritone) and Pater Profundus (bass) and the chorus of angels (women's voices).

The "Blessed Boys" singing *"Hände verschlinget"* introduce the second section. Here Goethe makes much use of symbolism:

the boys represent innocence, and the "Younger Angels" speak of roses, which are believed capable of repelling evil. No one yet can explain the allusion to asbestos in the song of the "More Perfect Angels."

The final section comes at the conclusion of Dr. Marianus's song. Mahler lets the violins state the slow opening theme over a murmured harp accompaniment. He follows this with the chorus of penitents, solos by Magna Peccatrix (Mary Magdalen), Mulier Samaritana (Samaritan Woman), and Maria Aegyptiaca (Mary of Egypt) and all three joining together, Gretchen's songs, the "Blessed Boys," and the Mater Gloriosa. At the end he brings forth the thrilling *"Chorus Mysticus,"* with its glorious affirmation of the eternal female.

FELIX
MENDELSSOHN

Born February 3, 1809, in Hamburg, Germany
Died November 4, 1847, in Leipzig, Germany

Felix Mendelssohn-Bartholdy (his full name) was one of the most gifted figures in the entire history of music—gifted in talent, in wealth, and in position. His grandfather was Moses Mendelssohn, a philosopher often hailed as the "German Plato," who worked for the emancipation of the Jews in Germany. His father, Abraham, was a much respected and highly successful banker who took every opportunity to foster and encourage his son's many talents—even though, when Felix began to achieve success, Abraham jokingly commented, "I have ceased to be the son of my father only to become the father of my son!"

As a child, Felix showed remarkable ability in art, poetry, foreign languages, and of course music. He performed as a pianist in a concert in Berlin at age nine, and that same year he heard his setting of Psalm 19 presented in public. At age sixteen he composed his Octet for Strings, and the following year he wrote the overture to the incidental music for Shakespeare's *A Midsummer Night's Dream*—works that show a maturity and musicality found in no other composer at a comparable age.

Widely performed and lionized as a leading composer of the age, Mendelssohn could boast many accomplishments that went beyond composing. His presentation of Bach's *St. Matthew Passion* in Berlin in 1829 led to the rediscovery of that master's music. As conductor, he made the Leipzig Gewandhaus Orchestra the leading orchestra of Europe. And he helped found the famed Leipzig Conservatory.

Mendelssohn's forebears were Jewish, but when he was seven years old his parents had him baptized as a Christian, not so much out of religious zeal as from a desire to allow him to partake more fully of German culture and to gain greater social acceptance. (Six years later his parents converted to Christianity.) Although they raised Felix as a Lutheran and he remained devoted to the church throughout his life, he was never fully accepted as a Christian by his contemporaries, nor was he ever fully cut off from his Judaic heritage.

Throughout Mendelssohn's career, the public considered him the leading musician of Germany. His compositions also appealed to British audiences; he made several long visits to England, spoke and wrote English perfectly, and composed several works—such as *A Midsummer Night's Dream* music, the "Scottish" Symphony, and the *Hebrides Overture*—that drew their inspiration from British sources. Thus, it is perfectly understandable that he wrote one of his three outstanding choral works—*Elijah*—with an English text for presentation in England. Mendelssohn wrote the others, *St. Paul* and *The First Walpurgis Night,* more for the public in his native Germany.

ST. PAUL, Op. 36
(Paulus)

2 hours

In 1831, the choir of the *Cäcilienverein* (St. Cecilia Society) of Frankfurt offered the young Mendelssohn his first commission for a large-scale choral work. Urged on by his father, Mendelssohn accepted the commission. By the following year he had decided to write an oratorio based on the story of St. Paul.

Some say Mendelssohn was attracted to St. Paul because Paul was, in effect, a converted Jew and Mendelssohn's family had also converted from Judaism to Christianity. Others ascribe his choice of subject to a visit to the Vatican in Rome and his powerful reaction to the paintings by Raphael that he saw there.

In December 1832, Mendelssohn sent a detailed outline of the oratorio he envisioned to his friend Pastor Julius Schubring, asking him to supply the text. Over the following months, letters went back and forth as they worked out the shape of the oratorio. From the beginning, both men decided that the music was to be primary, with the religious aspect playing a secondary role.

Mendelssohn began composing in March 1834; in November of the following year his father, who had been deeply involved in the work's creation, died, leading the composer to write to Schubring on December 6 that he had to finish the composition "because in his last letter, my Father insisted on it, being most impatient to see the work completed." Another letter said, "I must now devote all my efforts to finishing *St. Paul* as well as I can, and then imagine that he [his father] will hear it."

Mendelssohn completed *St. Paul* on April 18, 1836, and the *Cäcilienverein* in Frankfurt scheduled the premiere. Unfortunately, the choral director there fell ill, and the performance had to be postponed. Mendelssohn, who was then conducting in Düsseldorf, took advantage of the delay and introduced the work there on May 22, 1836.

St. Paul starts with an extended orchestral overture that the composer bases on the chorale *"Wachet auf, ruft uns die Stimme,"* undoubtedly in obeisance to Bach's eponymous cantata (No. 140). The choir sets the scene, after which the choir and soloists tell the story of Stephen, the first Christian martyr.

At the conclusion of the section dealing with Stephen, Mendelssohn relaxes the tension with the chorale *"Dir, Herr, dir will ich mich ergeben"* and begins the account of Saul, who became Paul, founder of the Christian church in the West. The first incident that he deals with is Paul's conversion on the road to Damascus, in which a four-part women's choir delivers the words of Jesus. According to Mendelssohn biographer Heinrich Jacob, the composer felt that a man singing that role would be the equivalent of a graven image, and therefore he gave the words to the women.

Instead of continuing with the narrative after the miracle of the conversion, Mendelssohn digresses with two of the most important choral numbers of the oratorio: a large-scale chorus

—*"Mache dich auf, werde Licht!"*—that includes a mighty fugue harking back to the fugues of Johann Sebastian Bach, and a chorale based on *"Wachet auf, ruft uns die Stimme,"* the melody originally heard in the overture. The first part of the oratorio now ends with Paul's encounter with the disciple Ananias.

The second part of *St. Paul* relates various incidents in Paul's work as a missionary and the persecution that he suffers. The oratorio ends with a magnificent chorus, *"Nicht aber ihm allein,"* which builds up to a glorious, ringing song of praise.

When Richard Wagner first heard *St. Paul* in 1840 he said, "Mendelssohn has presented us with a work representative of the highest flowering of art." But not all reactions were as kind. George Bernard Shaw said that he would as soon "talk Sunday school for two hours and a half to a beautiful woman with no brains as listen to *St. Paul* over again."

THE FIRST WALPURGIS NIGHT, Op. 60
(Die erste Walpurgisnacht)

40 minutes

Walpurgis Night, known in Germany as the Feast of St. Walpurgis, is a traditional celebration held on the eve of May Day, May 1, to greet the arrival of spring. According to legend, the witches gather on this night for their wild revels on Brocken, the highest peak in the Harz Mountains.

In 1799, Johann Wolfgang von Goethe wrote a poem that he hoped would become the text of a cantata, the music to be composed by Carl Friedrich Zelter, a composer who was both friend and later teacher to Mendelssohn. Goethe entitled the poem *"Die erste Walpurgisnacht"*—"The First Walpurgis Night"—to distinguish it from the Walpurgis Night scenes the poet describes in his *Faust*.

Zelter attempted the music in 1799, could not get started, put the project aside, tried again in 1812, and, still not able to make any progress, wrote to Goethe asking him to explain the poem's meaning. Goethe replied:

> A scholar of the German past wanted to justify the legend of the gathering of witches and devils on the Brocken, which has been known in Germany for ages, by giving it an historical origin. It seems that the pagan German priests and patriarchs, after they had been driven out of their sacred groves and Christianity had been forced upon the people, retreated with their faithful disciples to the wild and inaccessible Harz Mountains in the early days of Spring. There, according to ancient custom, they offered up their prayers and their fires to the incorporeal god of heaven and earth. To protect themselves against spying missionaries, they thought it good to disguise several of their number in order to frighten away their superstitious opponents; and thus protected by devils' masks, they carried out the purest service of their god.

Although the annual gathering of Druids on the mountaintop started as a pagan rite, it was replaced, over the years, by a Christian celebration dedicated to St. Walpurgis, an English nun who came to Germany in the eighth century—hence the celebration's current name.

In 1830, Mendelssohn decided to try his hand at setting Goethe's ballad. One can guess that he was attracted by the ghosts and goblins—as witness the marvelous music he was inspired to compose for *A Midsummer Night's Dream*—and he was always on the side of justice, sympathizing with the Druids in their oppression by the Christians. But the composing did not go easily. At one point he wrote to his sister that he had "half-composed it" in his head "but lacked the courage to write it down."

During 1831 and 1832, as he traveled throughout Europe, Mendelssohn was able to get the entire *Walpurgis Night* down on paper. Following a private performance on October 16, 1832, the work received its public premiere in Berlin on January 10, 1833. Although Mendelssohn was not satisfied with the score, he did not touch it for some seven years. Then, although his first thought was to make the piece the choral finale of a four-movement symphony, he ultimately decided against this scheme. On December 11, 1842, he wrote to his mother, "*The Walpurgis Night* will be resurrected, but garbed in a different habit than that before, which was lined too warmly with bones and was somewhat crude for the singers. For these reasons, I was compelled to rewrite the score from A to Z." The result was an extensively revised composition, the one we know today, which had its first performance on February 2, 1843, in Leipzig.

The First Walpurgis Night contains some of Mendelssohn's most fiery and exciting music. The lengthy overture starts with a very convincing portrayal of stormy winter weather, but by the end the harsh conditions give way to the warm breezes of spring. Mendelssohn then masterfully captures the mocking tone of Goethe's poem. Bold and daring in his writing, he is able to evoke the wild contortions of the "devils" as they frighten away the Christians, the Christians cowering in fear of the devils they themselves created, and the life-affirming rites of the Druids.

Most audiences agree with musicologist Alfred Einstein that *The First Walpurgis Night* is the best secular oratorio of the nineteenth century.

1. OVERTURE: ALLEGRO CON FUOCO

2. ALLEGRO VIVACE NON TROPPO. ALLEGRO ASSAI VIVACE.
(Tenor and Chorus)

Druid and Chorus of Druids

Es lacht der Mai!	May's in full bloom!
Der Wald ist frei	The forest's free
von Eis und Reifgehange.	of frost and ice.
Der Schnee ist fort	The snow is gone
am grunen Ort	on grassy ground
erschallen Lustgesange.	gay songs resound.
Ein reiner Schnee	Though high above
liegt auf der Hoh	it's white with snow
doch eilen wir nach oben	we hasten there

begehn den alten heil'gen Brauch.	to sing Great Father's
Allivater dort zu loben.	praise in ancient rites.
Die Flamme lod're durch den Rauch!	Let flames flare through the smoke!
Hinauf! Hinauf!	Arise! Arise!
So wird das Herz erhoben!	Our hearts are thus exalted!

3. ALLEGRETTO NON TROPPO (Alto and Women's Chorus)

Old Woman and Chorus of Druid Women

Konnt ihr so verwegen handeln?	Could you be so rash, so daring?
Wollt ihr denn zum Tode wandeln?	Wend your way to certain death?
Kennet ihr nicht die Gesetze	Don't you know the laws they made,
unsrer strengen Überwinder?	they who harshly conquered us?
Rings gestellt sind ihre Netze	Round about their snares are waiting
auf die Heiden auf die Sunder.	for the heathen, for the sinners.
Ach sie schlachten auf dem Walle	On the ramparts they are slaughtering
unsre Vater, unsre Kinder!	our fathers, our children!
Und wir alle nahen uns gewissem Falle.	And we're all approaching certain doom.
Auf des Lagers hohem Walle	High on the encampment's ramparts
schlachten sie uns unsre Kinder!	they are slaughtering our children!
Ach die strengen Überwinder!	Oh, those victors most severe!
Und wir alle nahen uns gewissem Falle.	And we're all approaching certain doom.

4. ANDANTE MAESTOSO (Baritone and Chorus)

Druid Priest and Chorus of Druids

Wer Opfer heut' zu bringen scheut	Whoever fears to sacrifice
verdient erst seine Bande.	today truly deserves his bondage.

Der Wald ist frei.	The forest is free.
Der Holz herbei	Bring on the wood
und schichtet es zum Brande!	and pile it high for burning!
Doch bleiben wir im Buschrevier	By day we'll stay quite still
am Tage noch im Stillen.	here in the shady thicket.
und Männer stellen wir zur Hut	and to allay your fears we'll place
um eurer Sorge willen.	some guards for your protection.
Dann aber lasst mit frischem Mut	But later on, our courage renewed,
Uns unsre Pflicht erfüllen!	let us fulfill our duty!

5. ALLEGRO LEGGIERO (Chorus)

Chorus of Druid Guards

Vertheilt euch, wackre Männer hier	Divide your forces, valiant men
durch dieses ganze Waldrevier.	spread out through the forest here
und wachet hier im Stillen	and keep a quiet watch
wenn sie die Pflicht erfüllen.	while they fulfill their duty.

6. RECITATIVE: ALLEGRO MODERATO
(Baritone and Men's Chorus)

Druid Guard and Chorus of Druid Guards

Diese dumpfen Pfaffenchristen,	Christians and their priests are witless,
lasst uns keck sie überlisten!	therefore let's outwit them boldly!
Mit dem Teufel den sie fabeln	Let us terrify them
wollen wir sie selbst erschrecken!	with the Devil they've invented!
Kommt! Kommt mit Zacken und mit Gabeln	Come! Come with prongs and pitchfork
und mit Gluth und Klapperstocken	and with embers and with rattles

lärmen wir bei nächt'ger Weile	fill the night with din and uproar
durch die engen Felsenstrecken.	through the rocky mountain passes.
Kauz und Eule heul' in unser Rundgeheule!	Come, you owls, join us in our noisy howls!

7. ALLEGRO MOLTO (Chorus)

Chorus of Druids

Kommt mit Zacken und mit Gabeln,	Come with prongs and pitchforks,
wie der Teufel denn sie fabeln,	like the Devil they've invented,
und mit wilden Klapperstocken	and with wildly roaring rattles
durch die engen Felsenstrecken!	through the rocky mountain passes!
Kauz und Eule heul' in unser Rundgeheule!	Come, you owls, join us in our noisy howls!

8. L'ISTESSO TEMPO: ANDANTE MAESTOSO
(Baritone and Chorus)

Druid Priest and Chorus of Druids

So weit gebracht dass wir bei Nacht	It's come so far that now by night
Allvater heimlich singen!	we praise Great Father in secret!
Doch ist es Tag	Still, it is day
sobald man mag ein reines Herz dir bringen.	wherever one may present you with a heart that's pure.
Du kannst zwar heut' und manche Zeit	Although today and for many days
dem Feinde viel erlauben	you let our enemy prosper
Die Flamme reinigt sich vom Rauch:	the flame is purified by the smoke:
so reinig unsern Glauben!	thus purify our faith!
Und raubt man uns den alten Brauch,	And if they rob us of our rite,
dein Licht wer will es rauben?	will any rob us of Your light?

9. ALLEGRO NON TROPPO (Tenor and Men's Chorus)

Christian Guard and Chorus of Christian Guards

Hilf, ach hilf mir, Kriegsgeselle!	Help, oh help me, comrades!
Ach, es kommt die ganze Holle!	Oh, all hell is loosed upon us!
Sieh wie die verhexten Leiber	See those witches, see those bodies
durch und durch von Flamme gluhen!	glowing in the flames!
Menschen-Wolf und Drachen-Weiber,	Werewolves, horrid dragon women,
die im Flug voruber ziehen!	see them passing by in flight!
Welch 'entsetzliches Getöse!	What a dreadful deafening din!
Lasst uns, lasst uns Alle fliehen!	Let's all flee from here, let's flee!
Oben flammt und saust der Böse.	Up above roar flaming devils,
aus dem Boden dampfet rings	from below hellish vapors
ein Höllen-Broden!	rise around us!
Lasst uns fliehen!	Let us flee!

10. ANDANTE MAESTOSO (Baritone and Chorus)

Druid Priest and Chorus of Druids

Die Flamme reinigt sich vom Rauch,	The flame is purified by smoke,
so reinig 'unsern Glauben!	thus purify our faith!
Und raubt man uns den alten Brauch,	And if they rob us of our rite,
dein Licht, wer kann es rauben!	could any rob us of Your light?

ELIJAH, Op. 70 (Elias)

2 hours, 30 minutes

Musicians have long debated whether Mendelssohn's three major choral works reflect his religious duality—born into what had been a Jewish family, but living as a Lutheran. The main subject of *St. Paul* is a figure from the New Testament who, although born as a Jew, became an early leader of Christianity. *The First Walpurgis Night* sympathetically describes pagan rituals and presents Christians in a poor light. And *Elijah* probes the wisdom of an Old Testament prophet from Israel.

After the resounding success of the May 1836 premiere of *St. Paul,* Mendelssohn's thoughts turned to the creation of another work in the same form. On August 12, 1836, less than three months later, the composer wrote to his good friend Karl Klingemann, saying that he was contemplating a second oratorio and wanted to make a biblical figure the subject. Klingemann was less than enthusiastic, and Mendelssohn dropped the project.

A letter Mendelssohn wrote in 1838, though, shows that he had decided to focus a new oratorio on Elijah: "I thought to myself of Elijah as a thorough prophet, such as we might again require in our own day, energetic and zealous, but also stern, wrathful, and gloomy; a striking contrast to the court rabble and the popular rabble—in fact, in opposition to the whole world, and yet borne on angels' wings."

Mendelssohn's hope of composing an oratorio on Elijah came closer to fruition on June 11, 1845, when he received a letter from Joseph Moore, manager of the Birmingham (England) Music Festival, asking him to conduct the 1846 festival and to "provide a new oratorio or other music for the occasion." Poor health impelled Mendelssohn to refuse the role of conductor, but he accepted the composing challenge and, in his own words, "began once again to plough up the soil" of the Elijah oratorio.

Mendelssohn turned to the Reverend Julius Schubring, the librettist of his earlier oratorio *St. Paul,* to prepare the text. There ensued many arguments between composer and librettist; the latter could best be described as a fundamentalist minister who tried to superimpose his New Testament beliefs on the Old Testament story. Schubring suggested, for example, that Christ appear at the climax of the oratorio as the fulfillment of Elijah's prophecies.

Mendelssohn, who had strong emotional ties to the biblical text, firmly rejected Schubring's theological revisionism, and eventually the two men agreed on the text. The composer began serious work on the music sometime after January 1846, working at a feverish pace until he completed the monumental work on August 11, 1846—a scant two weeks before the first scheduled performance.

The premiere, on August 26 in Birmingham, which Mendelssohn did conduct, brought the composer-conductor wild acclaim. Although audiences traditionally did not applaud at oratorio performances, *The Times* described the public's reaction on this occasion as a "unanimous volley of plaudits, vociferous and deafening." The listeners demanded that eight sections— four choruses and four arias—be repeated during the performance.

Mendelssohn, apologizing that he had a "dread disease" that made him revise even those compositions that won public approval, immediately started reworking *Elijah*. The changes included major alterations in numbers one, seven, eight, nine, fifteen, twenty-one, and forty-two, the addition of numbers twenty-four, twenty-five, twenty-eight, and thirty-six, and the omission of a few movements. The new version had its first hearing in London on April 16, 1847, again with Mendelssohn conducting.

Mendelssohn composed *Elijah* for four soloists—bass (Elijah), tenor (Obadiah, Master of the King's Palace, and Ahab, Israelite King), alto (Angel and Queen Jezebel), and soprano (Widow and Angel)—four-part mixed choir (variously the people, the followers of Baal, bringers of the word of God, narrators, and commentators), and orchestra.

The libretto of *Elijah* presents several key, dramatic incidents in the life of the prophet, including his warning that the terrible drought signaled God's wrath, his resurrection of the widow's son, his defeat of the priests of Baal and the coming of rain, his suffering under King Ahab, his vision of God on Mount Horeb, and his ascent into heaven.

Elijah opens with four solemn wind chords, which Mendelssohn later associates with the word of God; these chords lead to a recitative in which the prophet announces the start of the drought. Instead of continuing with the story, Mendelssohn interrupts at this point for an exciting, richly textured overture, which was the suggestion of William Bartholomew, who translated into English the original German text with which Mendelssohn worked. After building to a climax, the overture continues at the same level of intensity; it then leads, without pause, into the powerful opening chorus—"Help, Lord!"—after which the people lament their dreadful condition and plead for surcease. Two soprano soloists join the plaintive lament of the chorus until Obadjah introduces a note of hope in his recitative and very popular aria "If with all your hearts."

After another chorus, "Yet doth the Lord," an angel and then a double quartet of angels announce God's will that Elijah go into the wilderness, where a widow will care for him. In a highly theatrical duet between the Widow and Elijah, the prophet brings her dead son back to life, and the choir joins in praise of the Lord.

Elijah next returns to Israel, and the music moves toward the climactic contest between the priests of Baal and Elijah—the priests raging and ranting, Elijah taunting them—out of which comes Elijah's solemn prayer "Lord God of Abraham." In a musical high point, the solo quartet sings "Cast thy burden," followed by movements in which the people report that God sent flames to earth in response to Elijah's prayers and then unleashed a downpour to end the drought. The first part of the oratorio ends with the highly rhythmic chorus of thanksgiving "Thanks be to God!"

Mendelssohn opens Part II with the major soprano aria of *Elijah,* "Hear ye, Israel," a contemplative, elegiac song that ends strongly and flows directly into the equally forceful chorus "Be not afraid." Now Queen Jezebel incites the crowd to slay Elijah, and the people show their anger in the stirring chorus "Woe to him," which is soon followed by the most popular aria of the work, Elijah's "It is enough."

Surely the best-known choral number of *Elijah* is the a cappella "Lift thine eyes," which Mendelssohn added for the 1847 performance by completely reworking a duet from the first version. Although written for two sopranos and an alto, it is often sung either by all the women of the choir or a boys' choir. The noble, confident mood continues in the following chorus, "He, watching over Israel," after which an angel calls the despondent Elijah into the presence of God on Mount Horeb. The alto aria of consolation, "O rest in the Lord" (which Mendelssohn wanted to omit, saying, "It is too sweet"), gives way to "He that shall endure," a chorus in rather severe chorale style.

Another climactic point in the oratorio comes with the vivid, pictorial chorus "Behold, God the Lord passed by!" which ends in a highly charged stillness that the singers carry over into the prayer "Above Him stood the Seraphim." The voices of the people then bid Elijah to return to his people ("Go, return upon thy way"), which he does. Finally, the choir describes his vengeful actions in the name of the Lord, after which he ascends to heaven in a "fiery chariot."

The story of Elijah ends at this point. Probably at the urging of Schubring, Mendelssohn added five more movements of a pious, devout nature. As with the sanctimonious epilogue to *Don Giovanni,* one wonders if the work would not be better without the appended conclusion. Be that as it may, audiences around the world rank Mendelssohn's *Elijah* along with Handel's *Messiah* and Haydn's *The Creation* in the great choral triumvirate.

CLAUDIO MONTEVERDI

Born (baptized May 15) 1567, in Cremona, Italy
Died November 29, 1643, in Venice

Just as his life bridged the sixteenth and seventeenth centuries, so Claudio Monteverdi's music bridged the wide stylistic chasm that separated those two eras. A cappella vocal polyphony, usually with four or more voices weaving their independent lines, dominated the music of the sixteenth century—the Renaissance period of music history. The seventeenth century—the Baroque period—saw increased use of instruments and the rise of homophony, or accompanied melody (although polyphony soon returned to favor). In addition to mastering and employing these two different styles depending on his specific musical needs, Monteverdi infused all his music with great emotion and expression, two qualities which were somewhat limited in the older music. The composer is also acknowledged as one of the creators and first masters of opera.

Monteverdi's life may be considered in three distinct parts. He was born and began his music studies in what was then the small provincial town of Cremona. From about 1590 to 1612 he served at the court of Vicenzo Gonzaga, Duke of Mantua, the figure portrayed in Verdi's *Rigoletto*. While the duke appreciated Monteverdi's considerable talents, he was less than generous in his treatment of the composer. And finally Monteverdi served as *maestro di cappella* at St. Mark's Cathedral in Venice from 1613 until his death in 1643.

A highly prolific composer, Monteverdi wrote several operas and a plenitude of choral and vocal works, both sacred and secular. In recent years, with the rise of the early music movement, Monteverdi's music has been rescued from the often ill-considered transcriptions that were the only sources available in the past. As his works receive more exposure in authentic performances, they are gaining considerably in popularity and appreciation.

VESPRO DELLA BEATA VERGINE
(Vespers of the Blessed Virgin)

2 hours

In this extraordinary composition, Monteverdi brings together sixteenth-century polyphony and modal harmonies with the homophony and major and minor scales of the seventeenth century. Monteverdi not only integrates these disparate styles, but succeeds at making the music highly expressive and emotional as well.

Monteverdi published *Vespro* in September 1610 while on a visit to Rome. The Rome publication and the dedication to Pope Paul V led many to suspect that Monteverdi hoped this composition would earn him a position in either Rome or Venice and allow him to leave Mantua permanently. Scholars believe that his 1613 appointment to St. Mark's in Venice was due, in part, to the success of *Vespro*.

The monumental *Vespro della Beata Vergine* lasts about two hours and requires vast performing forces—six soloists, a choir divided into as many as eight parts, an orchestra, and continuo. An account book from the time shows that Monteverdi used twenty-five vocalists (with boys singing the soprano and alto parts) and an orchestra of twenty-six—huge numbers for those times.

Choirs traditionally sang *Vespro* on the Marian feast days, such as Nativity, Annunciation, and Assumption, but because Monteverdi's *Vespro* is so lengthy and has interpolations of nonliturgical text, he probably planned it, not for church use, but for performance in a noble's private chapel. Some, including musicologist Denis Stevens, even hold that this mammoth composition should not be performed as a single piece at all.

Monteverdi cast *Vespro* in thirteen movements:

1. *"Domine ad adiuvandum."* Choir and orchestra. The choir essentially chants the plainsong melody on one chord throughout.

2. *"Dixit Dominus."* Soloists, choir, and orchestra. Psalm 109; mostly fugal in texture, but including some chanting.

3. *"Nigra sum."* Solo tenor and continuo. A wonderful miniature, with text from the Song of Songs.

4. *"Laudate, pueri, Dominum."* Soloists, choir, and orchestra. Psalm 112; an extended polyphonic movement in several sections with changes of tempo and meter. Monteverdi divides the choir into two groups and treats them antiphonally.

5. *"Pulchra es, amica mea."* Two soprano solos and continuo. Text from the Song of Songs with highly melismatic vocal writing.

6. *"Laetatus sum."* Soloists, choir, and orchestra. Psalm 121; some delightful coloratura in the voices.

7. *"Duo seraphim clamabant."* Alto and two tenor soloists and continuo. The three voices interweave and interact in virtuosic display; Monteverdi took the text from a popular motet of the time.

8. *"Nisi Dominus."* Choir and orchestra. Psalm 126; antiphonal in both polyphonic and chordal textures.

9. *"Audi coelum."* Choir and orchestra. The obligatory "echo" song, though here handled musically and expressively, rather than mechanically.

10. *"Lauda Jerusalem, Dominum."* Choir and orchestra. Psalm 147; an intricate, jubilant movement in which the composer divides the choir into three groups (soprano, contralto, and bass I; soprano, contralto, and bass II; and altos and tenors). The treatment is largely antiphonal.

11. *"Sonata."* Choir sopranos and orchestra. Basically an in-

strumental movement with the sopranos repeating the simple plainsong melody over and over again.

12. *"Ave maris stella."* Soloists, choir, and orchestra. A hymn with seven verses, each verse set with a variant of the plainsong melody and separated by instrumental ritornelli (interludes).

13. *"Magnificat."* Soloists, choir, and orchestra. The crowning movement of *Vespro,* setting the traditional words of the Magnificat in twelve separate sections, with the same melody appearing in some form in each. Monteverdi subsequently prepared a simplified version of the "Magnificat" for voices and organ.

WOLFGANG AMADEUS MOZART

Born January 27, 1756, in Salzburg
Died December 5, 1791, in Vienna

By virtually every criterion, Mozart was the world's most gifted and talented musician. Legendary are his sensitive ear, musical memory, ability to compose entire works in his head, and skills as a performer on the piano, violin, and viola. As composer, he produced masterworks in every form—from massive choral works to miniatures for the keyboard, grandiose opera to intimate chamber music, symphonies for the concert hall to music of worship for church.

Yet, despite his many amazing attributes, Mozart never achieved the success and recognition in his lifetime that he so surely deserved. In part this may have been due to his abrasive personality and unattractive appearance. Accounts from the time describe him as tactless, supercilious, arrogant, temperamental, and obstinate. Also, his short, slight frame with overly large head and bushy hair, his smallpox-pitted face with yellowish complexion, his bulging blue eyes, and his large nose made a poor impression on the aristocrats who could offer him the court position he desired.

Musicians often cite Mozart's music as the very embodiment of the eighteenth-century Classical style, with its clarity, economy of means, balance, elegance, and grace. Although his music contains much that is impassioned and emotional, every note he wrote falls well within the boundaries of good taste. As he put it, music "must never offend the ear, but must please the hearer, or in other words, must never cease to be music."

During the thirty-six years of his brief life, Mozart composed over fifty choral works, almost all between the years 1766 and 1781 while employed by the onerous Hieronymous Colloredo, archbishop of Salzburg, who expected Mozart to provide music for special church occasions along with his many other duties.

In 1781, Mozart left Salzburg for Vienna. During the following years, with but three notable exceptions, he wrote neither church nor choral music, since he derived most of his income from composing music for the concert hall or opera stage.

From Mozart's Salzburg years, the "Coronation" Mass, K. 317, and the *Vesperae solennes de confessore,* K. 339, tower over his other choral compositions. Three choral works dominate the composer's production in Vienna—the Mass in C minor, K. 427 (417a), *Ave verum corpus,* K. 618, and the *Requiem,* K. 626, even though the *Ave verum corpus* was the only one he finished.

(The identifying K numbers derive from Ludwig Köchel's 1862 chronological catalog of Mozart's compositions. The K numbers in parentheses come from updated versions of Köchel's catalog.)

MASS IN C MAJOR, "CORONATION," K. 317

25 minutes

On January 15, 1779, Mozart returned home after over a year's trip to Munich, Paris, and Mannheim in search of a court appointment to replace his unpleasant employment with Hieronymous Colloredo, archbishop of Salzburg. As Mozart wrote to his father, "The Archbishop cannot pay me enough for the slavery in Salzburg! The Archbishop had better not start to lord it with me as he used to—I just might thumb my nose at him!"

In addition to his personal anger at the archbishop, Mozart was frustrated by the restrictions on the church music he wrote. Colloredo insisted that the celebration of Mass not last longer than forty-five minutes, which left the composer no more than twenty minutes or so for the musical portion.

It was against this burdensome background that Mozart composed his "Coronation" Mass, completing it on March 23, 1779. Scholars long believed that Mozart wrote the Mass for the annual festival to commemorate the 1751 crowning of the miraculous Blessed Virgin painting in the pilgrimage church at Maria Plain, just north of Salzburg. According to Alfred Beaujean, though, recent scholarship casts some doubt on this assertion. In any case, there is general agreement that the "Coronation" Mass is the finest Mass Mozart wrote while in Salzburg.

Throughout the Mass, the listener is aware of Mozart's religious fervor. Two particularly stunning moments come in the *"Credo"*—the awesome *"Descendit de coelis"* and the rapturous *"Et incarnatus est."*

Careful listening also reveals that Mozart uses symphonic techniques to structure the music. To mention a few examples: Mozart recapitulates the melody of the alto solo from the *"Kyrie"* in the *"Agnus Dei"*; likewise, he takes the theme of *"Dona nobis pacem"* from the *"Kyrie"*; he organizes both the *"Credo"* and *"Benedictus"* in free rondo form; he structures the *"Gloria"* in a modified sonata allegro form; and he unifies the *"Sanctus"* by means of a repeated orchestral ostinato.

At times, the "Coronation" Mass recalls Mozart's operatic style. For instance, the soprano solo in *"Agnus Dei"* bears a striking resemblance to the Countess's aria *"Dove sono"* in *The Marriage of Figaro*, and the theme of the *"Kyrie"* is similar to Fiordiligi's aria in *Cosi fan tutte*.

Mozart calls for a large orchestra in the "Coronation" Mass —two oboes, two horns, two trumpets, three trombones, timpani, strings minus violas, and organ. The vocal forces consist of the usual four soloists and mixed choir.

Standard Text (see Appendix)

VESPERAE SOLENNES DE CONFESSORE, K. 339

35 minutes

Little is known of the circumstances behind the composition of Mozart's *Vesperae solennes de confessore* beyond the fact that it was written in Salzburg, probably in August 1780, for some saint's day. Composed for four soloists, mixed choir, and an orchestra that includes trumpets, trombones, and timpani, the work is a setting of five psalms—numbers 110, 111, 112, 113, and 117—plus a grandiose concluding "Magnificat."

Perhaps the most striking feature of *Vesperae solennes* is the uniquely expressive and distinctive melodies Mozart creates for the five psalms. The melodies project the particular meaning and character of the individual texts with amazing insight and understanding.

Two settings deserve special mention. The music for the fourth psalm, *"Laudate, pueri,"* is fugal throughout, archaic in sound, and very much in the style of the older Baroque polyphony. The fifth psalm, *"Laudate Dominum,"* a stark contrast to what has come before, features a warm, affecting solo soprano line gently floating over the choir and orchestra.

Psalm 110: DIXIT DOMINUS

Dixit Dominus Dominus meo:	The Lord said to my God:
Sede a dextris meis donec ponam inimicos tuos scabellum pedum tuorum.	Sit by me on my right side until I shall make of your adversaries a footstool for your feet.
Virgam virtutus tuae emittet Dominus ex Sion; dominare	The Lord will extend the scepter of your authority

in medio inimicorum tuorum.

outside Zion; you will rule over your enemies.

Tecum principium in die virtutis tuae in splendoribus sanctorum ex utero ante luciferum genui te.

You will have first place on the day of your strength in the shining temples; I have made you to have the strength of your early youth.

Iuravit Dominus et non poenitebit eum; tu es sacerdos in aeternum secundum ordinem Melchisedech.

This solemn oath the Lord has sworn, and He will not retract it; you are his priest till the end of time, great as was Melchisedek.

Dominus a dextris tuis confregit in die irae suae reges.

The Lord, favoring you, has crushed the power of kings on the day of His wrath.

Iudacibit in nationnibus; implebit ruinas; conquassabit capita in terra multorum.

He will pass judgment against whole nations; He will spread desolation; He will topple rulers from their thrones far and wide.

De torrente in via bibet; propterea exaltabit caput.

He will drink the waters that rage in your path; thus will He magnify your power.

Psalm 111: CONFITEBOR

Confitebor, Domine, in toto corde meo, in consilio iustorum et congregatione.

Lord, I shall acknowledge your power in the depths of my heart, in the council hall, and in the marketplace.

Magna opera Domini, exquisita in omnes voluntatis eius.

Great are the works of the Lord and cherished by those who love Him.

Confessio et magnificentia opus eius; et iustitia eius manet in saeculum saeculi.

Honor and glory are his creations, and his justice has no end.

Memoriam fecit mirabilium suorum misericors,

As He is gracious, He has let us know the wonders He has wrought,

Et iustus escam dedit timentibus se.

And as He is just, He has given sustenance to those that stand in awe of Him.

Memor erit in saeculum testamenti sui;	He will be mindful of his covenant forever.
Virtutem operum suorum annuntiabit populo suo	He will proclaim the greatness of his works to his chosen people
Ut det illis hereditatem gentium.	So that they may rule the nations as his representatives.
Opera manuum eius veritas et iudicium.	The works of his hands are truth and impartiality.
Fidelia omnia mandata eius in veritate et aequitate.	His commandments do not deviate from truth and fair dealing.
Redemptionem misit Dominus populo suo;	The Lord has sent salvation to his people.
Mandavit in aeternum testamentum suum.	He has commanded that his covenant last forever.
Sanctum et terribile nomen eius.	Hallowed and awesome is his name.
Initium sapientiae timor Domini;	Who worships the Lord begins to learn wisdom;
Intellectus bonus omnibus facientibus eum;	A good understanding do they have who do his will.
Laudatio eius manet in saeculum saeculi.	His glory lives forever and ever.

Psalm 112: BEATUS VIR

Beatus vir qui timet Dominum, in mandatis eius volet nimis.	Blessed is he who fears the Lord and finds much joy in fulfilling his commandments.
Potens in terra erit semen eius: generatio rectorum benedicetur.	His seed will be powerful in the land; his line of righteous descendants will be blessed
Gloria et divitiae in domo eius: et iustitia eius manet in saeculum saeculi.	Honor and riches abound in his house, and his good name lives forever.
Exortum est in tenebris lumen rectis: misericors, et miserator, et iustus.	A light has risen in the darkness for the God-fearing—for him who is compassionate, understanding, and just.

Jucundus homo qui miseretur et
commodat, disponet sermones
suos in iudicio: quia in
aeternum non commovebitur.

That man lives a rewarding life
who feels for others and
shares with them, who
chooses his words wisely; he
will not let himself be moved.

In memoria aeterna erit justus:
ab auditione mala non
timebit.

A righteous man will never be
forgotten; he will not fear evil
tongues

Paratum cor eius sperare in
Domino, confirmatum est cor
eius: non commovebitur
donec despiciat inimicos suos.

For his heart is strong and
armored in the faith of the
Lord; he will not be shaken
but will look upon his
enemies with contempt.

Dispersit, dedit pauperibus:
iustitia eius manet in
saeculum saeculi: cornu eius
exaltabitur in gloria.

The man who has shared his
goods and gives to the poor,
his good name endures
forever; his head will be
exalted with honor.

Peccator videbit, et irascetur,
dentibus suis fremet et
tabescet: desiderium
peccatorum peribit.

The wicked man, seeing this,
will be filled with rage,
gnashing his teeth and
growing thin with envy, but
the ill will of the wicked will
come to nought.

Gloria Patri et Filio et Spiritui
Sancto

Glory to the Father and Son
and Holy Spirit

Sicut erat in principio et nunc et
semper et in saecula
saeculorum. Amen.

Forever and ever. Amen.

Psalm 113: LAUDATE, PUERI

Laudate, pueri, Dominum;
laudate nomen Domini.

Praise the Lord, O priests;
praise the name of the Lord.

Sit nomen Domini benedictum
ex hoc nunc et usque in
saeculum.

Blessed be the name of the Lord
forevermore.

A solis ortu usque ad occasum:
laudabile nomen Domin

From the rising of the sun to its
setting, may the name of the
Lord be praised.

Excelsus super omnes gentes
  Dominus et super caelos
  gloria eius.
Quis sicut Dominus Deus noster
  qui in altis habitat et humilia
  respicit in caelo et in terra?

Suscitans a terra inopem et de
  stercore erigens pauperem

Ut collocet eum cum
  principibus, cum principibus
  populi sui;
Qui habitare facit sterilem in
  domo, matrem filiorum
  laetantem.

Gloria Patri et Filio et Spiritui
  Sancto
Sicut erat in principio et nunc et
  semper et in saecula
  saeculorum. Amen.

For the Lord is exalted over all
  nations and his glory is above
  the heavens.
Who is like the Lord, our God,
  that dwells on high yet sees
  every little thing on the earth
  and in the sky?

He raises the needy from the
  ground and lifts the poor
  man from his dung hill

So that he may be seated beside
  the rulers, the rulers of his
  people;

He has turned the barren
  woman into mistress of a
  house and a happy mother of
  children.

Glory to the Father, the Son,
  and the Holy Spirit
Now and forevermore. Amen.

Psalm 117: LAUDATE DOMINUM

Laudate Dominum, omnes
  gentes, laudate eum, omnes
  populi,
Quoniam confirmatus est super
  nos misericordia eius et
  Veritas Domini manet in
  aeternum.
Gloria Patri et Filio et Spiritui
  Sancto
Sicut erat in principio et nunc et
  semper in saecula saeculorum.
  Amen.

Praise the Lord, all you nations;
  praise Him, all you peoples,

For his compassion is a shield
  and support, and his Truth
  continues without end.

Glory to the Father, the Son,
  and the Holy Spirit
Now and forevermore.

Amen.

MAGNIFICAT

Magnificat anima mea
Dominum et exsultavit
spiritus meus in Deo, Salutari
meo,

My soul exalts the Lord, and
my spirit has rejoiced in God,
my Savior,

Quia respexit humilitatem
ancillae suae; ecce enim ex
hoc beatum me dicent omnes
generationes.

For He has looked from his
height on me who am but his
handmaiden, and on this
account all the races of men
shall call me blessed.

Quia fecit mihi magna qui
potens est, et sanctum nomen
eius.

For He who is omnipotent and
whose name is holy has
wrought much in my behalf.

Et misericordia eius a progenie
in progenies timentibus eum.

And his mercy will reach those
who worship Him from
generation to generation.

Fecit potentiam in braccio suo;
dispersit superbos mente
cordis sui.

He has shown the strength of
his arm; He has scattered as
chaff the aggressors in their
arrogance.

Deposuit potentes de sede et
exaltavit humiles.

He has put down the mighty
from their seats and exalted
the meek and humble.

Esurientes implevit bonis et
divites dimisit inanes.

He has filled the hungry with
nourishing foods and has sent
the rich away empty-handed.

Suscepit Israel puerum suum,
recordatus misericordiae suae.

He has raised his servant Israel,
mindful that He is a God of
mercy.

Sicut locutus est ad patres
nostros, Abraham et semini
eius in saecula.

This was his everlasting
covenant with our fathers,
with Abraham and all his
descendants.

Gloria Patri et Filio et Spiritui
Sancto.

Glory to the Father and Son
and Holy Spirit

Sicut erat in principio et nunc et
semper et in saecula
saeculorum. Amen.

Now and forevermore. Amen.

MASS IN C MINOR, "THE GREAT,"
K. 427 (K. 417a)

1 hour

Before May 1781, while in the employ of the archbishop of Salzburg, Mozart composed nearly twenty Masses for various special church functions. After leaving that position, he devoted himself almost exclusively to instrumental music and operas.

In the summer of 1782, though, just about when he announced his engagement to Constanze Weber, Mozart began composing a large-scale Mass. Later, in a January 4, 1783 letter to his father, Mozart wrote that he had "promised to his heart" to compose a Mass if she would accompany him to Salzburg as his wife. They were indeed married in Vienna on August 4, and just over a year later they went to Salzburg to introduce Constanze to Mozart's parents.

The composer was eager to have the Mass performed on that occasion, but he had only completed the *"Kyrie," "Gloria," "Sanctus," "Benedictus,"* and part of the *"Credo";* he had not even begun *"Agnus Dei."* Nevertheless, Mozart put together a performance of an entire Mass, probably substituting movements borrowed from his earlier Masses for the missing sections. The premiere of the Mass in this form was given on October 23, 1783 (not August 25, as once believed) at St. Peter's Church, Salzburg. (Most modern performances include only the parts Mozart wrote for the C minor Mass.)

Shortly before beginning the Mass, Mozart was introduced to the music of Johann Sebastian Bach at the Sunday concerts in the home of the Viennese aristocrat Baron Gottfried van Swieten, and he was much impressed by what he heard. The C minor Mass, and a few of Mozart's other works from this period, show the strong influence of Bach and late seventeenth-century Baroque style, especially in the much greater use of fugues and imitative counterpoint. As Mozart said of this older technique, "True church music lies in attics almost eaten by worms."

The grandly conceived Mass in C minor lasts much longer and is more monumental than any of Mozart's earlier works in the form, and it features much fugal writing. He scored it for four soloists—two sopranos (or soprano and mezzo-soprano), tenor, and bass—a mixed chorus (which at times is divided into as many as eight separate parts), and a full Mozart orchestra, minus clarinets, but including trombones.

Due to its powerful impact and strong theatricality, the C minor Mass does not easily fulfill the traditional role of the Mass in church ritual. In fact, the solo sections are more akin to the styles of contemporary opera than contemporary liturgical music.

Noted Mozart scholar Alfred Einstein wrote, "Mozart's church music . . . is 'catholic' in a higher sense of the word, namely in that all art is 'devout.' And so in this higher sense the 'catholicism' of Mozart's church music lies . . . in its humanity, in its appeal to all devout and childlike hearts, in its directness."

The intense writing and impressive dimensions have won for the C minor Mass the nickname "The Great" and have earned it a welcome place in the musical repertoire. Musicologist Karl Geiringer summed up the quality of this incredible work when he wrote, "The C Minor Mass marks a peak of artistic achievement which Mozart was to exceed only in his very last work [the *Requiem*]."

Standard Text (see Appendix)

AVE VERUM CORPUS, K. 618

5 minutes

By 1791, the last year of his life, Mozart suffered from ill health, poverty, and a lack of any opportunity to advance his career significantly. On June 4, his wife Constanze, pregnant for the sixth time and also ailing, went to Baden, a spa just outside of Vienna, to take the waters.

Less than a fortnight later, Mozart joined Constanze, and in just two days he completed an absolutely exquisite, miniature choral gem, the motet *Ave verum corpus*. He dedicated it to Anton Stoll, music director at the tiny parish church in Baden and an old friend, who looked after Constanze on her rather frequent visits to Baden. Stoll probably gave the first performance at the Feast of Corpus Christi in Baden on June 23, 1791.

Recognizing the limited resources of the Baden church, Mozart wrote *Ave verum corpus* for an orchestra made up only of strings and organ to accompany the mixed choir. Yet in the forty-six measures of this sublime composition Mozart achieves a model of Classical beauty and simplicity that he manages to infuse with intense fervor and deep spirituality.

Ave, verum corpus, natum de Maria virgine:	Hail, true Body born of the Virgin Mary:
Vere passum, immolatum in cruce pro homine;	That suffered truly and was crucified for mankind;
Cujus latus perforatum unda fluxit et sanguine.	Whose pierced side poured forth water and blood.
Esto nobis praegustatum in mortis examine.	Grant that we taste of it before we pass death's door.
O Jesu dulcis! O Jesu pie! O Jesu, fili Mariae.	O sweet Jesus! Holy Jesus! O Jesus, son of Mary.

REQUIEM, K. 626

55 minutes

The full circumstances surrounding the composition of Mozart's *Requiem* have been the subject of many fictionalized accounts (the play and film *Amadeus,* for example) and much scholarly research. Little wonder—it is one of the most intriguing stories in the entire history of music, raising questions that may never be answered.

The tale of the *Requiem* begins in July 1791, when a tall, lean stranger (now known to be Franz Anton Leitgeb, steward to Count Franz Walsegg-Stuppach) comes to visit Mozart, who is already sick and weak. The stranger, masked and wearing a large gray cloak, hands Mozart an unsigned letter and warns him at the same time to make no effort to discover the sender's name. The letter is a commission for a Requiem Mass at a fee to be set by Mozart.

Mozart agrees, and a few days later the messenger returns with fifty ducats (the equivalent of about $4,500 today), one half of the fee, the remainder to be paid on completion.

The composer immediately sets to work on the *Requiem,* but with fatalistic fervor, convinced that the messenger was, in effect, the Grim Reaper. Mozart is positive that he has been asked to write a Mass for his own death at the hands of an unknown murderer who has given him a slow-acting poison.

Soon after starting, though, Mozart interrupts work on the *Requiem* to write the opera *La clemenza di Tito* for the September 6 coronation of Emperor Leopold II in Prague. He also has to prepare *The Magic Flute* for its premiere on September 30.

Growing ever more feeble, Mozart resumes work on the *Requiem.* In September he writes to his librettist, Lorenzo Da Ponte: "My head is confused. It is only with difficulty that I can keep my thoughts collected. The image of that stranger will not part from my eyes. I always see him before me; he asks, he urges me, he impatiently demands the work from me. I continue because composing tires me less than rest. Otherwise there is nothing more at which I need tremble. I feel it, my condition tells me: my hour has struck! I shall have to die. And so I am finishing my funeral dirge. I must not leave it incomplete."

Now confined to bed, Mozart feverishly carries on. Eager to adumbrate his monumental conception, he sketches in entire sections while simultaneously writing the full score of the opening movement. When too ill to put pen to paper, he dictates the music to his friend and pupil Franz Xaver Süssmayr (not Antonio Salieri, as in *Amadeus*) and describes how he wants the music to end.

About these last days, Mozart's sister-in-law, Sophie Haibel, wrote, "Süssmayr was at Mozart's bedside. The well-known Requiem lay on the quilt, and Mozart was explaining to him how, in his opinion, he ought to finish it when he was gone. His last movement was to attempt to express with his mouth the drum passages in the Requiem. That I can still hear."

When death comes on December 5, 1791, Mozart has fully finished only the first of the *Requiem*'s eight sections, along with vocal parts, an outline of the harmony, and a few fully scored passages for movements two through five, although he has only done eight measures of the *"Lacrimosa"* section of the *"Sequentia."*

Eager to collect the remainder of the commission, Constanze, Mozart's widow, asks the young court composer Joseph von Eybler to complete the work. (Why she did not ask Süssmayr, the obvious choice, is a mystery.) Eybler, overwhelmed by the responsibility, refuses, and only then does Constanze ask Süssmayr to finish the parts Mozart has left incomplete and to supply the missing sections.

The discovery in 1962 of some sketches Mozart had prepared and given to Süssmayr raises questions about exactly how much of the music was Süssmayr's. But most everyone now agrees that Süssmayr completed the *"Lacrimosa"* beyond the eight measures Mozart had written, composed the entire *"Sanctus,"* *"Benedictus,"* and *"Agnus Dei,"* orchestrated *"Dies irae"* and

"Offertorium," and based the concluding *"Communion"* on the music Mozart had composed for the *"Kyrie."* Since Süssmayr's handwriting closely resembled his master's, Constanze had no trouble passing off the entire *Requiem* as Mozart's work.

Walther Brauneis, the Austrian historian, recently unearthed some documents showing that on December 10, 1791, a Requiem Mass was held for Mozart in St. Michael's Church in Vienna—at which time, according to a newspaper report, "the Requiem, which he composed in his last illness, was executed." Since Süssmayr had not yet started to complete the piece, probably only the fragment was performed, with some minor additions to give it a satisfactory ending.

Some two years later, on December 14, 1793, at the Cistercian monastery of Neukloster at Wiener Neustadt, Count Walsegg-Stuppach, who had originally commissioned the *Requiem,* conducted a performance of a Requiem that he claimed he had composed in memory of his recently departed wife. It soon came to light, though, that the composer of the Requiem was indeed Mozart, and that Count Walsegg-Stuppach had merely copied over and signed his name to the music.

Whether Süssmayr's additions followed suggestions and sketches that Mozart had given him, as he later insisted, or were completely original is still a matter for conjecture. Experts point to several passages that are not in the "true" Mozart style. But almost everyone agrees that the resulting work is a composition of sheer genius—a highly romantic, awestruck view of the mysteries of life and death. As Beethoven put it, "If Mozart did not write the music, then the man who wrote it was a Mozart."

Standard Text (see Appendix)

CARL ORFF

Born July 10, 1895, in Munich
Died March 29, 1982, in Munich

Carl Orff's early years gave no hint of the direction his life and music were to take. Born to a wealthy, cultured family, Orff displayed his musical abilities at an early age, had his first compositions published at age fifteen, and graduated from the Munich Academy of Music when he was nineteen years old. For several years, while continuing to compose in what can be termed a post-Romantic style, he held various conducting and coaching positions at opera houses in Munich, Mannheim, and Darmstadt.

Then came the turning. In 1920, Orff began studying with Heinrich Kaminski, a reclusive, mystic composer. Collaboration with dancer Mary Wigman at about the same time led to an interest in the eurhythmics of Émile Jaques-Dalcroze, who focused his attention on the physical elements involved in the creation and perception of music. Then, in 1925, with Dorothee Günther, Orff founded the Güntherschule, a music school that put into practice his evolving ideas on music education—that music should generate physical movement, that physical movement should generate music, and that improvising on simple percussion instruments, starting with the rhythmic patterns of everyday speech, should be a central part of every child's education. Out of his experience at the Güntherschule came Orff's five-volume teaching course, *Schulwerke*—an important publication, still in active music education use, that links music, speech, and gesture.

The first work by Orff that showed the influence of his rethinking of the fundamental concepts of music was *Carmina burana,* a scenic cantata he composed in 1935 and 1936. On its completion he disowned all of his previous music, making *Carmina burana,* in effect, his first composition.

Over the following years Orff wrote exclusively for the stage, since he believed that the potential of concert music had been largely exhausted. *Catulli carmina* (1943) and *Trionfo di Afrodite* (1952) are dramatic cantatas that Orff later added to *Carmina burana* to form a trilogy, which he entitled *Trionfi*. Neither the two later works nor his more operatic stage creations have had nearly the impact or the popularity of *Carmina burana*.

CARMINA BURANA

1 hour

In 1935, while Carl Orff was still teaching at the Güntherschule, a friend told him about a collection of thirteenth-century poems that had been discovered in 1803 at the Benediktbeuern monastery in the Bavarian Alps and were published in 1847 by Andreas Schmeller, who gave them the title *Carmina burana*— "Songs of Beuren."

The contents of *Carmina burana* varied widely, from finely wrought poetic lyrics to simple, rhyming minstrel ditties. The languages were varied, too; most of the poems were in medieval Latin, but with liberal use of Old German and Old French.

The poems of *Carmina burana* stimulated Orff's imagination. He saw them as an opportunity to adapt his new concept of music to a serious composition, and he spent the better part of two years—1935 and 1936—realizing his vision. The result was what he called a "scenic cantata" for soprano, tenor, and baritone soloists, a large mixed choir, and an orchestra with a huge percussion section that includes two pianos and five timpani! Although he intended the work to be danced and staged, with the orchestra, choir, and soloists in the pit, he gives no specific directions, preferring to leave the actualization in the hands of the performers. Most often, however, *Carmina burana* is heard in unstaged, concert form.

Orff groups the twenty-five separate numbers of *Carmina burana* into three major clusters—"Spring," "In the Tavern," and "The Court of Love." The thread that runs throughout is the working of Fortuna, the goddess of fate.

The work opens with two introductory choral numbers: a chorus, "O Fortuna," musing on the fickleness of human fate ("O Fortune, variable as the moon, always dost thou wax and wane"), followed by a chorus bemoaning the cruelty of fate.

The "Spring" section follows, with its several individual selections extolling the varied joys of the vernal season. The rough and gruff second part, "In the Tavern," uses only the male soloists and choristers and is essentially a series of drinking songs. Orff explores the many facets of love from both the woman's and man's viewpoint in "The Court of Love." This section builds in intensity toward a final hymn to *"Venus generosa."* And the work concludes with a repeat of the opening chorus, "O Fortuna."

The premiere of *Carmina burana* in Frankfurt on June 8, 1937, caused an absolute sensation. Nothing quite like this had ever been heard before. It seemed as though Orff had reduced music to its most basic elements of rhythm and melody, particularly the former. He built up both the rhythm and melody from small units that he subjected to huge numbers of repetitions without change and without passing the units through any development or transformation. The composer utilized the simplest harmonies and eliminated virtually all counterpoint and polyphony. Almost always he treated the dynamics in terraces, moving from soft to loud or loud to soft in a single leap without gradually shifting from one to the other. In place of one of the traditional forms, Orff organized the music in blocks. Each block is complete in itself, yet the blocks follow each other with an inner logic that impels the music forward throughout the entire composition.

GIOVANNI PIERLUIGI DA PALESTRINA

Born between February 1525 and February 1526, in
Palestrina, Italy
Died February 2, 1594, in Rome

Born Giovanni Pierluigi, the composer added *"da Palestrina"*
("from Palestrina") to his name, a reference to the small town
east of Rome where he was born. Curiously enough, he is uni-
versally known today by the name of his birthplace.

Although Palestrina worked for some time as a church musician in the town of his birth, he spent many more years in
Rome, most of that time singing, conducting, and composing
for various churches, including St. Peter's and the Sistine
Chapel. While it is hard to imagine how he found the time,
Palestrina also operated a fur business that his second wife had
inherited.

Palestrina's lifetime coincided with the latter years of the Renaissance, the amazing period of human creativity that began in
the fifteenth century with significant advances in the arts, the
sciences, learning, and voyages of exploration—along with a
new philosophical perspective, called humanism, which focused
on the realities of human existence rather than the world of the
spirit and the afterlife. Palestrina's years also span the decades
following the Protestant Reformation, when the newly established Protestant churches challenged the central, supreme position of the Catholic church.

The impact of all of these incredible changes on music was, of
course, immense. The dominant musical texture of the centuries
preceding the Renaissance was monophony—a single line of
melody without accompaniment or countermelody. But by the

thirteenth century, music in several parts, or polyphony, appeared. Almost always, however, composers built their music on a cantus firmus, a preexisting melody, to which they added other lines.

By the Renaissance, polyphony was the predominant texture, and music was typically written with several parts of equal importance. Even though many Renaissance composers continued to use a cantus firmus, the practice became much freer, with the cantus firmus also coming from popular melodies and folk songs instead of exclusively from Gregorian chant.

The emerging polyphony was a reflection of the new beliefs of the Renaissance. Monophony represented a world outlook which held that everything flowed from God, a single source, with only one man, the priest, able to communicate with God. Renaissance polyphony, on the other hand, could be conceived as music of equals, with everyone the same before God and therefore able to worship individually. The music is made up of several independent voices of comparable importance and value. As English musicologist Wilfrid Mellers summed it up, "Monody [monophony] is man in relation to God; polyphony is man in relation to his fellow man."

Around the middle of the sixteenth century, the Catholic church began to take steps to win back some of the adherents it had lost as a result of the Reformation. Through the Counter-Reformation and the Council of Trent, church officials tried to correct problems and difficulties within Catholicism as a way of making the religion more appealing and attractive. In their effort to improve church music, the authorities often pointed to Palestrina as the composer who best exemplified the ideals of the Catholic church and whose music served as an ideal model.

Palestrina produced so much music—one hundred Masses, nearly two hundred motets, over a hundred hymns and offertories, and thirty-five Magnificats—that a complete edition of his works fills thirty-three volumes. Of this vast body of music, perhaps a dozen compositions remain in the current repertoire. And of these, the most widely performed and frequently recorded is surely the *Pope Marcellus Mass.*

Virtually every single composition in Palestrina's vast oeuvre is religious in nature. He wrote about eighty secular madrigals, but their musical style and spirituality of tone closely resemble that of his other works.

POPE MARCELLUS MASS
(Missa Papae Marcelli)

30 minutes

Pope Marcellus II was distressed at the music he heard in St. Peter's at the observances of Holy Week 1555. He complained of difficulty in understanding the text, the lack of serious tone in the music, and the excessive length of the musical selections. Following the Good Friday services he summoned the Papal Choir and told them of his concerns. *"Primo le parole e poi la musica"* ("First the words and then the music"), he declared.

Palestrina, who was singing with and composing for the Papal Choir at the time, took Pope Marcellus's words very much to heart. Probably the very next year, Palestrina composed a Mass dedicated to the Pope, in which the composer tried to correct the abuses that offended Pope Marcellus.

Palestrina wrote the *Pope Marcellus Mass* for six voices a cappella, or unaccompanied; the particular voices, however, are not clearly identified. Two common voicings are soprano, alto, two tenors, and two basses, or two sopranos, alto, tenor, and two basses.

A striking characteristic of the *Pope Marcellus Mass* is the perfection of the melodies. Nothing intrudes, nothing upsets, everything is in balance and in proportion, creating a wonderful sense of otherworldly beauty and heavenly repose. Palestrina's polyphonic treatment of the six lines has the different voices blending and interweaving seamlessly and effortlessly, effectively hiding the skill and technique necessary to achieve such results.

Although the music floats along, without any strong rhythmic impulse or interruption to the gentle flow, careful listening reveals a fervor, a powerful religious quality, behind the apparent restraint and control. Though the music never shouts or pounds, it convincingly conveys the composer's strong religious beliefs and unquestioning acceptance of a Divine Being.

The predominant texture of *Pope Marcellus Mass* is polyphony, more particularly imitative polyphony, in which the various voices repeat a melody, each voice starting at a different time and often on a different pitch. The opening movement, *"Kyrie,"* is an excellent example of imitative polyphony: the four-note opening phrase passes through voices three, one, six, and two, followed somewhat later by voices four and five stating the same melody.

While *Pope Marcellus Mass* is predominantly polyphonic, some movements are much more chordal in texture; that is, all the voices form chords as they move along in the same rhythmic pattern. The second movement, *"Gloria,"* is an example of a chordal movement. Although there are any number of minor exceptions, all the voices move along in virtually identical rhythm throughout.

Since *Pope Marcellus Mass* was written over four hundred years ago, church officials have cited it time and again as the most perfect example of Catholic sacred music and the finest example of music from that era, which is known as the Golden Age of A Cappella Vocal Polyphony. Whether in church or the concert hall, for Christians or not, *Pope Marcellus Mass* continues to thrill audiences. Like all true masterpieces, it is both timeless and universal in its appeal.

Standard Text (see Appendix)

FRANCIS POULENC

Born January 7, 1899, in Paris
Died January 30, 1963, in Paris

For the first two decades of his composing career, Francis Poulenc almost exclusively wrote music for fun and entertainment. His name was closely associated with an informal group of equally irreverent young French composers known as *Les Six* (Louis Durey, Arthur Honegger, Darius Milhaud, Germaine Tailleferre, Georges Auric, and Poulenc). Their major influence was Erik Satie, the wonderful musical iconoclast who, as an example, numbered his first composition Op. 62 and who, when accused of writing music without form, wrote *Three Pieces in the Form of a Pear*.

Poulenc was probably the most skillful and successful member of the group in realizing the aims of *Les Six*. His music represented a reaction against the seriousness and solemnity of the music of both French Impressionism and German Romanticism. His compositions are endowed with delicacy and lightness, touches of jazz, great lucidity and clarity, and a full measure of charm and humor to replace the emotional and expressionist content of the older composers.

A major change in Poulenc's life came in 1936 when his good friend, the composer Pierre Octave Ferroud, died in an auto accident. The incident brought Poulenc back to the Catholic church, where he had been so deeply involved as a child. And his music took on a much more serious and spiritual quality.

The new religiosity first appears in *Litanies à la vierge noire de Rocamadour* ("Litanies to the Black Virgin of Rocamadour") of 1936. Other works displaying the reawakening of Poulenc's faith followed: *Mass* (1937), *Stabat Mater* (1951), the opera *Dialogues des Carmélites* (1956), and *Gloria* (1959), the best known of his choral compositions.

Despite the solemn, devotional intent of Poulenc's later religious music, he was never fully capable of repressing the wit and charm of his earlier style. As he put it, he was "half monk, half bounder." This mingling of styles makes these more serious works all the more attractive and appealing.

GLORIA

25 minutes

Poulenc's religious convictions were, as he put it, "instinctive and hereditary." Although born to a pietistic father and subject to rigorous church training as a child, he gave no indication of his deep religious faith in his musical compositions until the death of his friend Pierre Octave Ferroud in 1936.

Over the following decades, Poulenc wrote a number of major liturgical works, of which the most familiar is *Gloria*. He composed *Gloria* from May to December 1959 on a commission from the Koussevitzky Foundation of the Library of Congress, and he dedicated the composition to the memories of Serge Koussevitzky (former conductor of the Boston Symphony) and Koussevitzky's wife, Natalie.

The *"Gloria"* is the joyous second part of the Ordinary of the Mass, the most solemn rite of the Roman Catholic church. Poulenc, however, treats this section as an independent work, complete in itself. His style strikes a balance between the traditional solemnity of church music, the exultancy of the message of the *"Gloria,"* and the Gallic high spirits that he seemed incapable of expunging from his music.

Poulenc's comments on the *Gloria* give an insight into the approach he favored. He once said, "I like the spirit of religion to be expressed clearly in the sun." On another occasion he wrote that he tried to make the *Gloria* "a joyous hymn to the glory of God." And he described the tone colors of the *Gloria* as "very clear, primary colors—rude and violent like the Provence chapel of Matisse."

Some critics have remarked that perhaps the exuberant, jazzy elements overpower the underlying religious and devotional aspects of the *Gloria*. To these reproofs, Poulenc responded, "The second movement caused an uproar. I wonder why? In writing it, I simply thought of those frescoes of Gozzoli [Benozzo Gozzoli, fifteenth-century Italian painter] in which the angels are sticking out their tongues and also of those serious Benedictine monks whom I spotted one day playing soccer."

Poulenc organizes the *Gloria* into six major sections. The first, *"Gloria in excelsis Deo,"* is a bold, declamatory song of praise.

"Laudamus te," the second, is lively and rhythmic, a joyful, exultant affirmation of faith that evoked the most criticism. Here, the composer separates the choir into two groups—sopranos and tenors introducing the individual lines of text, mezzo-sopranos and basses singing the same lines in imitation.

"Domine Deus, Rex coelestis," a serene, spiritual prayer of supplication, introduces the soprano soloist.

The following *"Domine Fili unigenite,"* a movement virtually bursting with glee and rapture, makes the fervor of Poulenc's religious convictions most readily apparent.

Poulenc assigns a particular melodic shape to each phrase of the text in the next section. *"Domine Deus"* leaps dramatically upward; *"Agnus Dei"* goes down two steps and up one; *"Rex coelestis"* and *"Qui tollis"* both start with repeated notes on one pitch; and so on.

An impassioned introduction for a cappella choir with violent orchestral interjections opens the final movement, *"Qui sedes ad dexteram Patris;"* this opening leads to the faster body of the movement with its exciting, dramatic sweep, which brings the entire work to a conclusion.

Poulenc composed the *Gloria* for soprano soloist, four-part mixed choir, and orchestra. (He calls the second female choral part "mezzo-soprano," instead of the more customary "alto"; there is, however, no noticeable difference in the vocal range or style of writing.) The premiere of *Gloria* was given on January 20, 1961, performed by the Boston Symphony under Charles Munch.

Standard Text (see Appendix)

SERGEY PROKOFIEV

Born April 23, 1891, in Sontsovka, Russia
Died March 5, 1953, in Moscow

"And as far as politics, they don't concern me," Prokofiev once wrote. "It is none of my business." Ironically, his life was changed and shaped to a remarkable extent by the political turmoil that raged around him.

Prokofiev showed his amazing musical talent when still very young. His mother, an excellent amateur pianist, started giving him lessons before he was five years old. By age thirteen he was enrolled in the St. Petersburg Conservatory, where his outstanding musical gifts were often obscured by his harsh, abrasive personality, an obvious lack of respect for his teachers, and an ill-concealed contempt for the other students. One of his least endearing traits was to compile lists of all the mistakes made in class by his fellow students!

Prokofiev feared that the Communist government, which came to power a few years after his 1914 graduation from the conservatory, would not be sympathetic to composers and would make it difficult, if not impossible, for him to develop a career in Russia. His insecurity impelled him to leave the country, settling first in New York and then in Paris. Homesick and sympathetic to the Communist ideals, however, Prokofiev returned to Russia on two extended concert tours as pianist. Both times, though, he hesitated to settle permanently in Russia.

It was not until 1933 that Prokofiev finally decided to go back home. For the remaining years of his life, government authorities subjected every one of his compositions to evaluation to see if it met the criteria of "social realism" that all music should display. Sometimes Prokofiev was in favor, and his compositions were widely performed. Other times he was sternly criticized, and his music disappeared from concert programs.

The final irony of Prokofiev's life is that he died on the exact same date as Joseph Stalin, the Russian dictator who so completely dominated Prokofiev's personal and professional life.

ALEXANDER NEVSKY, Op. 78

40 minutes

In the years following the Russian Communist revolution of 1917, many of Russia's leading artists left the country. Among those who fled were composer Sergey Prokofiev and film director Sergey Eisenstein. After some work in Hollywood and Mexico, Eisenstein returned in 1932, and one year later Prokofiev also came back, following fifteen years of living in Western Europe and the United States. During his self-imposed exile, Prokofiev had been asked by Walt Disney to write some film scores. He refused, but he did spend some time at the Disney studios, becoming familiar with the techniques of composing for movies.

Although both Prokofiev and Eisenstein were drawn irresistibly to their beloved homeland, they had grave concerns about their ability to function as creative artists under Stalin's repressive regime. These were the circumstances when Eisenstein, in May 1938, asked Prokofiev to compose the music for his planned epic motion picture on Alexander Nevsky. Prokofiev, long an admirer of Eisenstein's work, immediately agreed.

The hero of Eisenstein's film, Alexander Nevsky (1220–63), was prince of the city of Novgorod during the period of the Mongolian conquest of Russia (1240–1480). He first came to attention in 1240 when he led his army in a stunning victory over an invading Swedish army. Then, two years later, he defeated an invasion by the crusading army of the Teutonic Order of the Sword from Germany, which was attacking with the approval and blessing of the Pope. The climactic battle took place on frozen Lake Chud (Peipus), where the heavily armored Teutons fell through the ice and drowned.

Both Eisenstein and Prokofiev realized that the subject was

perfect for the time, serving as a metaphor for the all but inevitable upcoming war with Germany and the hoped-for defeat of the Germans by Stalin. Eisenstein wrote that if "the might of the people's spirit" could avenge itself so successfully on an enemy even when the country was still exhausted from the fetters of the Tartar yoke, "then what force could be strong enough to destroy this country today, now that it has thrown off all chains of oppression? For today our country has become a socialist Motherland and is led to unprecedented victories by the greatest strategist in world history—STALIN!"

Prokofiev's general approach to composing the musical score was to watch the rushes at the end of each day's shooting, time each scene to the second, go home, write the music in a piano score, and deliver it to Eisenstein by noon of the next day. The composer would then accompany a showing of the new part of the film on the piano and, if necessary, make changes in the score. So close and sympathetic was the relationship between director and composer, though, that on occasion Prokofiev wrote the music for a scene *before* it was filmed, and Eisenstein would tailor the action and images to the music.

Right from the start, Prokofiev decided against quoting thirteenth-century music: "Original musical material from the 13th century has become so alien to us in an emotional sense that it cannot supply sufficient food for the spectator's imagination. I thought that it would be best to write the music for the Teutons, not as it actually sounded at the time of the Battle on the Ice, but as we now imagine it. I adopted the same approach in working on the Russian music. It is cast in a modern mold rather than in the style of 700 years ago." He used the word "recomposed" to describe his approach.

Prokofiev's score, though, went far beyond "background music." In addition to the orchestra, the composer called for a chorus (at times representing the peasants of Novgorod, at other times the Teutonic Knights) and a mezzo-soprano soloist (a Russian maiden mourning her slain lover). Prokofiev wrote the texts for the vocal selections.

The first showing of the film took place in Moscow on December 1, 1938, where it won the immediate and enthusiastic approval of the authorities and critics, and it became a popular hit with the Russian public. Early in 1939, Prokofiev decided to arrange the music into a dramatic cantata for mezzo-soprano soloist, mixed choir, and orchestra. Most of the score, he found, worked perfectly in this new concert version. Only "The Battle on the Ice" and "Alexander's Entry into Pskov" required some reworking. Prokofiev conducted the premiere of the *Alexander Nevsky* cantata in Moscow on May 17, 1939.

The composer separated the cantata into seven individual numbers:

"Russia Under the Mongolian Yoke." A bleak, hollow-sounding orchestral prelude that evokes the desolation and gloom of the Russian people during the brutal Tartar invasion. Eisenstein used these words of description: "Woeful traces of the ravages wrought on Russia by the Mongols—heaps of human bones, swords, rusty lances. Fields overgrown with weeds and ruins of buried villages."

"Song About Alexander Nevsky." The peasants sing of Nevsky's earlier military success against the Swedes ("We shall never yield native Russian land") and of the Russians' determination to overcome all enemy invaders. Brief reminders of the recent fray interrupt.

"The Crusaders in Pskov." The Germans pillage the city. A sinister and clashing military theme sounds before and between statements of a Latin hymn ("As a foreigner, I expected my feet to be cymbal-shod"). The hymn characterizes the cruel Teutonic warriors hiding behind their religious pretensions.

"Arise, ye Russian people." Novgorod peasants marching off to war sing a stirring, heroic call to battle ("Arise to arms, ye Russian folk, in battle just, in fight to death").

"The Battle on the Ice." Nearly half the film—and the major movement of the cantata—are devoted to this musical depiction of the climactic battle on the frozen lake: the chilly mists of dawn, the advancing armies, the fury of the conflict, the drowning of the Teutons, and the return of quiet. Prokofiev includes

an elaboration of the earlier chant "As a foreigner, I expected my feet to be cymbal-shod."

"The Field of the Dead." A Russian girl laments her lover who has been slain in battle: "He who fell for Russia in noble death shall be blest by my kiss on his dead eyes."

"Alexander's Entry into Pskov." Nevsky's triumphant return. "Celebrate and sing, native mother Russia! In our native land foes shall never live."

HENRY PURCELL

Born between June and November, 1659, in London
Died November 21, 1695, in London

Biographers know precious little of the life of Henry Purcell. They believe that his father was Thomas Purcell, a musician in the king's service. By age ten young Henry was already composing and singing as a boy soprano in the Chapel Royal. Eight years later Purcell became composer for the king's orchestra, and a decade after that he was appointed organist at Westminster Abbey. In 1682 he was chosen as one of the organists of the Chapel Royal.

Throughout his tenure in the various posts, Purcell functioned as a sort of unofficial composer to the royal court. As such, he turned out an immense amount of choral music to celebrate weddings, birthdays, festivals, visits by dignitaries, church holidays, and significant national events. These choral works are variously entitled odes, anthems, welcome songs, cantatas, hymns, and psalms. Purcell also produced a considerable body of songs, instrumental compositions, and theater music of exceptionally high quality—which is all the more remarkable when one realizes that Purcell died in his thirty-sixth year.

Great rhythmic energy and freshness of melodic creation fill Purcell's music. With an ease that hides the skill involved, his choral writing passes effortlessly from the accompanied melody of homophony to the most complex interweavings of polyphony. Commentators are largely in accord, though, that most outstanding is his ability to set the English language. With remarkable skill he captures the natural rhythms and inflections of English speech, at the same time adapting the prosody to his own artistic purposes.

Seventeenth-century Purcell set a level of musical composition in England that was not equaled until two hundred years later, with such composers as Elgar, Delius, Vaughan Williams, Walton, Tippett, and Britten.

ODE TO ST. CECILIA
(Hail, Bright Cecilia)

57 minutes

St. Cecilia, a saint of the Roman Catholic church, was martyred around A.D. 230. Since she was famous for singing the praises of God, St. Cecilia has long been considered the patron saint of music; her feast day is November 22.

The earliest known musical celebration of St. Cecilia's Day dates back to 1570 at Evreux, Normandy. The tradition of having musical performances on St. Cecilia's Day began in England in 1683, and Purcell wrote two odes—*Laudate Ceciliam* and *Welcome to All the Pleasures*—for that occasion. Neither of these odes holds a place in the modern repertoire.

It was for the festival in 1692 that Purcell wrote his third and most famous ode to St. Cecilia, the one known as either *Ode to St. Cecilia* or *Hail, Bright Cecilia*. A contemporary magazine, *Gentleman's Journal*, described the celebration in London:

> The 22nd November, being St. Cecilia's Day, is observed through all Europe by the lovers of Music. On that Day, or the next when it falls on a Sunday, most of the lovers of Music, whereof many are persons of the first rank, meet at Stationers' Hall in London, not through a principle of superstition but to propagate the advancement of that divine science. A splendid entertainment is provided and before it always a performance of Music by the best voices and hands in town: the words which are always in the patroness's praise, are set by some of the greatest Masters in town. The feast is one of the genteelest in the world; there are no formalities nor gatherings like at others, and the appearance there is always very splendid. While the company is at table the Hautbois [oboes] and Trumpets play successively.

Using a poem by Nicholas Brady, who was chaplain to Queen Mary II, Purcell composed his ode for six soloists, mixed choir, and orchestra. The premiere was given on St. Cecilia's Day, November 22, 1692, in London.

The *Gentleman's Journal* report on the performance has led to some confusion. The article said, "The following Ode was admirably set to Music by Mr. Henry Purcell, and performed twice with universal applause, particularly the second Stanza [" 'Tis nature's voice"], which was sung with incredible Graces [ornaments] by Mr. Purcell himself."

Yet, in the autograph score, the name of Mr. Pate, a well-known singer of the time, appears next to that verse, and in the roster of singers who performed at the coronation of James II in 1685, Purcell is listed as a bass, while the stanza in the ode called for a countertenor. Could the writer for *Gentleman's Journal* have made a note that a "Mr. P" sang the stanza, meaning Mr. Pate, but when he wrote the article he mistakenly substituted Mr. Purcell's name?

The *Ode to St. Cecilia* opens with an instrumental "Symphony," which is in five sections, alternately slow and fast in tempo. The following twelve movements are all vocal, featuring the choir and the soloists. The unifying thread in all these stanzas is praise for music, for Cecilia, and for the various musical instruments—the "sprightly violin," "noble organ," "lofty viol," "am'rous flute," and "soft guitar."

For listeners—and for choristers as well—*Ode to St. Cecilia* contains some very special moments: "Soul of the world," with its expansive opening on a sustained pedal tone; the striking trembling effect to the words "The jarring seeds"; and the concluding "Hail! bright Cecilia," replete with its stirring instrumental fanfares and thrilling shouts of "Hail!" from the choir.

1. Symphony	With love of thee and thy celestial art,
2. Soli and Chorus: "Hail! Bright Cecilia"	That thine, and Music's sacred love
Hail! bright Cecilia, fill ev'ry heart	May make the British forest prove

As famous as Dodona's vocal grove.

3. Duet: "Hark, Each Tree"

Hark, each tree its silence breaks,
The box and fir to talk begin,
This in the sprightly violin,
That in the flute distinctly speaks.
'Twas sympathy their list'ning brethren drew.
When to the Thracian lyre with leafy wings they flew.

4. Alto Solo: " 'Tis Nature's Voice"

'Tis nature's voice, thro' all the wood and creatures understood, the universal tongue, to none of her num'rous race unknown.
From her it learned the mighty art
To court the ear, or strike the heart,
At once the passions to express or move,
We hear, and straight we grieve or hate, rejoice or love.
In unseen chains it does the fancy bind.
At once it charms the sense and captivates the mind.

5. Chorus: "Soul of the World"

Soul of the world, inspired by thee,

The jarring seeds of matter did agree.
Thou didst the scattered atoms bind
Which by the laws of true proportion joined,
Made up of various parts, one perfect harmony.

6. Soprano Solo and Chorus: "Thou Tun'st This World"

Thou tun'st this world below, the spheres above,
Who in the heavenly round to their own music move.

7. Trio: "With That Sublime Celestial Lay"

With that sublime celestial lay can any earthly sounds compare?
If any earthly music dare, the noble organ may.
From heav'n its wondrous notes were giv'n,
Cecilia oft conversed with heav'n.
Some angel of the sacred quire
Did with this breath the pipes inspire,
And of the notes above the just resemblance gave,
Brisk without lightness, without dullness, grave.

8. Bass Solo: "Wond'rous Machine"

Wond'rous machine, to thee the
warbling lute,
Tho' used to conquest, must be
forced to yield,
With thee unable to dispute.

9. Alto Solo: "The Airy Violin"

The airy violin and lofty viol
quit the field.
In vain they tune their speaking
strings
To court the fair or praise
victorious kings.
While all thy consecrated lays
Are to more noble uses bent.
And every grateful note to
heav'n repays
The melody it lent.

10. Duet: "In Vain the Am'rous Flute"

In vain the am'rous flute and
soft guitar jointly labour
To inspire wanton heat and
loose desire,
While thy chaste airs to gently
move
Seraphic flames and heav'nly
love.

11. Alto Solo: "The Fife and all the Harmony of War"

The fife and all the harmony of
war in vain attempt the
passions to alarm.

Which thy commanding sounds
compose and charm.

12. Duet: "Let These Among Themselves Contest"

Let these among themselves
contest
Which can discharge its single
duty best.
Thou summ'st their diff'ring
graces up in one.
And art a consort of them all
within thyself alone.

13. Great Chorus: "Hail! Bright Cecilia"

Hail, bright Cecilia, hail to
thee!
Great Patroness of us and
Harmony!
Who whilst among the quire
above
Thou dost thy former skill
improve.
With rapture of delight dost see
Thy fav'rite art make up a part
Of infinite felicity.

TE DEUM AND JUBILATE

17 minutes

Scholars believe that Purcell composed five festal odes for celebrations of St. Cecilia's Day—two in 1683, the famous one in
1692, the undated *Raise, Raise the Voice,* and the final one, *Te
Deum and Jubilate,* in 1694. (See the entry concerning Purcell's
Ode to St. Cecilia for background on St. Cecilia's Day celebrations.)

As in all of the previous odes—with the exception of *Laudate
Ceciliam,* which had no soloists—Purcell composed *Te Deum
and Jubilate* for soloists, choir, and orchestra. Since the vocalists
and instrumentalists who would be performing were among the
best of the day, Purcell felt free to write extremely florid, virtuosic parts for the soloists, as well as elaborate choral parts and
brilliant, demanding instrumental parts.

Te Deum and Jubilate received a very warm reception at its
first performance and was repeated at subsequent St. Cecilia
celebrations. It was also performed annually for the Festival of
the Sons of the Clergy at St. Paul's Cathedral from 1697 to
1713. After that it was offered every other year, alternating with
Handel's *Utrecht Te Deum* until 1743, when it was replaced by
Handel's *Dettingen Te Deum.* Further, *Te Deum and Jubilate*
received frequent performances at celebrations of British military victories.

Purcell organized his *Te Deum and Jubilate* into a series of
twenty-two very short movements that explore the full range of
performing media possible with the five soloists, mixed choir,
and orchestra of trumpets and strings. The textures of the choral writing, for example, include varied textures: four-part
counterpoint, imitative polyphony, antiphonal singing by the
divided choir, and completely chordal singing.

Despite the fragmentary approach, though, Purcell gives the

work a lavish sweep and magnificence. The trumpets, in particular, add great brilliance and splendor to the overall sound.

TE DEUM

Soprano, Alto, Bass: We praise Thee, O God, we acknowledge Thee, to be the Lord.

CHORUS: All, all the earth doth worship Thee, the Father everlasting.

Verse or (Semi Chorus): To Thee All Angels cry aloud, the Heav'ns, and all the Pow'rs there-in

To Thee Cherubim and Seraphim continually do cry,

CHORUS: Holy, continually do cry, Holy, Lord God of Sabaoth;

Verse or (Semi Chorus): Heaven and earth

CHORUS: are full of the Majesty of Thy Glory.

Alto: The glorious company of the Apostles praise Thee,

Tenor: The goodly fellowship of the Prophets praise Thee,

Bass: The noble army of Martyrs praise Thee.

CHORUS: The holy Church, throughout all, all the world doth acknowledge Thee.

The Father of an infinite Majesty,

Thine honourable, true, Thine true, and only Son;

Also the Holy Ghost, the Comforter.

Thou art the King of Glory, O Christ.

Thou art the everlasting Son of the Father.

When Thou took'st upon thee to deliver man,

Thou didst not abhor the Virgin's womb,

When Thou hadst overcome the sharpness of death,

Thou didst open the Kingdom of Heav'n to all believers.

Thou sittest at the right hand of God, in the Glory of the Father.

We believe that Thou shalt come to be our Judge.

We therefore pray Thee, help Thy servants,

Whom Thou hast redeemed with Thy precious blood.

Make them to be number'd with Thy Saints in glory everlasting.

Oh Lord, save Thy people and bless Thine heritage.

Govern them, and lift them up forever.
Day by day we magnify Thee;
And we worship Thy Name, ever World without end.
Vouchsafe, Oh Lord, to keep us this day without sin,

Oh Lord, let Thy mercy lighten upon us, as our trust is in Thee.
Oh Lord, in Thee have I trusted,
Let me never be confounded.

JUBILATE

Oh, be joyful in the Lord, all ye lands
Serve the Lord with gladness
Oh, be joyful in the Lord, all ye lands,
and come before His presence with a song.
Serve the Lord with gladness, and come before
His presence with a song.
Be ye sure that the Lord He is God;
it is He that hath made us, and not we ourselves;
we are His people, and the sheep of His pasture.

O go your way into His gates with thanksgiving, and into His courts with praise.
be thankful unto Him, and speak good of His Name.
For the Lord is gracious, His mercy is everlasting.
and His truth endureth from generation to generation.
Glory be to the Father,
Glory be to the Son, and to the Holy Ghost,
As it was in the beginning is now and ever shall be,
World without end, Amen.

SERGEY RACHMANINOFF

Born April 1, 1873, in Semyonovo, Russia
Died March 28, 1943, in Beverly Hills

Rachmaninoff came to musical maturity in this century, but his musical roots were firmly embedded in late nineteenth-century Romantic tradition. Critics describe his style as "Universal Romanticism," a highly emotional approach that espouses no particular ism or creed. Some say that Rachmaninoff began composing at the point where Tchaikovsky—whom he held in the very highest regard—left off.

At age nineteen, right after graduation from the Moscow Conservatory, Rachmaninoff won international renown with his Prelude in C sharp minor for Piano. As a result, he was invited to conduct and perform programs of his own works—as both pianist and conductor—in London and elsewhere. But at this crucial point in his career, he developed a severe writing block that made it impossible for him to put pen to paper. With the help of psychiatrist Dr. Nikolai Dahl, who used the technique of autosuggestion to convince him that he could compose and be successful, Rachmaninoff regained his confidence and began to write again. Nevertheless, for the rest of his life, composing required extraordinary amounts of mental energy.

Perhaps Rachmaninoff best summed up his approach to music when he wrote, "I compose music because I must give expression to my feelings, just as I talk because I must give utterance to my thoughts." His deeply affecting, moving music is characterized by melodies of powerful emotional impact supported by rich, lush harmonies.

THE BELLS, Op. 35

35 minutes

Even though modern audiences have chosen Rachmaninoff's Second Piano Concerto as their favorite, the composer considered his choral symphony, *The Bells,* to be his finest work. He wrote *The Bells* early in 1913 while living in Italy. Up until that time Rachmaninoff, an active pianist, conductor, and leading figure in Russian musical circles, was essentially a "summer composer." That is, he wrote music while on holiday; during the concert season he had no time because of his full and busy schedule. For the 1912–13 season, however, Rachmaninoff decided to devote more time to composing. To accomplish this, he cut back on his concertizing and resigned as vice president of the Imperial Russian Musical Society (presumably because of the society's anti-Jewish policy). After fulfilling a few conducting dates early in the season, Rachmaninoff journeyed leisurely through Germany and Switzerland with his family, arriving in Rome in February 1913. Curiously enough, his apartment, on the Piazza di Spagno, had once been occupied by Tchaikovsky's brother, Modest.

Soon after his arrival, Rachmaninoff received an unsigned letter from a cello student at the Moscow Conservatory. The young woman included Konstantin Balmont's Russian translation of Edgar Allan Poe's poem "The Bells," suggesting that the poetry called out for a musical setting. The composer found the idea intriguing, especially since he had many happy childhood memories of church bells and realized the many different emotions that pealing bells can convey.

Balmont's free reworking of "The Bells" kept only some of Poe's all-important repetition and none of his meter, but he did retain the poet's four-verse organization. The arrangement suggested to Rachmaninoff the four movements of a symphony, despite the problem of the slow tempo implied by the final section, "The Mournful Iron Bells."

Rachmaninoff worked quickly and well in the Rome apartment, always mindful that the revered Pyotr Ilich Tchaikovsky had spent some time composing there. "All day long I spent at the piano or writing table," Rachmaninoff wrote, "and not until the sinking sun gilded the pines of the Monte Pincio did I put away my pen."

Despite the great temptation, Rachmaninoff resisted the excessive use of orchestral bells. Instead, his instrumentation and writing for the voices suggest even more tellingly the character of the different kinds of bells—the crisp tinkle of the silvery sleigh bells, the burnished richness of the mellow wedding bells, the brazen clamor of the bells of alarm, and the dark gloom of the funereal bells.

Rachmaninoff composed *The Bells* for three soloists—soprano, tenor, and baritone—mixed choir, and large orchestra. The composer led the first performance in Moscow on February 8, 1914; he revised the work in 1936.

GIOACCHINO
ROSSINI

Born February 29, 1792, in Pesaro, Italy
Died November 13, 1868, in Passy, near Paris

For the decades from 1810, when he composed his first opera, *La cambiale di matrimonio,* until 1829, when he wrote his final opera, *William Tell,* Rossini dominated the operatic stages of Europe. Perhaps the principal reason was his unfailing ability to produce attractive, memorable melodies that fit the operatic situations perfectly, that expressed the full range of human emotions, and that described all sorts of situations from sensuous lovemaking to farcical humor. The best of these melodies had the uncanny capacity to remain permanently in the listeners' ears. Richard Wagner, perhaps ironically, said Rossini's operas were built on "naked, ear-delighting, absolutely-melodic melody, that is, melody that was just melody and nothing else."

At age thirty-seven, after completing *William Tell* and winning recognition as the greatest opera composer of the age, Rossini inexplicably stopped composing! The only major works he wrote in the remaining thirty-nine years of his life were the two choral compositions *Stabat Mater* and *Petite messe solennelle.*

Scholars have come up with a few possible explanations for the sudden cessation. Perhaps it was because he no longer needed the income his music brought him. Rossini was immensely wealthy; on his death, his estate was valued at nearly $1.5 million, a staggering sum in 1868. Perhaps it was his ill health; as he put it, "I have all of women's ills. All that I lack is the uterus." Perhaps it was out of sheer laziness. According to one oft-repeated story, Rossini was composing in bed one day when the music paper fell to the floor. Rather than bestir himself and pick up the paper, Rossini simply wrote another piece!

While opera lovers can bemoan the fact that the composer of *The Barber of Seville* put down his pen so early in his life, lovers

PETITE MESSE SOLENNELLE

1 hour, 30 minutes

On the autograph score of *Petite messe solennelle* Rossini wrote this description:

> *Petite messe solennelle,* in four voices with accompaniment of 2 pianos and harmonium, composed during my country stay at Passy. Twelve singers of three sexes—men, women, and *castrati*—will be enough for its performance: that is, eight for the chorus, four for the solos, a total of twelve cherubim. God, forgive me the following comparison. Twelve also are the Apostles in the celebrated *coup de mâchoire* ["jaw-stroke"] painted in fresco by Leonardo, called *The Last Supper:* who would believe it! Among Thy disciples there are those who strike false notes!! Lord, rest assured, I swear to Thee that there will be no Judas at my supper and that mine will sing properly and *con amore* Thy praises and this little composition, which is, alas, the last mortal sin of my old age.

On the last page Rossini added a personal letter to the Deity: "Dear God, here it is finished, this poor little mass. Is this sacred music [*musique sacrée*] that I have written or damned music [*sacrée musique*]? I was born for *opera buffa,* as you well know! A little skill, a little heart, that's all I have. Be merciful, then, and admit me to Paradise. G. Rossini. Passy 1863."

This description and letter demonstrate Rossini's fabled wit and wonderful sense of humor. Other examples abound. He once commented, for example, that *Petite messe solennelle* (literally "Small Solemn Mass") is "a long, only intermittently solemn, Mass." And what is one to make of the tempo marking for the *"Credo"*—Allegro cristiano ("Christian allegro")? Perhaps his statement "My most sacred music is always just *semiserious!"* best sums up his attitude.

Semiserious or not, there is no question that *Petite messe* is the work of a religious man—not necessarily a fanatical believer, but one with a strong personal trust in God. A few years after completing *Petite messe,* when Rossini was on his death-bed, the priest administering the last rites asked if he had always accepted God. Rossini replied, "Would I have been able to write the *Stabat* and the *Messe* if I had not had faith?"

A lifetime spent writing operas, including light, comic operas, shaped Rossini's compositional style. When he wrote sacred music, no matter how deeply he felt the religious significance, elements of his operatic style would appear, and the sacred piece would be no less reverent or pious because of this influence. According to Rossini biographer Francis Toye, the composer held that laughter is the best preventive for tears and that there is nothing too serious for humor.

Rossini composed *Petite messe solennelle* in the summer of 1863 for the consecration of the private chapel in the Paris home of Countess Louise Pillet-Will. Here it was first performed on March 14, 1864, before a small audience that included several leading composers, all of whom were most enthusiastic about the work.

As word of this exciting new piece spread throughout Paris, there was a demand for Rossini to prepare a concert edition. In particular, musicians called for a full-sized orchestra accompaniment instead of the two pianos and harmonium that Rossini had probably chosen to fit into the limited space of the countess's chapel. But, complaining that he was old and tired, Rossini refused.

Then, in 1866, Rossini changed his mind and began the orchestration. "You should know that I did the score for the vocal parts of this modest work some time ago," Rossini told Emil Naumann, who visited the composer in April 1867. "If it were to be found among my effects, there would be Monsieur Sax [Adolphe Sax, inventor of the saxophone] with his saxophone or Monsieur Berlioz with another monstrous modern orchestra, and they'd want to orchestrate my Mass, killing all my vocal lines, and thus killing me also."

Done more out of obligation than conviction, the orchestration of *Petite messe* sounds rather conventional, lacking the astringency and piquancy of the original, but it was nonetheless necessary to meet the requirements of a large choral group. Both versions are heard today.

In *Petite messe solennelle* Rossini shows his mastery of fugal writing in such movements as *"Christe eleison," "Gratias,"* and *"Cum Sancto Spiritu,"* along with demonstrating throughout his general skill in contrapuntal writing. Some of the solo sections—*"Domine Deus"* (tenor), *"Quoniam"* (bass), *"Crucifixus"* (soprano)—are reminiscent of beautiful, melodic, operatic arias, but at the same time they are perfectly suited to their places in the Mass.

Here, then, is the genius of *Petite messe solennelle:* it brings together Rossini's ability to craft contrapuntal music in the traditional ecclesiastical mode with his unquestioned supremacy in writing for the human voice, his flow of glorious melody, and his underlying religious faith—a combination that is hard to beat.

Standard Text (see Appendix)

ARNOLD
SCHOENBERG

Born September 13, 1874, in Vienna
Died July 13, 1951, in Los Angeles

Surely no composer's music underwent such complete and dramatic transformations as that of Arnold Schoenberg. Judged by his early works—the music he composed until 1908—Schoenberg would be considered a Romantic or expressionist. His passionate and expressive music, filled with surging melodies and rich, lush harmonies, was an extension and intensification of the style of Brahms, Wagner, and Mahler.

Then, starting in 1908, Schoenberg began composing atonal music—music without the strong feeling of tonal center that had been basic to music for hundreds of years. At the same time that Wassily Kandinsky was turning out the first paintings that showed no real objects, Schoenberg was producing analogous music, compositions that were not in any particular key and had no specific tonality.

About fifteen years later, Schoenberg went even further when he created a style of composition that he called "method of composing with twelve tones." This style, known as dodecaphony, not only did away with tonality, but also eliminated melody in the traditional sense. The composer organized the music around a tone row, a particular arrangement of the twelve tones that make up the chromatic scale. The twelve tones could be sounded sequentially, simultaneously, in reverse order, and so on. Dodecaphony imposed a positive structure on atonality, which had the negative connotation of avoiding a feeling of key.

Aside from the unfinished oratorio *Die Jakobsleiter* ("Jacob's Ladder"), Schoenberg's only major choral composition is

Gurre-Lieder. This monumental creation, which dates from the early period in his career, can be considered one of the last significant outpourings of nineteenth-century Romanticism.

GURRE-LIEDER
(Songs of Gurre)

2 hours

Arnold Schoenberg based his *Gurre-Lieder* on a retelling of an ancient Danish legend by poet Jens Peter Jacobsen (the composer used a German translation by Robert Franz Arnold). The hero, King Waldemar, falls in love with Tove and builds the castle of Gurre for her. Waldemar's wife, though, seeks vengeance; she has the door to Tove's bathroom bolted shut with Tove inside and fills the room with hot steam, killing her rival.

The tale has some historical basis: King Waldemar I, "the Great" (not the fourteenth-century Waldemar IV, as is sometimes stated), who ruled Denmark from 1157 to 1182, had a mistress, Tove. Tove mothered his two sons and was later killed by Helvig, Waldemar's wife. The castle at Gurre, though, was probably built later, around 1375.

In conceiving *Gurre Lieder,* Schoenberg expanded what could have been a simple song cycle into an overwhelmingly dramatic creation. Not only does the work last a full two hours, but it calls for immense performing forces—six soloists (including one speaker); a gigantic orchestra of eight flutes, five oboes, seven clarinets, five bassoons, ten horns, seven trumpets, seven trombones, tuba, six timpani, a huge percussion section that includes "several large iron chains," four harps, celesta, forty violins (divided into twenty different parts), sixteen violas (divided into eight), sixteen cellos (divided into eight), and twelve basses; three men's choirs composed of eight each of tenor I, tenor II, bass I, and bass II; and an eight-part mixed choir composed of twelve each of soprano I, soprano II, alto I, alto II, tenor I, tenor II, bass I, and bass II!

Schoenberg began writing *Gurre-Lieder* in March 1900—right after completing his best-known piece, *Verklärte Nacht*—and finished exactly one year later. Because of the pressure of other work, though, the composer did not conclude the orchestration until 1911. The first performance took place in Vienna on February 23, 1913, with Franz Schreker conducting. While the concert was a success, the composer remained embittered by the public's slow recognition of his abilities. In fact, after conducting a performance of *Gurre-Lieder* in Leipzig, Schoenberg refused to acknowledge the listeners' enthusiastic ovation, bowing only to the applauding performers!

The composer divides *Gurre-Lieder* into three unequal parts. After a lovely orchestral prelude that conjures up a bucolic twilight scene with the two lovers, Schoenberg devotes Part I to the love songs of Waldemar (tenor) and Tove (soprano), which are pervaded with many images of death. The duets are soon followed by the famous "Song of the Wood Dove" *("Waldtaube"),* which touchingly describes the death of Tove.

In the very brief Part II, Waldemar complains and rails against the God who has treated him so cruelly.

In Part III, *Die wilde Jagd* ("The Wild Hunt"), Waldemar leads his retainers (men's choirs) on a mad ride through the countryside seeking his lost Tove. The Peasant (bass) and Klaus-Narr, or Fool (tenor), sing their solos.

An orchestral prelude leads to *"Des Sommerwindes wilde Jagd"* ("The Wild Chase of the Summer Wind"), a fanciful tale of the wind's passage through the landscape. Here Schoenberg introduces the speaker, who uses a delivery known as *Sprechgesang* (literally, "spoken melody"). The composer explains this technique: "The rhythm and the intensity of sound (in relation to the accompaniment) should be absolutely respected. The pitches should only be regarded as 'difference of level', which means that the particular place (not the single tone!!!) is to be spoken higher or lower."

At the end of the speaker's melodrama, the mixed choir enters, singing of the rising sun and bringing the entire work to its climax and conclusion.

FRANZ SCHUBERT

Born January 31, 1797, in Vienna
Died November 19, 1828, in Vienna

Franz Schubert, to a very large extent, personifies the popular image of the composer: unrecognized and unperformed; ill clothed, penniless, and often hungry; completely unworldly in everything from getting paid for his music to keeping appointments with his friends; driven to compose by some inner demon; and dying at a young age—thirty-one in Schubert's case.

Schubert was born in Lichtenthal, then a suburb of Vienna, now within the city limits. When he finished school, his father, a schoolteacher and amateur cellist, encouraged his son to join him as an assistant teacher, a position the young man detested. After leaving that job, Schubert drifted into a sort of Bohemian existence, joining up with a small group of friends who admired his music and were perfectly willing to share what meager money and possessions each could contribute. Despite Schubert's incredible talent and fecundity, his music was rarely performed and almost none was published during his lifetime; he earned virtually nothing from his composing until near the very end of his life.

Although he played the violin and piano, Schubert never mastered either instrument well enough to become a performer. All he could do was compose, which he did superbly well. As he once commented to a friend, "The state should keep me. I have come into the world for no purpose but to compose."

And compose he did. Schubert produced an amazing quantity of music in virtually every form—songs (he wrote over six hundred!), operas, symphonies, piano pieces, chamber music, and choral works. Only concertos are missing from this list; could it be that not being a virtuoso performer on any instrument made him uncomfortable in this form?

In order to produce as much music as he did, Schubert had to be able to compose at great speed. A friend, Franz Schober, reported that if someone called on Schubert when he was working on a score, the composer would say, "Hello, how are you? Good!" and immediately turn back to his music.

Another friend, Josef Edler von Spaun, tells of being present when Schubert first read Goethe's poem *"Erlkönig,"* which was to become the text of one of the composer's best-known songs: "He paced up and down several times with the book, suddenly he sat down, and in no time at all (just as quickly as you can write) there was the glorious ballad finished on the paper."

Schubert composed a total of six Masses. Of these, three hold important positions in the current choral repertoire—No. 2 in G (D. 167), No. 5 in A flat (D. 678), and No. 6 in E flat (D. 950). All three are discussed in this book.

The D numbers refer to the listing in the chronological catalog of Schubert's music prepared by Otto Erich Deutsch. A numbering system is necessary because so few compositions were published during Schubert's lifetime that it is difficult to place them in sequential order.

A curious—and striking—fact about the Schubert Masses is that each one omits the phrase *"Et unam sanctam catholicam et apostolicam Ecclesiam"* ("And [I believe] in one holy catholic and apostolic church") from near the end of *"Credo."*

This omission has led to much speculation. Some offer a simple explanation: in those pre–duplicating machine days, Schubert copied over the text of the Mass by hand and inadvertently left out the missing section. This is not too credible because Schubert probably knew the text by heart, and while this might explain one omission, it is inconceivable that it would happen six times.

Others suggest that the omission is Schubert's way of saying that, while deeply committed in his devotion to and belief in God, he does not fully accept the role of the church. Finally, a few hold that the composer dropped the phrase for strictly musical reasons—that his conception of the music of the *"Credo"* did not allow for setting those particular words.

For now, until more evidence is uncovered, the puzzle of the missing line remains unsolved. Occasionally, when used for a liturgical purpose, the *"Credos"* of the Schubert Masses are rearranged to allow for the insertion of the missing text.

MASS NO. 2 IN G MAJOR, D. 167

25 minutes

In 1808 the Vienna court choir admitted eleven-year-old Franz Schubert to its ranks, and he entered the "Konvict," the choir's training school. Five years later, soon after his voice changed, he left the school. Because young men were customarily conscripted into the army right after school, Schubert decided to attend a teacher-training school and to take a position as assistant teacher at the school where his father taught.

Since he lacked both the interest and the ability to be a good teacher, Schubert suffered in this position. The only advantage, he found, was that it allowed him plenty of time for composing. It was during this period that Schubert wrote four Masses for the local (Lichtenthal) parish church; the second, in G major, is perhaps the most popular of the six Masses he was eventually to compose.

In writing the Mass in G, Schubert crafted a small-scale work intended for liturgical, rather than concert, use. The predominantly choral piece uses a small orchestra of strings and organ and makes minimal use of the three soloists—soprano, tenor, and bass. The composer keeps the general tone light and almost cheery, with an abundance of graceful melody and scarcely any polyphony or imitative writing. The simplicity and good spirits of the music, and the fact that Schubert composed it in the amazingly short period of five days—from March 2 to 7, 1815 —led musicologist Alfred Einstein to comment, "Once again Schubert's lack of reverence for the church makes itself evident."

The *"Kyrie"* is a quiet, subdued movement, homophonic in

texture, with a brief soprano solo at the beginning of the *"Christe eleison."*

In the central section of the exultant *"Gloria,"* Schubert creates a striking textural contrast by pitting short soprano and bass solos against the choral altos and tenors.

The hushed, reverential tone of the opening of the *"Credo"* comes from the long, sustained chords in the choir over the brisk, ever-moving pizzicato line in the cellos and double basses.

Short in length, *"Sanctus"* ends with an exciting fugue to the words *"Osanna in excelsis."*

Only the *"Benedictus"* features the three soloists, whose parts are sometimes treated in imitation. The choir enters for the conclusion—which is identical to the fugue in the preceding *"Sanctus."*

Most commentators consider the concluding *"Agnus Dei"* the finest movement in the Mass. Slow in tempo, sensitive and delicate in expression, it features solos for soprano and bass that contrast with the choir's solemn intoning of *"Miserere nobis"* until the end, where the choir uses the same melody for *"Dona nobis pacem."*

Most likely the Mass in G was performed in the Lichtenthal parish church during the spring of 1815, but there are no records to confirm this fact. In an egregious case of plagiarism, Robert Führer, *Kapellmeister* at the Cathedral of St. Veit in Prague, in 1846 passed off Schubert's Mass as his own!

Standard Text (see Appendix)

MASS NO. 5 IN A FLAT MAJOR, D. 678
(Missa solemnis)

45 minutes

In a letter dated December 7, 1822, regarding his Mass in A flat, Schubert wrote to a friend, "My Mass is finished and is shortly to be performed. I still have my old idea of dedicating it to the Emperor [Franz I] or Empress [Carolina Augusta], as I think it has turned out so well." Schubert proposed the dedication because he considered the Mass special enough to win him a position in the imperial court. Sad to say, he never received any sort of official position or even recognition.

Schubert wrote his starting date, November 1819, at the top of the Mass manuscript. He continued working on the Mass from time to time over the following three years, marking the date September 1822 at the end. Over the following years he substituted two completely new sections—"*Cum Sancto Spiritu*" and "*Osanna*"—and, atypically, made numerous minor changes and revisions. (Some editions of the Mass in A flat include both the first and second versions of the two sections, allowing choral directors their choice.)

In 1825, on the death of Antonio Salieri, who had been *Hofkapellmeister* of the imperial court, his assistant, Joseph von Eybler, moved up, leaving the post of *Vice-Hofkapellmeister* open. Schubert submitted his Mass in A flat in application for the position.

After a few weeks, the emperor dropped Schubert from consideration. The reason? The emperor had described very specifically how a Mass should be written: there were to be no tenor or bass solos; fugues should be expertly worked out, but not be too long; and the "*Sanctus*" and "*Benedictus*" should be very short. Since Schubert's Mass did not meet these criteria, he could not be engaged! The composer, as one would expect, reacted angrily, saying, "Well, so I am not fortunate enough to be able to write in the imperial style."

The gentle *"Kyrie"* that opens the Mass conveys what one critic has described as "pious resignation rather than prayer." The four soloists carry most of the burden of the brief middle section, the *"Christe eleison."*

After the subdued *"Kyrie,"* the *"Gloria"* bursts forth in a blaze of musical exultation. Over racing passages in the orchestra, the choir cries out its phrases of adoration. The concluding section, the vigorous *"Cum Sancto Spiritu,"* emerges as a magnificent extended fugue—in both the original and revised versions.

Two wind chords open the *"Credo"* before the a cappella choir intones, *"Credo in unum Deum, Patrem omnipotentem, factorem coeli et terrae"* ("I believe in one God, the Father Almighty, maker of heaven and earth"). Schubert fills this remarkable movement with a wide variety of choral textures—antiphony (with men and women alternating), homophony (at *"Credo, per quem omnia facta sunt"),* an eight-part choir (at *"Et incarnatus est"),* and a long, sustained vocal line over the onward-rushing orchestra (for the final "Amens"). Mention must be made of that incredible moment at the word *"mor tuos,"* or "dead," as the sopranos eerily slither up the chromatic scale and the basses slide down in contrary motion.

It is interesting to compare Schubert's reworking of *"Osanna,"* the last part of *"Sanctus,"* with the original. The composer set the first in a rocking rhythm (6/8), which gives the comparatively simple melody a folk-song quality; in the second version, he keeps the same melody and harmony but changes the meter (to 4/4) and alters the note lengths to impart a much more foursquare, serious mien to the same notes.

Three soloists—soprano, alto, and tenor—alternate with and join with the choir in *"Benedictus."* For the ending, *"Osanna,"* Schubert uses the original version of the fugal *"Osanna"* from *"Sanctus."*

After creating a moving, haunting melody for the *"Agnus*

Dei," Schubert ends the Mass by giving the *"Dona nobis pacem"* the character of a poised, confident recessional.

Scholars disagree on the first hearing of the Mass in A flat. Otto Deutsch believes it was sometime in 1822 at Alt-Lerchenfelder Church in Vienna; Wilhelm Altmann holds that the first performance was not until 1863, that being the earliest documented performance.

Standard Text (see Appendix)

MASS NO. 6 IN E FLAT MAJOR, D. 950

1 hour

When Stravinsky was asked whether the length of some of Schubert's works did not put him to sleep, he replied, "What does it matter if, when I awake, it seems to me that I am in Paradise." Stravinsky's remark applies with particular relevance to Schubert's Sixth Mass. It is indeed a lengthy work, but it is so finely crafted and so deeply felt that at the end one longs for more.

In the first eight and one-half months of 1828, before his death on November 19, Schubert produced an absolutely astonishing series of masterpieces—the Ninth Symphony (called the "Great C Major"), the string quintet in the same key, the final three monumental piano sonatas in C minor, A major, and B flat major, the fourteen songs that are known as *Schwanengesang,* or "Swan Song," and his sixth and final Mass (in E flat major). Looking at this accomplishment makes one wonder if the thirty-one-year-old composer somehow knew his end was near and rushed to set down on paper all the music that was welling up inside him.

Scholars know little about the composition of this Mass beyond the fact that it was begun late in the spring of 1828 and completed by the end of the summer. While most composers write Masses with a specific performance in mind, whether it be in church or concert hall, Schubert wrote this Mass with no such prospect. Indeed, the Mass was not performed until November 4, 1829, a year after his death, at the Church of the Holy Trinity in Alser, a suburb of Vienna, under the direction of Schubert's brother Ferdinand. Since then, critics have given the Mass an honored place among the great works of the composer's last year; many rank it as his finest church composition. Johannes Brahms, an early admirer of this Mass, showed his high esteem by arranging the orchestra part for piano to encourage more performances.

Although Schubert calls for five soloists—soprano, alto, two tenors, and bass—the Mass is essentially a choral Mass. The composer calls for a large orchestra, including three trombones, but he omits the flutes and keeps the violins in their lower register, thereby giving the piece a dark, shaded tone.

Schubert cast the *"Kyrie"* in the usual three-part form, starting with the tender, lyrical *"Kyrie eleison,"* going on to the highly dramatic *"Christe eleison,"* and ending with a return of the opening, this time considerably expanded in length and dynamic range.

"Gloria" begins with a full-voiced a cappella cry of *"Gloria in excelsis Deo."* Twice more this bold opening phrase erupts, with music of great emotion and variety coming between the repetitions. Schubert makes the last section, *"Cum Sancto Spiritu,"* an extended fugue on a theme he borrowed from the E major Fugue of Bach's *Well-Tempered Clavier,* Book II.

"Credo" opens mysteriously with a hushed timpani roll and a whispered choir entrance. In time, the dynamics rise as the choir affirms, *"Credo in unum Dominum Jesum Christum."* Schubert bases the middle section, *"Et incarnatus est,"* on a lyrical melody of ravishing beauty, which he mostly entrusts to the soprano and two tenor soloists. The character of the opening returns at *"Et resurrexit,"* which also employs a good deal of imitative writing.

Most composers are restrained in the joy they express in *"Sanctus"*—but not Schubert! In this intense, concentrated, high-energy movement, Schubert, after the first *"Sanctus,"* keeps the choir singing at full volume throughout. The tempo picks up for the concluding fugue on *"Osanna."*

Tender and calm, the *"Benedictus"* ushers in a period of repose after the excitement of the *"Sanctus."* Four soloists alternate with the choir in the presentation until the final section, which is a choral fugue identical to the ending of *"Sanctus."*

Schubert bases the *"Agnus Dei"* on two musical ideas he derived from the C sharp minor Fugue of Bach's *Well-Tempered Clavier,* Book I. The mood he creates is somber, if not despairing, due in part to the ongoing, restless bass line. In the last section, *"Dona nobis pacem,"* he introduces a note of calm confidence; a brief reminder of the *"Agnus Dei"* interrupts before the section returns to its earlier, confident character, which brings the entire Mass to an end with feelings of peace and hope.

Standard Text (see Appendix)

IGOR STRAVINSKY

Born June 17, 1882, in Oranienbaum, Russia
Died April 6, 1971, in New York City

Igor Stravinsky, one of the great seminal figures of twentieth-century music, created three ballets—*The Firebird, Petrouchka,* and *The Rite of Spring*—that burst with explosive force on the musical world in the years from 1910 to 1913. With harsh fragments of melody repeated over and over again, brutal, throbbing rhythms, sharp dissonances, and brilliant colors and tonal effects, Stravinsky drew the curtain on nineteenth-century Romanticism and provided a glimpse of the wonderful new possibilities of twentieth-century music.

Despite the instant, worldwide fame that came to Stravinsky with these ballets, the composer completely changed his musical course in the following years—which coincided with World War I. With the onset of hostilities, Stravinsky fled Russia for Switzerland and, missing his homeland very much, began writing in what music commentators call his Russian style: melodies based on old Russian folk songs, rhythms from Russian peasant dances, and words and stories from Russian legends and myths.

Meanwhile, Stravinsky stripped his compositions down to their barest essentials, using minimal forces to achieve his musical goals. This trimming of his musical sails might also have been a practical necessity. The disruption of the war cut music budgets, and large performing forces were virtually impossible to assemble. It was under these straitened circumstances that Stravinsky composed the first of his choral masterpieces, *Les Noces.*

By the mid-1920s, Stravinsky left his Russian phase and entered what many call his neoclassical period—a term that Stravinsky insisted means "absolutely nothing." Transparency of texture, restraint of emotion, elimination of any extramusical references, and clear, symmetrical structural organization are the hallmarks of this new phase. *Symphony of Psalms* belongs to this period.

Until about 1950, Stravinsky underwent no major stylistic change, although his music explored any number of different approaches to the neoclassical style. In the 1950s he struck off in a new direction, taking up the twelve-tone method, or dodecaphony, that Arnold Schoenberg had introduced in the 1920s. Simply put, the twelve-tone method requires that the composer organize the twelve tones of the chromatic scale into an order, called the tone row. Then, the composer must sound all twelve tones before repeating any of them. The result destroys any feeling of tonality, since one of the factors that gives a composition a tonal center is the repetition of the home tonality. With *Canticum sacrum* and *Threni,* Stravinsky made two important contributions to the body of twelve-tone music.

Many music lovers are convinced that Stravinsky's greatest works were his early ballets—that they were on a level he never achieved subsequently. Others, though, believe that his later works include some of his most interesting compositions, and that they amply repay any extra effort required to become familiar with their style and content.

LES NOCES
(The Wedding)

23 minutes

In his book *Expositions and Developments,* Stravinsky traces the genesis of *Les Noces:*

> I became aware of an idea for a choral work on the subject of a Russian peasant wedding early in 1912; the title, *Svadebka, Les Noces,* occurred to me almost at the same time as the idea itself. As my conception developed, I began to see that it did not indicate the dramatization of a wedding or the accompaniment of a staged wedding spectacle with descriptive music. My wish was, instead, to present actual wedding material through direct quotations of popular —i.e., non-literary—verse.

Individual roles do not exist in *Les Noces,* but only solo voices that impersonate now one type of character and now another. Thus the soprano in the first scene is not the bride, but merely a bride's voice; the same voice is associated with the goose in the last scene.

I began the composition of *Les Noces* in 1914 in Clarens [Switzerland]. The music was composed in short score form by 1917, but it was not finished in full score until three months before the premiere, which was six years later [in Paris on June 13, 1923, conducted by Ernest Ansermet]. No work of mine has undergone so many instrumental metamorphoses. I completed the first tableau for an [extremely large] orchestra, and then decided to divide the various instrumental elements—strings, woodwinds, brass, percussion, keyboard (cimbalom, harpsichord, piano)—into groups and to keep these groups separate on the stage. In still another version I sought to combine pianolas [mechanical pianos] with bands of instruments that included saxhorns and flugelhorns. Then, one day in 1921, I suddenly realized that an orchestra of four pianos would fulfill all my conditions. It would be at the same time perfectly homogenous, perfectly impersonal, and perfectly mechanical.

Stravinsky began the composition of *Les Noces* in Switzerland in May or June of 1914. In July he traveled to Kiev, where he obtained the texts of some old Russian wedding songs collected by poet P. V. Kireievsky; these became Stravinsky's principal source for the text. Because he interrupted *Les Noces* to work on other compositions, the score—without orchestration —was not done until October 1917. Then, over the next five and a half years, the composer experimented with the orchestration before arriving at the final version in April 1923.

Stravinsky composed *Les Noces* for four solo voices—soprano, alto, tenor, and baritone—chorus, and an instrumental ensemble of four pianos and a large percussion battery that includes four timpani, bells, xylophone, tambourine, cymbals, small cymbals, triangle, bass drum, snare drum, and drum without snares. Since the composer envisioned *Les Noces* as being danced as well as played and sung, he directed that the singers and instrumentalists be in the pit and the dancers on the stage.

Les Noces is made up of four separate tableaux:

1. *"The Bride's Chamber."* Set in the bride's house, with her

companions binding her tresses. Much of it is lamenting in tone as the bride mourns the end of her freedom and girlhood. Stravinsky makes use of a pentatonic scale, which gives the music an oriental quality; he also limits the melodic range and features much repetition of short snatches of melody.

2. *"At the Bridegroom's House."* More forceful and wilder, although always clear and spare in texture, this movement features moments of quiet contemplation in contrast with the generally bright tone.

3. *"The Bride's Departure."* A brief scene that continues tableau one. The mothers of the bride and groom grieve over the symbolic loss of their children.

4. *"The Wedding Feast."* By far the longest section, it opens with the choir singing the song of the berries. After a bit of the marriage ceremony the choir sings the song of the goose. The assemblage chooses a couple to warm the bridal bed. More songs of celebration, fun, and good wishes follow until the couple go to the bed and *Les Noces* ends.

SYMPHONY OF PSALMS
(Symphonie des psaumes)

25 minutes

In 1929 Serge Koussevitzky, conductor of the Boston Symphony, invited four composers—Sergey Prokofiev, Arthur Honegger, Albert Roussel, and Igor Stravinsky—to write major works honoring the orchestra's fiftieth anniversary the following year. Stravinsky gladly accepted the commission, since for some time he had been contemplating "a work of considerable scope."

The composer first thought to write a symphony, but he did not want to write it in traditional symphonic form. "Symphonic form as bequeathed to us by the 19th century," he wrote in his *Autobiography,* "held little attraction for me. . . ." Slowly a vision of the kind of piece he wanted to write took shape. "My idea was that my symphony should be a work with great contrapuntal development, and for that it was necessary to increase the media at my disposal. I finally decided on a choral and instrumental ensemble in which the two elements should be on equal footing, neither of them outweighing the other." He continues, "I sought for my words, since they were to be sung, among those which had been written for singing. And quite naturally my first idea was to have recourse to the psalms."

Stravinsky began the *Symphony of Psalms* early in 1930, but with many interruptions for concert appearances as conductor and pianist. Starting at the beginning of that summer he devoted himself fully to the symphony, and he completed the work on August 15 in Nice, France. Just before finishing, Stravinsky wrote in a letter the best brief description of the composition: "It is not a symphony in which I have included psalms to be sung. On the contrary, it is the singing of the psalms that I am symphonizing."

The score calls for mixed choir and large orchestra, including two pianos but without clarinets, violins, or violas. The composer requested that, if possible, boys sing the soprano and alto parts, though he expressed a willingness to accept women; he also asked that it be sung in Latin.

In 1948, Stravinsky revised the symphony, the major change being a considerably slower tempo for the final section, the coda, of the third movement. Curiously enough, most performances, including the composer's 1963 recording, do not observe the change but maintain the earlier tempo. And along those lines, although he asks for children's voices if possible, women sing the soprano and alto parts on his recordings.

On the manuscript the composer wrote, "This Symphony, composed to the glory of GOD, is dedicated to the Boston Symphony Orchestra on the occasion of the fiftieth anniversary of its existence." Because of a postponement of the Boston Symphony concert, the Brussels Philharmonic under Ernest Ansermet actually gave the premiere on December 13, 1930, with the first Boston performance following six days later.

The three movements of *Symphony of Psalms* are played without pause. Movement one is a setting of Psalm 38, verses 13 and 14 in the Vulgate (corresponding to Psalm 39, verses 12 and 13 in the King James Version). Movement two is Psalm 39, verses 2 to 4 (Psalm 40, verses 1 to 3 in King James). And movement three is the entire Psalm 150 in both versions, although Stravinsky omitted the sixth line—"Praise Him with the timbrel and dance."

Stravinsky made these comments regarding his choice of texts: "The juxtaposition of the three psalms is not fortuitous. The prayer of the sinner for divine pity (prelude), the recognition of grace received (double fugue), and the hymns of praise and glory are the basis of an evolutionary plan. The order of the three movements presupposes a periodic scheme and in this sense realizes a 'symphony.' For a periodic scheme is what distinguishes a 'symphony' from a collection of pieces with no scheme but one of succession, as in a suite."

The symphony opens with an uninflected line in the oboe and bassoon that is punctuated by short, sharp chords, creating a remote, austere sonic environment. A piano picks up the oboe-bassoon line, leading to the alto entrance, which obsessively rocks back and forth between two adjacent notes. The character changes at *"Quoniam advena,"* with the entire choir singing leaping parts until the tenors and then the sopranos take up the two-note rocking and the movement ends.

A solo oboe starts the second movement, a double fugue, with the angular, deliberate theme or subject. After working this up to five voices, Stravinsky has the sopranos state the subject of the choral fugue, which soon involves the entire choir. The two fugues continue their own development until near the end, when choir and orchestra come together for the conclusion.

In explaining why he chose Psalm 150 as the text of the third movement, Stravinsky wrote that a "compelling reason was my eagerness to counter the many composers who had abused these magisterial verses as pegs for their own lyrico-sentimental feelings." To a large extent, Stravinsky did eliminate lyricism and sentiment in his treatment, thereby forcing listeners to hear the words of this familiar psalm in a completely new way and to gain a fresh new understanding of their meaning. He achieved this result by his unique setting of the text. For example, the opening "Alleluia" is a slow wail instead of a joyous shout; the usually exultant *"Laudate Dominum"* ("Praise God") sounds restrained and distant. Stravinsky builds up the excitement and intensity in the faster middle section of the movement, but after an ascending scale in the flutes, oboe, and sopranos he returns to a slower tempo and gives the sopranos a quiet four-note ostinato figure that brings the entire symphony to a close.

I

Exaudi orationem meam, Domine,	Hear my prayer, O Lord,
Et deprecationem meam;	And give ear unto my cry;
Auribus percipe lacrimas meas:	Hold not Thy peace at my tears:
Ne sileas,	For I am
Ouoniam advena ego sum apud te,	A stranger with Thee,
Et peregrinus,	And a sojourner,
Sicut omnes patres mei.	As my fathers were.
Remitte mihi, ut refrigerer	O spare me, that I may recover strength,
Prius quam abeam,	Before I go hence,
Et amplius non ero.	And be no more.

(Psalms 38:13–14)

II

Expectans eexpectavi Dominum,	I waited patiently for the Lord;
Et intendi mihi	And He inclined to me,
Et exaudivit preces meas;	And heard my cry.
Et eduxit me de lacu miseriae,	He brought me up also out of an horrible pit,
Et de luto farcis.	Out of the miry clay,
Et statuit super petram pedes meos:	And set my feet upon a rock:

Et direxit gressus meos.

Et immisit in os meum canticum novum,

Carmen Deo nostro.

Videbunt multi et timebunt:

Et sperabunt in Domino.

And established my goings.

And He hath put a new song in my mouth,

Even praise unto our God:

Many shall see it, and fear,

And shall trust in the Lord.

(Psalms 39:2–4)

III

Alleluia.

Laudate Dominum in sanctis Eius.

Laudate Eum in firmamento virtutis Eius.

Laudate Eum in virtutibus Eius.

Laudate Eum secundum

Multitudinem magnitudinis Eius.

Laudate Eum in sono tubae,

Laudate Eum in cordis et organo.

Laudate Eum in cymbalis bene sonantibus

Laudate Eum in cymbalis iubilationbus

Omnis spiritus laudet Dominuum.

Hallelujah.

Praise God in His sanctuary,

Praise Him in the firmament of His power.

Praise Him for His mighty acts.

Praise Him according to

His excellent abundant greatness.

Praise Him with the sound of the trumpet,

Praise Him with stringed instruments and organs.

Praise Him with the loud cymbals;

Praise Him with the clanging cymbals;

Let everything that hath breath praise the Lord.

(Psalms 150)

MASS

17 minutes

Stravinsky had particularly strong opinions about his *Mass* and other religious music. It was his hope that his *Mass* would challenge the two-hundred-year decline of the role of music in the church and that it would find a place in the liturgy. He realized that the church knew, as the psalmist knew and as he knew, that music is better able to praise God than the most highly decorated church building.

When asked whether one had to be a believer in order to compose music for the church, Stravinsky replied, "Certainly, and not merely a believer in 'symbolic figures,' but in the person of the Lord, the person of the devil, and the miracles of the church."

In light of his convictions, it is interesting to note that Stravinsky chose to compose a Roman Catholic mass, even though he was a member of the Russian Orthodox church, and knew that his *Mass* could not be performed there.

The immediate impulse to compose the *Mass* came in 1948, when Stravinsky picked up a used copy of some Mozart Masses in a bookshop in Los Angeles, where he was then living, and decided to "write a Mass of [his] own, but a real one." He set it for soloists, mixed choir—with children singing the treble parts if possible—and an orchestra of double wind quintet: two oboes, English horn, two bassoons, two trumpets, and three trombones.

The opening *"Kyrie"* sounds highly dissonant and chromatic, with the vocalists and instrumentalists of equal importance. Two treble soloists emerge from the choir in the *"Gloria."* The many meter changes in this movement do not create a strong rhythmic impulse, as in Stravinsky's *The Rite of Spring*, but rather weaken the rhythmic drive, giving the *"Gloria"* the chantlike sound of medieval plainsong.

The *"Credo"* starts with the Priest intoning the plainsong melody. Although the orchestra plays throughout, it supports the voices so discreetly that the effect is of a cappella singing, even though the term only truly applies to the final "Amen." By utilizing repeated notes, Stravinsky gives the *"Credo"* the same chantlike character as the *"Gloria."*

In *"Sanctus,"* Stravinsky uses all four soloists and gives them a brief fugal section before the entire choir joins in, loudly crying, "Hosanna"; the choir returns after *"Benedictus"* to end the movement. The concluding *"Agnus Dei"* alternates instrumental sections with sections of pure, restrained a cappella singing.

Ernest Ansermet led the first performance of Stravinsky's *Mass* in Milan on October 26, 1948.

Standard Text (see Appendix)

CANTICUM SACRUM
(Canticum Sacrum ad honorem Sancti Marci Nominis, "Sacred Cantata in Honor of St. Mark")

17 minutes

Early in the 1920s, Arnold Schoenberg introduced a radically new approach to composing that he called "method of composing with twelve tones." Simply put, it structured its music around a particular arrangement of the twelve tones of the chromatic scale (the tone row) and mandated that all twelve tones had to be sounded before any could be repeated. A number of composers adopted Schoenberg's system. Alban Berg and Anton Webern were early followers; Milton Babbitt, Karlheinz Stockhausen, and Pierre Boulez came later.

For some thirty years after the introduction of the twelve-tone method, Stravinsky found no use for this approach. Then, in 1955, four years after Schoenberg's death, Stravinsky wrote *Canticum sacrum,* a major choral work, using his interpretation of the twelve-tone method. Could the death of Schoenberg have freed Stravinsky to adapt the system to his own musical needs?

Stravinsky composed *Canticum sacrum* in 1955 on a commission from the Venice Biennial Festival of Contemporary Music. He scored it for tenor and baritone soloists, mixed choir, and an orchestra of flute, two oboes, English horn, two bassoons, contrabassoon, three trumpets, bass trumpet, three trombones, bass trombone, organ, violas, and double basses. The text, which comes from both the Old and New Testaments of the Bible, is sung in Latin. The composer conducted the first performance in St. Mark's Cathedral in Venice on September 13, 1956.

Stravinsky starts *Canticum sacrum* with a brief musical dedication "To the city of Venice, in praise of its patron saint, the blessed Mark the Apostle," which is sung by the tenor and baritone soloists against a background of three trombones. The writing here does not follow the twelve-tone method but rather exhibits some qualities of Gregorian chant.

The first movement, *"Euntes in mundum,"* is not in twelve tone either. Instead it is organized in blocks of sound: three loud passages of choir and full orchestra separated by two quiet passages for bassoons and organ. Since the acoustics in St. Mark's are extremely resonant, Stravinsky may have written it this way to allow the air to clear between loud sections.

"Surge, aquilo," the second movement, does employ the twelve-tone method. The solo tenor states the tone row on which Stravinsky bases the movement. (The tone row is A flat, G, F, D, F sharp, E, E flat, D flat, B flat, C, B, A.) The choir does not sing here at all, and the composer restricts the orchestra to flute, English horn, harp, and three double basses.

Central to the entire work is the third movement, *"Ad Tres Virtutes Hortationes,"* a glorification of the three virtues—love, faith, and hope. Stravinsky structured this section in a tripartite division, with "Faith" serving as the keystone; the organ presents the new, but related, tone row of the movement and introduces each of the sections with a transposition of the row.

The fourth movement, *"Brevis Motus Cantilenae,"* bears a resemblance to the second movement in that it is a short movement in which a solo voice, here the baritone, states the tone row. The choir also participates, echoing and imitating the soloist.

The text of the fifth movement, *"Ille autem profecti"* ("And they went forth, and preached everywhere") follows after the first-movement text, "Go ye into all the world and preach." Also, Stravinsky makes the last movement an almost literal copy of the first—but in reverse, going from finish to start!

Thus, Stravinsky creates a symmetry that runs through the

entire work. Movement one is performed backward for movement five; movements two and four feature a solo voice; and movement three is internally symmetrical, with a central middle part. Musicologist Dika Newlin points out that the five sections of *Canticum sacrum* also correspond to the five symmetrical gold domes of St. Mark's, a relationship that might well have been in Stravinsky's mind.

Rarely can the casual listener—or even the trained professional—catch the many intricacies of *Canticum* on first exposure. Repeated listening, though, reveals the structural scheme, as well as the musical worth of this unique composition. Realizing that it is difficult to grasp the music in one hearing, Stravinsky performed it twice on the same program at the premiere—a practice followed by a number of other conductors since then, and one that is most helpful to the audience.

DEDICATIO

Urbi Venetiae, in laude Sancti sui Presidis, Beati Marci Apostoli.

To the City of Venice, in praise of its Patron Saint, the Blessed Mark the Apostle.

I

Euntes in mundum universum, praedicate evangelium omni creaturae.
(Vulgata. Evang. secunum Marcum, XVI. 7.)

Go ye into all the world and preach the gospel to every creature.

II

Surge, aquilo; et veni auster; perflahortum meum, et fluant aromata illius. Veniat dilectus meus in hortum suum, et comedat fructum pomorum suorum. Veni in hortum meum, soror mea, sponsa;

Awake, O north wind; and come, thou south; blow upon my garden, that the spices thereof may flow out. Let my beloved come into his garden, and eat his pleasant fruits. I am come into my garden, my

messui myrrham meam cum
aromatibus meis; comedi
favum meum cum melle meo;
bibi vinum meum cum lacte
meo. Comedite, amici, et
bibite; et inebriamini,
carissimi.
(Vulgata. Canticum
Canticorum IV. 16, V.)

sister, my spouse; I have
gathered my myrrh with my
spice; I have eaten my
honeycomb with my honey; I
have drunk my wine with my
milk; eat, O friends, drink,
yea, drink abundantly, O
beloved.

III

Caritas

Diliges Dominum Deum tuum
ex toto corde tuo, et ex tota
anima tua, et ex tota
fortitudina tua.
(Vulgata. Deuter. VI, 5.)

Thou shalt love the Lord thy
God with all thine heart, and
with all thy soul, and with all
thy might.

Diligamus nos in vicem, quia
charitas ex Deo est; et omnis
qui diligit ex Deo natus est, et
cognoscit Deum.
(Vulgata. Prima Epistola Beati
Joannis Apostoli. IV, 7.)

Beloved, let us love one
another: for love is of God:
and everyone that loveth is
born of God, and knoweth
God.

Spes

Qui confidunt in Domino, sicut
mons Sion; non
commovebitur in aeternum,
qui habitat in Jerusalem.
Sustinuit anima mea in verbo
ejus; speravit anima mea in
Domino, a custodia matutina
usque ad noctem.
(Vulgata. Libr. Psalm,
CXXV.I.CXXIX. 4–5.
CXXIV.I.)

They that trust in the Lord,
shall be as Mount Zion,
which cannot be removed but
abideth for ever. My soul
doth wait, and in His word
do I hope. My soul waiteth
for the Lord more than they
that watch for the morning.

Fides

Credidi proctor quod locutus
sum; ego autem humiliatus
sum nimis.
(Vulgata. Libr. Psalm, CXXV,
10.)

I believed, therefore have I
spoken: I was greatly
afflicted.

IV

Jesus autum aït illi: Si potes
credere, omnia possibilia sunt
credenti. Et continuo
exclamans pater pueri, cum
lacrimis aïebat: Credo,
Domine; adjuva
incredulitatem meam.
(Vulgata. Ev. secundum
Marcum, IX, 22–23.)

Jesus said unto him, if thou
canst believe, all things are
possible to him that believeth.
And straightway the father of
the child cried out, and said
with tears, Lord I believe;
help Thou my unbelief.

V

Ille autem profecti
praedicaverunt ubique,
Domino cooperante et
sermonem confirmante,
sequentibus signis. Amen.
(Vulgata. Ev. secundum
Marcum, XVI, 20.)

And they went forth, and
preached everywhere, the
Lord working with them, and
confirming the word with
signs following. Amen.

THRENI
(Threni id est Lamentationes Jeremiae prophetae, "Tears, That Is, Lamentations of the Prophet Jeremiah")

35 minutes

Stravinsky first used the twelve-tone method in his 1955 *Canticum sacrum*. In *Threni*, which he composed in 1957 and 1958, he again followed the twelve-tone method but here applied it much more rigorously. He employs it throughout (instead of just in three of the five movements); the tone row is the same for the entire work (instead of a different tone row for each section); and he sounds the notes of the tone row simultaneously as well as sequentially (instead of just sequentially). *Threni,* therefore, is much closer than *Canticum sacrum* to the ideals of twelve-tone writing as stated by Arnold Schoenberg, creator of the twelve-tone method.

For *Threni,* which was commissioned by North German Radio, Stravinsky chose his text from chapters 1, 3, and 5 of the Lamentations of Jeremiah. He set the work for six soloists— soprano, alto, two tenors, bass, and basso profundo—mixed choir, and orchestra.

Although Stravinsky organized *Threni* around a tone row, his frequent use of the highly dissonant minor second interval (F and F sharp), both melodically (sequentially) and harmonically (simultaneously), is most striking to the ear. Stravinsky always insisted that music was incapable of "expressing" anything—as he said, "Composers combine notes. That is all." Still, some commentators hear in this piercing interval some of the anguish and pain of Jeremiah's laments.

Structurally, Stravinsky made the work very sectional; each section is introduced by a choral setting of a letter of the Hebrew alphabet—*Aleph, Beth, He,* and so on. Within each unit the composer divides the writing into short phrases, which gives the work a certain austere, ritualistic character. Stravinsky uses the orchestra very sparingly, seldom having more than a few of the many instruments playing at the same time.

The composer conducted the premiere on September 23, 1958, at the Venice Biennial Festival of Contemporary Music. Extremely difficult for the choristers and equally challenging for the listeners, *Threni* is far from a popular favorite—yet a good number of music lovers find this an intriguing and stimulating work.

DE ELEGIA PRIMA

ALEPH. Quomodo sedet sola civitas plena populo! Facta est quasi vidua domina gentium: princeps provinciarum facta est sub

How doth the city sit solitary, that was full of people! How is she become as a widow! she that was great among the nations, and princess among tributo.

the provinces, how is she become tributary!

BETH. Plorans ploravit in nocte, et lacrymae ejus in maxillis ejus.

She weepeth sore in the night, and her tears are on her cheeks.

HE. Facti sunt hostes ejus in capite, inimici ejus locupletati sunt. Quia Dominus locutus est super eam propter multitudinem iniquitatum ejus.

Her adversaries are the chief, her enemies prosper; for the Lord hath afflicted her for the multitude of her transgressions.

CAPH. Vide, Domine, et considera, quoniam facta sum vilis.

See. O Lord, and consider; for I am become vile.

RES. Vide, Domine, quoniam tribulor, conturbatus est venter meus, subversum est cor meum in memetipsa quoniam amaritudine plena sum. Foris interficit gladius, et domi mors similis est.

Behold, O Lord, for I am in distress: my bowels are troubled: mine heart is turned within me; for I have grievously rebelled: abroad the sword bereaveth, at home there is as death.

DE ELEGIA TERTIA

(1) Querimonia • Complaint

ALEPH. Ego vir videns paupertatem meam in virga indignationis ejus.

I am the man that hath seen affliction by the rod of his wrath.

Me menavit, et adduxit in tenebras, et non in lucem.

He hath led me, and brought me into darkness, but not into light.

Tantum in me vertit, et convertit manum suam tota die.

Surely against me is he turned; he turneth his hand against me all the day.

BETH. Vetustam fecit pellem meam et carnem meum, contrivit ossa mea.

My flesh and skin hath he made old; he hath broken my bones.

Aedificavit in gyro meo, et circumdedit me felle et labore.

He hath builded against me and compassed me with gall and travail.

In tenebrosis collocavit me, quasi mortuos sempiternos.

He hath set me in dark places, as they that be dead of old.

VAU. Et fregit ad numerum dentes meos, cibavit me cinere.

He hath also broken my teeth with gravel stones, he hath covered me with ashes.

Et repulsa est a pace amima mea, oblitus sum bonorum.

And thou hast removed my soul far off from peace; I forgat prosperity.

Et dixi: Periit finis meus, et spes mea a Domine.

And I said, My strength and my hope is perished from the Lord.

ZAIN. Recordare paupertatis, et transgressionis meae, absinthii et fellis.

Remembering mine affliction and my misery, the wormwood and the gall.

Memoria memor ero, et tabescet in me anima mea.

My soul hath them still in remembrance, and is humbled in me.

Haec recolens in corde meo, ideo sperabo.

This I recall to my mind, therefore have I hope.

(2) Sensus Spei • Perceiving Hope

HETH. Misericordiae Domini, quia non sumus consumpti; quia non defecerunt miserationes ejus.

It is of the Lord's mercies that we are not consumed, because his compassions fail not.

Novi diluculo, multa est fides tua.

They are new every morning: great is thy faithfulness.

Pars mea Dominus, dixit anima mea; propterea exspectabo eum.

The Lord is my portion, saith my soul; therefore will I hope in him.

TETH. Bonus est Dominus sperantibus in eum, animae quaerenti illum.

The Lord is good unto them that wait for him, to the soul that seeketh him.

Bonum est praestolari cum silentio salutare Dei.

It is good that a man should both hope and quietly wait for the salvation of the Lord.

Bonum est viro, cum portaverit jugum ab adolescentia sua.

It is good for a man that he bear the yoke in his youth.

LAMED. Ut contereret sub pedibus suis omnes vinctos terrae;

To crush under his feet all the prisoners of the earth,

Ut declinaret judicium viri in conspectu vultus Altissimi;

To turn aside the right of a man before the face of the most High.

Ut perverteret hominem in judicio suo, Dominus ignoravit.

To subvert a man in his cause, the Lord approveth not.

NUN. Scrutemur vias nostras, et quaeremus, et revertamur ad Dominum.

Let us search and try our days, and turn again to the Lord.

Levemus corda nostra cum manibus ad Dominum in coelos.

Let us lift up our hearts with our hands unto God in the heavens.

Nos inique egimus, et ad iracundiam provocavimus; incirco tu inexorabilis es.

We have transgressed and have rebelled: thou hast not pardoned.

SAMECH. Operuisti in furore, et percussisti nos; occidisti, nec pepercisti.

Thou hast covered with anger and persecuted us; thou hast slain, thou hast not pitied.

Opposuisti nubem tibi, ne transeat oratio.

Thou hast covered thyself with a cloud, that our prayer should not pass through.

Eradicationem et abjectionem posuisti me in medio populorum.

Thou hast made us as the offscouring and refuse in the midst of the people.

AIN. Oculus meus afflictus est, nec tacuit, eo quod non esset requies.

Mine eye trickleth down, and ceaseth not, without any intermission.

Donec respiceret et videret Dominus de coelis.	Till the Lord look down, and behold from heaven.
Oculus meus depraedatus est animam meam in cunctis filiabus urbis meae.	Mine eye affecteth mine heart because of all the daughters of my city.
TSADE. Venatione ceperunt me quasi avem inimici mei gratis.	Mine enemies chased me sore, like a bird, without cause.
Lapsa est in lacum vita mea, et posuerunt lapidem super me.	They have cut off my life in the dungeon, and cast a stone upon me.
Inundaverunt aquae super caput meum; dixi: Perii.	Waters flowed over mine head; then I said, I am cut off.
COPH. Invocavi nomen tuum, Domine, de lacu novissimo.	I called upon thy name, O Lord, out of the low dungeon.
Vocem meam audisti; ne avertas aurem tuam a singultu meo et clamoribus.	Thou hast heard my voice: hide not thine ear at my breathing, at my cry.
Appropinquasti in die quando invocavite; dixisti: Ne timeas.	Thou drewest near in the day that I called upon thee: thou saidst, Fear not.

(3) Solacium • Compensation

RES. Judicasti, Domine, causam animae meae, redemtor vitae meae.	O Lord, thou hast pleaded the causes of my soul; thou hast redeemed my life.
Vidisti, Domine, iniquitatem illorum adversum me.	O Lord, thou hast seen my wrong.
Vidisti omnen furorem, universas cogitationes eorum adversum me.	Thou hast seen all their vengeance and all their imaginations against me.
SIN. Audisti opprobrium eorum, Domine, omnes cogitationes eorum adversum me:	Thou hast heard their reproach, O Lord, and all their imaginations against me.

Labia insurgentium mihi, et
meditationes eorum adversum
me tota die.

The lips of those that rose up
against me, and their device
against me all the day.

Sessionem eorum, et
resurrectionem eorum vide,
ego sum psalmus eorum.

Behold their sitting down and
their rising up; I am their
musick.

THAU. Reddes eis vicem,
Domine, juxta opera manuum
suarum.

Render unto them a
recompense, O Lord,
according to the work of
their hands.

Dabis eis scutum cordis,
laborem tuum.

Give them sorrow of heart, thy
curse unto them.

Persequeris in furore, et
conteres eos sub coelis,
Domine.

Persecute and destroy them in
anger from under the heavens
of the Lord.

DE ELEGIA QUINTA
Oratio Jeremiae Prophetae
The prayer of the Prophet Jeremiah

Recordare, Domine, quid
acciderit nobis; intuere et
respice opprobrium nostrum.

Remember, O Lord, what is
come upon us; consider, and
behold our reproach.

Tu autem, Domine, in aeternum
permanebis, solium tuum in
generationem et
generationem.

Thou, O Lord, remainest for
ever: thy throne from
generation to generation.

Converte nos, Domine, ad te, et
convertemur; innova dies
nostros, sicut a principio.

Turn thou us unto thee, O
Lord, and we shall be turned;
renew our days as of old.

RANDALL THOMPSON

Born April 21, 1899, in New York City
Died July 9, 1984, in Boston

Many composers in the twentieth century have felt the need to identify with one compositional ideology or another—serial or dodecaphonic, minimalist or aleatoric, neoromantic or neoclassical. Randall Thompson chose to stay above the fray. He stated his fundamental philosophy very succinctly: "A composer's first responsibility is, and always will be, to write music that will reach and move the hearts of listeners in his own day." In line with this outlook, he wrote highly expressive music, achieving his ends with a wonderful simplicity and economy of means, and without identifying with any of the fashionable fads of modern music.

Even though he was born in New York City, Thompson did not think of his compositions as "American" music; he preferred to think of himself as an American who wrote music of universal appeal.

While his Second and Third Symphonies still occasionally appear on orchestral programs, it is Thompson's choral works that have proved to have the greatest staying power. In addition to the four works discussed in this book, which have won the most secure places in today's repertoire, Thompson's choral compositions include *The Last Words of David* (1949), *Requiem* (1958), and *The Passion According to St. Luke* (1965).

Thompson received his training at Harvard University and the Eastman School of Music, with additional study under Ernest Bloch. Over the following years he held a number of prestigious teaching posts for short periods of time until he was appointed to the faculty at Harvard University, where he taught from 1948 until his retirement in 1966.

AMERICANA

18 minutes

In the fall of 1931, Randall Thompson was appointed conductor of the Dessoff Choirs in New York City, and the League of Composers commissioned him to write a choral composition that the group could perform at one of the league concerts. Thompson had some difficulty finding a suitable text and was browsing in the New York Public Library when he came upon bound volumes of H. L. Mencken's magazine, *The American Mercury*. His attention was drawn to a monthly column, called "Americana," which contained items of special interest culled from various newspapers and magazines around the country.

Thompson chose five of the items to set for mixed choir and piano, which he later expanded to mixed choir and orchestra. Appropriately enough, he named it *Americana*.

On the score, Thompson wrote this prefatory note:

The different parts of the work are satirical and, at moments, mirth-provoking, but the music was written with compassion. The five texts represent five characteristics of this nation and doubtless of various other nations at different stages in their history. The texts were set to music with a keen sense of the emotional quality which lay behind each excerpt. The music is not meant to point the finger of scorn, but only to underline the pathos inherent in those whose ideas about life lead to extraordinary and sometimes extreme conclusions.

The composer also wrote these brief descriptions of the five movements:

1. "May Every Tongue" [from the *Seattle Post-Intelligencer*] is the impassioned anathema of the preacher, discrediting science. It is vehemently chanted by the chorus, the accompaniment supplying a hymn-like background to heighten the effect.
2. "The Staff Necromancer" [from the *New York Evening*

Graphic] treats each question and answer according to the character of each questioner. Desperate, misguided humanity seeking the Delphic Oracle, the Sybils, soothsayers!

3. "God's Bottles" [from the Women's Christian Temperance Union] suitably enough, is set for women's voices. Dare one hope that this music will do for Prohibition what *Uncle Tom's Cabin* did for slavery?

4. "The Sublime Process of Law Enforcement" [from *Startling Detective Adventures*] is for mixed voices, mostly in unison. This is not "pleasant" music. It is a short, one-act opera, deliberate and macabre—intentionally so.

5. "Loveli-lines" [from an ad for a book of verse in the *California Literary Intelligence*] is a glorification of our love of Beauty and Uplift in poetry—and advertising. The words, "Each one will lift you to the Heights of Consciousness," and those following, are set as a round with the chorus divided into seven parts.

Since the text was all important in *Americana*, Thompson took great care to ensure clarity of diction by following natural speech rhythms; he achieved this clarity by frequent changes of meter and accentuation. The settings are all witty and ironic, often depending for their humor on the contrast between the mock seriousness of the musical treatment and the ingenuousness of the text.

Thompson conducted the premiere in New York City on April 4, 1932.

MAY EVERY TONGUE

[WASHINGTON—Christian sentiment of the Rev. Dr. Mark Matthews, veteran instrument of the Lord in Seattle, as reported by the *Post-Intelligencer*.]
May every tongue be paralyzed and every hand palsied that utters a word or raises a finger from this pulpit in advocacy of Modernism.

THE STAFF NECROMANCER

[NEW YORK—*The Staff Necromancer* of the *Evening Graphic* comes to the aid of troubled readers of that great family newspaper.]

[Q.]—Will I ever recover my stolen jewelry? . . . A.M.

[A.]—*Your jewelry was taken to New Orleans and sold. You can recover it in part.*

[Q.]—My children made me break up my home and come to New York from Massachusetts; and now I am so lonesome, and can't pay my room rent. What can I do? . . . E.T.

[A.]—*You will get a position as nurse to three small children in Pelham, N. Y. It will give you a source of income, and something easy to do. I see you will marry again later and go back to Massachusetts.*

[Q.]—Is my husband, Charles W——, alive? . . . A.W.

[A.]—*No, he is not. I see him drowning in deep water.*

[Q.]—Will it be advisable for me to go into the laundry business with my boy friend before we are married? . . . F.I.B.

[A.]—*Yes, the two of you will be very successful. I see you will marry very soon.*

[Q.]—Will I ever have any children? I have been married nearly two years. . . . A.F.W.

[A.]—*You will have three children, the first one in about two years. That is plenty of time.*

GOD'S BOTTLES

[Leaflet Issued by the N.W.C.T.U.]

APPLES ARE GOD'S BOTTLES: The sweet juice of the apple God has placed in His own bottle. What a beautiful rosy-red bottle it is! These red bottles hang on the limbs of a tree until they are all ready for us to use. Do you want to open God's bottle? Bite the apple with your teeth and you will taste the sweet juice God has put in His bottle for you.

GRAPES ARE GOD'S BOTTLES: These purple and green bottles you will find hanging on a pretty vine. See! So many little bottles are on a single stem! Put a grape in your mouth and open God's bottle. How nice the juice tastes! Some men take the juice of apples and grapes and make drinks, that will harm our bodies. They put the drinks in glass bottles, but we will not drink from such bottles. We will DRINK FROM GOD'S BOTTLES.

THE SUBLIME PROCESS OF LAW ENFORCEMENT

[ARKANSAS—*The Sublime Process of Law Enforcement,* described by Joseph B. Warger, deathhouse reporter of Little Rock *Gazette,* in *Startling Detective Adventures.*]

One scene in the death chamber was particularly unpleasant, even gruesome. That occurred the morning four white men were executed a few minutes apart. The condemned men were Duncan Richardson, Ben Richardson, F. G. Bullen and Will DeBord. The first three had been convicted of the murder of one man; DeBord was condemned for murdering an old couple.

Preparations for this unusual execution were not as complete as they might have been. There were no accommodations for the undertaker who was to take the four bodies away. The death chamber was too small for the four coffins and the augmented crowd of witnesses, and there was no other room convenient.

Hence the four coffins were deposited in the run-around of the death house, directly in front of the cells in which the four men were confined awaiting their turn in the chair. It was an unintentional cruelty on the part of the officials. If the doomed men looked through the doors of their cells, the grim row of coffins was directly in view. If they looked out the windows, they could see the hearses waiting to carry them away after the execution. So they sat on their bunks with their faces in their hands and waited the execution.

Duncan Richardson was the first to go. After it was all over for him, his body was carried back and laid in the coffin where the other three could see it if they lifted their heads. And when Ben Richardson started his death march, he passed by the row of coffins, one of which contained all that remained of his brother.

LOVELI-LINES
[CALIFORNIA—Literary intelligence: *Announcing*]

LOVELI-LINES

by Edna Nethery

Loveli-Lines is composed of thirty-three Individualistic Verse poems all abrim with Joy, Love, Faith, Abundance, Victory, Beauty and Mastery.
Each one will lift you to the Heights of Consciousness.
Bound in cloth of Happy blue: trimmed and lettered in gold.
Order from
Edna Nethery
Riverside, Calif.
One Dollar

THE PEACEABLE KINGDOM

16 minutes

As with his earlier work, *Americana*, *The Peaceable Kingdom* was a commission for Randall Thompson from the League of Composers, this one for a piece to be performed by the combined Harvard Glee Club and Radcliffe Choral Society. As with the previous work, Thompson had some difficulty finding a suitable text.

Thompson set out on the trail that led to *The Peaceable Kingdom* after reading in a newspaper that the Worcester, Massachusetts, Art Museum had just bought a painting with that name by the Pennsylvania Quaker preacher and painter Edward Hicks (1780–1849). The painting, in primitive style, was inspired by Isaiah, chapter 11, verses 6 through 9; the right side shows wild and domestic animals living happily together and being led by a young child, while the left side shows William Penn speaking to the Indians. Thompson went to Worcester to see the painting and decided then to create a choral work on the same theme.

As a first step, Thompson read and reread Isaiah, selecting passages that would lend themselves to the musical work he was planning. He finally chose a number of verses from throughout Isaiah and organized them into eight comparatively brief choruses for single or double mixed choir a cappella.

The first chorus draws a dramatic contrast between the melodies of the righteous, who "sing for joy of heart," and the wails of the wicked, who "howl for vexation of spirit."

"Woe unto them" elaborates on the lot of the wicked, with agitated declamatory lines in single voices interrupted by shouts of "Woe!" from the others.

There is no real melody in the third chorus; rather, it essentially presents an exciting arrangement of plateaus of sound at different pitch and dynamic levels.

Following without pause, "Howl ye" describes a climactic movement that requires a double choir to hurl out, with the utmost force and power, the warning to the wicked.

The focus, which had largely been on the wicked until now, begins to shift to the righteous with the quiet and calm fifth chorus.

Calling for a double choir, and including brief passages for solo soprano and tenor, the sixth chorus continues with the theme of the joy of the righteous.

Short and loud throughout, "Have ye not known?" is the culminating final chorus, which pits the men of the double choir against the women antiphonally as they sing with great fervor of the triumph of the righteous. The text "Ye shall have a song" refers back to the song of the righteous from the opening section.

Thompson composed *The Peaceable Kingdom,* which many consider his finest choral work, in 1936. It received its premiere in Cambridge, performed by the combined Harvard Glee Club and Radcliffe Choral Society, on March 3, 1936, under G. Wallace Woodworth. A reproduction of Hicks's *The Peaceable Kingdom* appeared in the program.

I

Say ye to the righteous, it shall be well with him:
  for they shall eat the fruit of their doings.
Woe unto the wicked! it shall be ill with him:
  for the reward of his hands shall be given him.
Behold, my servants shall sing for joy of heart,
  but ye shall cry for sorrow of heart and shall howl for vexation of
  spirit.

II

Woe unto them that draw iniquity with cords of vanity and sin as it
  were with a cart rope!
Woe unto them that call evil good and good evil; that put darkness for

light and light for darkness; that put bitter for sweet and sweet for bitter!

Woe unto them that are wise in their own eyes and prudent in their own sight!

Woe unto them that are mighty to drink wine and men of strength to mingle strong drink!

Woe unto them that rise up early in the morning, that they may follow strong drink; that continue till night, till wine inflame them! And the harp, and the viol, and the tabret, and pipe and wine are in their feasts;

But they regard not the work of the Lord, neither consider the operations of his hands.

Woe to the multitude of many people, which make a noise like the noise of the seas!

Woe unto them that join house to house, that lay field to field, till there be no place, that they may be placed alone in the midst of the earth.

Woe!

III

The noise of a multitude in the mountains, like as a great people; a tumultuous noise of the Kingdoms of nations gathered together; the Lord of hosts mustereth the host of the battle. They come from a far country, from the end of Heaven, even the Lord and the weapons of his indignation, to destroy the whole land. Their bows also shall dash the young men to pieces; and they shall have no pity on the fruit of the womb; their eye shall not spare children. Everyone that is found shall be thrust through; and everyone that is joined unto them shall fall by the sword. Children also shall be dashed to pieces before their eyes; their houses shall be spoiled and their wives ravished. Therefore shall all hands be faint and every man's heart shall melt: they shall be afraid: pangs and sorrow shall take hold of them: they shall be in pain as a woman that travaileth: they shall be amazed at one another: their faces shall be as flames.

IV

Howl ye; for the day of the Lord is at hand.
Howl, O gate; cry, O city; thou art dissolved.

V

The paper reeds by the brooks, by the mouth of the brooks, and everything sown by the brooks shall wither, be driven away, and be no more.

VI

But these are they that forsake the Lord, that forget my holy mountain.
For ye shall go out with joy, and be led forth with peace: the mountains and the hills shall break forth before you into singing and all the trees of the fields shall clap their hands.

VII

Have ye not known? Have ye not heard?
Hath it not been told you from the beginning? Have ye not understood from the foundations of the earth?
Ye shall have a song, as in the night when a holy solemnity is kept, and gladness of heart, as when one goeth with a pipe, to come into the mountain of the Lord.

ALLELUIA

5 minutes

Some may argue whether the very short *Alleluia,* with a text of only that word, should be considered a choral masterpiece, but none can doubt its position as one of the most exciting, noble, and frequently performed pieces in the entire choral repertoire.

Just three weeks before the July 8, 1940, opening of the Berkshire Music Center in Lenox, Massachusetts, Serge Koussevitzky, conductor of the Boston Symphony, commissioned Thompson to compose a brief choral work for the opening ceremonies. In that short time, Thompson had not only to compose the music but to allow time for copies to be printed for the 250-voice Tanglewood Choir.

The copies of *Alleluia* were sent out from Philadelphia on Saturday morning, July 6, and arrived at Tanglewood at five minutes before two on Monday afternoon. The choir, under G. Wallace Davison, had about forty-five minutes to rehearse, then went on to give the very successful premiere at three-thirty that very afternoon! Davison later commented, "So sure was Thompson's technique, so expert his craftsmanship, and so masterly his grasp of the true genius of choral singing" that the choir was able quickly to master the music and the work was of such exceptional quality that it has become a favorite of both choirs and audiences.

THE TESTAMENT OF FREEDOM

26 minutes

Randall Thompson composed *The Testament of Freedom* in 1943 to honor the two hundredth anniversary of Thomas Jefferson's birth. He wrote it for four-part men's choir and piano (which he later orchestrated) and used Jefferson's prose writings as the text. The University of Virginia Glee Club, under Stephen D. Tuttle, gave the first performance, with the composer at the piano. Serge Koussevitzky and the Boston Symphony introduced the orchestral version in Boston on April 6, 1945.

Honoring Jefferson with a major musical work was particularly fitting, since he was probably the most musical of all United States presidents. As he once wrote in a letter, "Music is the favorite passion of my soul." Thompson selected the text from three sources: section one from *A Summary View of the Rights of British America, 1774;* sections two and three from *Declaration of Causes and Necessity of Taking Up Arms, July 6, 1775;* and section four from a letter to John Adams, September 12, 1821.

The unifying core of the entire work is expressed in the text of the first section—"The God who gave us life gave us liberty at the same time; the hand of force may destroy but cannot disjoin them." This line is repeated at the very end.

Thompson kept the choral writing very simple, with much use

of unison and many folklike melodies. The accompaniment, too, stays on the simple side, with a good number of drum figures and fanfares giving the work a somewhat military-patriotic cast.

The composer treats the first part like a hymn, and he harmonizes it in a very straightforward manner. The second part, according to composer and critic Virgil Thomson, sounds as though it was derived from an accompanied chant of the Russian Orthodox church. The martial spirit comes to the fore in section three, which includes some melodies that might have been inspired by Revolutionary War songs. Thompson casts a contemplative, meditative mood in the final section before concluding with a reprise of the opening.

1. The God who gave us life gave us liberty at the same time; the hand of force may destroy but cannot disjoin them.
— *A Summary View of the Rights of British America*, 1774

2. We have counted the cost of this contest, and find nothing so dreadful as voluntary slavery. Honor, justice and humanity forbid us tamely to surrender that freedom which we received from our gallant ancestors and which our innocent posterity have a right to receive from us. We cannot endure the infamy and guilt of resigning succeeding generations to that wretchedness which inevitably awaits them if we basely entail hereditary bondage upon them.

Our cause is just. Our union is perfect. Our internal resources are great. . . . We gratefully acknowledge, and signal instances of the Divine favor toward us, that this Providence would not permit us to be called into this severe controversy until we were grown up to our present strength, had been previously exercised in warlike operation, and possessed of the means of defending ourselves. With hearts fortified with these animating reflections, we most solemnly, before God and the world, declare that, exerting the utmost energy of those powers which our beneficent Creator hath graciously bestowed upon us, the arms we have been compelled by our enemies to assume we will, in defiance of every hazard, with unabating firmness and perseverance, employ for the preservation of our liberties; being with one mind resolved to die freemen rather than to live as slaves.

—*Declaration of Causes and Necessity of Taking Up Arms,*
July 6, 1775

3. We fight not for glory or conquest. We exhibit to mankind the remarkable spectacle of a people attacked by unprovoked enemies, without any imputation or even suspicion of offense. They boast of their privileges and civilization, and yet proffer no milder conditions than servitude or death.

In our native land, in defense of the freedom that is our birthright and which we ever enjoyed till the late violation of it; for the protection of our property, acquired solely by the honest industry of our forefathers and ourselves; against violence actually offered; we have taken up arms. We shall lay them down when hostilities shall cease on the part of the aggressors and all danger of their being renewed shall be removed, and not before.

—*Declaration of Causes and Necessity of Taking Up Arms,*
July 6, 1775

4. I shall not die without a hope that light and liberty are on steady advance. . . . And even should the cloud of barbarism and despotism again obscure the science and liberties of Europe, this country remains to preserve and restore light and liberty to them. . . . The flames kindled on the 4th of July, 1776, have spread over too much of the globe to be extinguished by the feeble engines of despotism; on the contrary, they will consume these engines and all who work them.

—letter to John Adams, September 12, 1821

MICHAEL TIPPETT

Born January 2, 1905, in London

Beginning when he was a child, Michael Tippett has always been a most caring and concerned person. Social and economic inequities troubled and saddened him; an inalterable opposition to violence and killing turned him against all wars. This warm, compassionate quality pervades his music and affects his choice of subject.

One of Tippett's first compositions after graduation from the Royal College of Music in London was a ballad opera, *Robin Hood,* which he wrote for production by unemployed coal miners. In this, and in other works from that period, Tippett composed in a style best described as neoromantic—using the rich harmonies and melodies of the late nineteenth century in a more modern and advanced setting.

In the mid-1930s, though, Tippett disowned all that he had written until then and started off in a new direction, combining the Romantic traits from the past with an eloquent polyphonic texture, a freer use of more complex rhythms, and a greater lyrical quality. The first work in the new style to receive wide attention was his oratorio, *A Child of Our Time,* from 1939.

In the years since then, Tippett has produced an impressive body of works, including operas and symphonies, that are widely performed. His many accomplishments have earned him a knighthood in England and membership in the American Academy of Arts and Letters.

A CHILD OF OUR TIME

1 hour, 7 minutes

Michael Tippett's *A Child of Our Time* developed from a germ of an idea for an opera on the Irish rebellion of Easter, 1916, that came to him during the social upheaval in Europe of the

1930s. His enthusiasm for that subject waned, however, as he became "emotionally affected" by growing tensions in central Europe and the increasing likelihood of the outbreak of a world war. The escalating chain of events, which reached a peak in September 1938 and continued unabated, seemed to influence Tippett profoundly. To quote the composer, "When in November of that year the cruelest and most deliberate of the Nazi pogroms was launched on the pretext of an incident in Paris, the personal amalgam of general compassion for all outcasts and particular susceptibility to the Nazi horror fused into a clear artistic image."

The incident to which Tippett refers was the shooting in Paris of the German diplomat Ernst von Rath by a teenage Jewish refugee from Poland, Herschel Grynszpan; this led directly to "Crystal Night," during which Nazis and their sympathizers smashed the windows of Jewish homes and businesses throughout central Europe. Grynszpan became Tippett's symbolic hero.

Tippett approached his friend, poet T. S. Eliot, and asked him to write the text for an oratorio based on this incident. The poet agreed, asking only that Tippett provide a precise scheme of the length and content of each of the sections the composer felt necessary for the work. Tippett prepared what he called "Sketch for a Modern Oratorio," which he submitted to Eliot. After considering the "Sketch" for some weeks, Eliot surprised the composer by suggesting that he should write the words himself. Thus, Tippett said, "I began the somewhat unusual task for a composer: to invent or find the necessary words for my own musical scheme."

From studying Handel's The Messiah Tippett was aware of the older composer's use of a tripartite arrangement. His analysis of The Messiah found: "The first part is all prophecy and preparation. The second part is epic: from the birth of Christ to the second coming . . . and world's end. The third part is meditative. . . ."

Tippett favored this tradition and decided to structure A Child of Our Time the same way. His plan was to keep the first part entirely general, to restrict the epic material to the second part, and to use the third part for what he called "consequential comment."

In addition, Tippett was intrigued by the arrangement he found in the Lutheran *Passions*. Careful study revealed that these works are quite unitary, with narrational recitatives, descriptive choruses, contemplative arias, and congregational hymns or chorales all focused on the same theme.

While he foresaw no difficulty in adapting most of these older forms to his oratorio, the obvious difficulty lay in finding a twentieth-century analog of the congregational hymn. For a long time Tippett was at a loss on how to proceed. Then, one day he heard someone sing the spiritual "Steal Away." Struck by the powerful effect of this music, he chose five spirituals for their melodies and their texts, saying that they provided "the exact 'congregational' metaphor for five calculated situations in my scheme."

Tippett began writing the music for *A Child of Our Time* in September 1939, two days after the start of World War II, and he finished two years later. Because of his extremely compassionate views and his consequent pacifist convictions, Tippett became a conscientious objector during the war. So strong were his antiwar views that he refused full-time farm work in lieu of military service, and he was imprisoned for three months at the end of 1943. On his release he arranged for the first performance of *A Child of Our Time*, which was given at the Adelphi Theatre, London, on March 19, 1944, under the direction of Walter Goehr.

The overall scheme of *A Child of Our Time* follows the journey from the cold and gloom of Part I—starting with the opening chorus, "The world turns on its dark side"—through the shooting and the terror that follow in Part II, to the warmth and consolation of the spiritual "Deep River" which ends Part III. Tippett takes us on this deeply moving and affecting journey with four soloists, mixed choir, and orchestra, which are treated much the same way as they are treated in the great Bach Passions.

In his remarks for the 1975 recording of *A Child of Our*

Time, Tippett produced a succinct summary of the work: "*A Child of Our Time* is indeed a Passion; not of a god-man, but of man whose god has left the light of the heavens for the dark of the collective unconscious. The work asks the question: What happens to this man as the confusion deepens and the collective forces become evermore undiscriminating and unjust? Indeed what happens when individual actions of apparently righteous protest produce colossal ensuing catastrophes? As the text says somewhere: 'God [that is, the collective] overpowered him—the child of our time.'"

RALPH VAUGHAN WILLIAMS

Born October 12, 1872, in Down Ampney, England
Died August 26, 1958, in London

"Art, like charity, should begin at home. It is because Palestrina and Verdi are essentially Italian and because Bach, Beethoven and Wagner are essentially German that their message transcends their frontiers. The greatest artist inevitably belongs to his country as much as the humblest singer in a remote village." This statement by Ralph (pronounced "Rayf" in England) Vaughan Williams effectively sets forth the basic ideal for which he was striving in his music.

After receiving his musical training (mostly at the Royal College of Music and Trinity College, Cambridge), Vaughan Williams was turning out music of little distinction or originality; it owed most to the influence of Johannes Brahms. His transformation into a truly English composer began in the early years of the century, when he spent some time in the field collecting folk songs in Essex, Norfolk, and Sussex and, in 1903, became a member of the newly formed English Folk Song Society. Preparing the music for a new Anglican hymnbook and publishing a book of Christmas carols and songs of praise further enriched his background by introducing him to the treasure trove of English national and religious music.

Vaughan Williams's folk-music research familiarized him with the music of Tudor England—the glorious sixteenth century, which reached its artistic climax during the reign of Elizabeth I at the end of that period. From the music of that time Vaughan Williams assimilated a number of stylistic elements that became an integral part of his personal musical vocabulary.

Instead of organizing his melodies and harmonies exclusively around the major and minor scales, Vaughan Williams crafted melodies and used harmonic schemes based on the ancient modes—Dorian, Phrygian, Lydian, and so on—a practice that gave his music a somewhat archaic flavor.

Among the outstanding features of old English folk music are its great clarity, its emotional restraint, and the solidity and regularity of its rhythmic underpinnings. All the traits became part of Vaughan Williams's music—without any conscious borrowing or quotation on his part.

Over time, Vaughan Williams grafted the various characteristics he acquired from his study of English national music—and a natural predilection for mysticism and introspection—onto his own richly Romantic style. The result is a body of music of great beauty and distinction.

In addition to such popular favorites as the *Fantasia on Greensleeves* and the *Fantasia on a Theme by Thomas Tallis,* the public knows Vaughan Williams today for his nine symphonies, *Norfolk Rhapsody* for orchestra, the song cycle *On Wenlock Edge,* and an impressive list of choral works, which includes (in addition to those discussed here) *O Clap Your Hands* (1920), *Te Deum* (1928), *Magnificat* (1932), *Dona nobis pacem* (1936), *An Oxford Elegy* (1949), *The Sons of Light* (1950), *Three Shakespeare Songs* (1951), *The Old Hundredth Psalm Tune* (1953), and *Hodie* (1954).

SYMPHONY NO. 1, "A SEA SYMPHONY"

1 hour, 5 minutes

While Vaughan Williams was at Cambridge University in the 1890s, fellow student Bertrand Russell introduced him to the poetry of Walt Whitman, who was quite popular in England at the time. The young composer was much taken with Whitman, and over the following years he bought several editions of Whitman's works, including a pocket-sized one that he kept with him at all times.

By 1903, Vaughan Williams had selected several passages from Whitman's *Leaves of Grass* that he planned to set for choir and orchestra in a work he called *Songs of the Seas*. The composing did not go easily, and Vaughan Williams interrupted it for other work—including writing the music for part of Whitman's *Whispers of Heavenly Death* for choir and orchestra (which Vaughan Williams entitled *Toward the Unknown Region*)—before returning to his original idea, which he now called *The Ocean*. He composed, discarded, asked friends for advice, studied briefly in Paris with Ravel, and finally finished the work in 1910, giving it the title Symphony No. 1, "A Sea Symphony." He scored the symphony for soprano and baritone soloists, choir, and orchestra. The composer conducted the premiere at the Leeds Festival on October 12, 1910.

Vaughan Williams drew the text from various Whitman poems. The first three movements relied on poems in *Sea Drift*—"Songs of the Exposition," "A Song for All Seas, All Ships," "On the Beach at Night, Alone," "After the Sea-ship." The longer fourth movement used "The Explorers" from *Passage to India*. To suit his musical needs, however, Vaughan Williams dropped some lines and repeated some others of Whitman's original.

Each movement explores a different aspect of the sea. Throughout, though, Vaughan Williams uses the sea as metaphor for humans who are driven to undertake journeys toward self-discovery, much as they are driven to probe the secrets of the vast oceans. In his book *An Introduction to the Music of Ralph Vaughan Williams,* A. E. F. Dickinson summarizes the message of the poetry in each movement:

I. "Behold the sea itself." Limitless, indomitable. And not less indomitable the sailors, the "unnamed heroes . . . whom fate can never surprise nor death dismay. . . ."

II. To the philosophic mind, the sea is a symbol of all human life.

III. (Descriptive digression.) Look at it! That wonderful panorama of a myriad waves, following the great ship as ceaselessly as they are displaced by it.

IV. Now I begin to see the meaning of it all. These restless explorations will lead to a Reality of some kind. . . . "We too take ship, O Soul . . . steer for the deep waters only . . . where mariner has not yet dared to go. . . . O farther, farther sail!"

"A Sea Symphony" must be considered a choral symphony, since the choir sings throughout. Every movement strikes a balance between traditional symphonic forms, the requirements of the poetic structure, and the character and mood that the music portrays. The first movement, in modified sonata allegro form, opens magnificently, as though one suddenly sights the sea in all its stunning, overwhelming immensity. After that, the orchestra states the broad, expansive principal theme, which is then taken up by the choir. The tempo quickens and the mood lightens to introduce the second, contrasting theme, which Vaughan Williams entrusts to the solo baritone, followed by the choir. After developing and expanding the two themes, Vaughan Williams brings back only the first one and proceeds to a quiet ending.

The slow second movement for baritone soloist and semichoir retains some melodic figures carried over from the first movement. It is divided into three parts. The opening has the baritone soloist largely confined to a single note, with the melodic burden carried by the choir. The middle section, following the choir's "I think a thought of the clef of the universes and of the future," contains a melody related to the first movement's second theme. And finally there is a reminder of the opening that starts with the baritone's mysterious, monotone chanting, "On the beach at night, alone."

The subtitle of the Scherzo third movement, "The Waves," accurately describes the visions of the hearty, roiling sea that Vaughan Williams conjures up; he even includes hints of the melodies from two old English sea shanties—"The Golden Vanity" and "The Bold Princess Royal"—to underline the movement's nautical character.

Vaughan Williams treats the finale as a giant synthesis: a bringing together of motifs that have been heard in varied forms throughout the symphony, as well as an amalgamation of the philosophical threads—that man is truly the "great vessel" mentioned in the Scherzo and that the sea represents the infinite human realm.

1. A Song for All Seas, All Ships

Baritone, Soprano, Chorus
Behold, the sea itself,
And on its limitless, heaving
    breast, the ships;
See, where their white sails,
    bellying in the wind, speckle
    the green and blue,
See, the steamers coming and
    going, steaming in or out of
    port,
See, dusky and undulating, the
    long pennants of smoke.
Behold, the sea itself,
And on its limitless, heaving
    breast, the ships.
(Baritone)
Today a rude brief recitative,
Of ships sailing the seas, each
    with its special flag or ship-
    signal,
Of unnamed heroes in the
    ships—of waves spreading
    and spreading far as the eye
    can reach,
Of dashing spray, and the
    winds piping and blowing,
And out of these a chant for
    the sailors of all nations,
Fitful, like a surge,
Of sea-captains young or old,
    and the mates, and of all
    intrepid sailors,
Of the few, very choice,

taciturn, whom fate can
    never surprise nor death
    dismay,
Picked sparingly without noise
    by thee old ocean, chosen by
    thee,
Thou sea that pickest and
    cullest the race in time, and
    unitest the nations,
Suckled by thee, old husky
    nurse, embodying thee,
Indomitable, untamed as thee.
(Soprano)
Flaunt out, O sea, your
    separate flags of nations!
Flaunt out visible as ever the
    various flags and ship-signals!
But do you reserve especially
    for yourself and for the soul
    of man one flag
    above all the rest,
A spiritual woven signal for all
    nations, emblem of man elate
    above death,
Token of all brave captains and
    of all intrepid sailors and
    mates,
And all that went down doing
    their duty,
Reminiscent of them, twined
    from all intrepid captains
    young or old,
(Baritone)
A pennant universal, subtly

waving all time o'er all brave
  sailors,
All seas, all ships.

2. On the Beach at Night, Alone

Baritone, Chorus
On the beach at night, alone,
As the old mother sways her to
  and fro singing her husky
  song,
As I watch the bright stars
  shining, I think a thought of
  the clef of the universes and
  of the future,
A vast similitude interlocks all,
All distances of space however
  wide,
All distances of time,
All souls, all living bodies
  though they be ever so
  different,
All nations, all identities that
  have existed or may exist,
All lives and deaths, all of the
  past, present, future,
This vast similitude spans them,
  and always has spanned,
And shall forever span them
  and shall compactly hold and
  enclose them.

3. [Scherzo] The Waves

Chorus
After the sea-ship, after the
  whistling winds,
After the white-gray sails taut
  to their spars and ropes,
Below, a myriad, myriad waves

hastening, lifting up their
  necks,
Tending in ceaseless flow
  toward the track of the ship,
Waves of the ocean bubbling
  and gurgling, blithely prying,
Waves, undulating waves,
  liquid, uneven, emulous
  waves,
Toward that whirling current,
  laughing and buoyant with
  curves,
Where the great vessel sailing
  and tacking displaced the
  surface,
Larger and smaller waves in the
  spread of the ocean
  yearnfully flowing,
The wake of the sea-ship after
  she passes, flashing and
  frolicsome under the sun,
A motley procession with many
  a fleck of foam and many
  fragments,
Following the stately and rapid
  ship, in the wake following.

4. The Explorers

Baritone, Soprano, Chorus
O vast Rondure, swimming in
  space,
Covered all over with visible
  power and beauty,
Alternate light and day and the
  teeming spiritual darkness,
Unspeakable high processions
  of sun and moon and
  countless stars above,

Below, the manifold grass and
  waters,
With inscrutable purpose, some
  hidden prophetic intention,
Now first it seems my thought
  begins to span thee.
Down from the gardens of Asia
  descending,
Adam and Eve appear, then
  their myriad progeny after
  them,
Wandering, yearning, with
  restless explorations, with
  questionings, baffled,
  formless, feverish, with never-
  happy hearts, with that sad
  incessant refrain,—
'Wherefore unsatisfied soul?
  Whither O mocking life?'
Ah who shall soothe these
  feverish children?
Who justify these restless
  explorations?
Who speak the secret of the
  impassive earth?
Yet soul be sure the first intent
  remains, and shall be carried
  out,
Perhaps even now the time has
  arrived.
After the seas are all crossed,
After the great Captains have
  accomplished their work,
After the noble inventors,
Finally shall come the poet
  worthy that name,
The true son of God shall come
  singing his songs.
O we can wait no longer,
We too take ship O Soul,

Joyous we too launch out on
  trackless seas,
Fearless for unknown shores on
  waves of ecstasy to sail,
Amid the wafting winds (thou
  pressing me to thee, I thee to
  me, O Soul),
Caroling free, singing our song
  of God,
Chanting our chant of pleasant
  exploration.
O Soul thou pleasest me, I thee,
Sailing these seas or on the
  hills, or waking in the night,
Thoughts, silent thoughts, of
  Time and Space and Death,
  like water flowing,
Bear me indeed as through
  regions infinite,
Whose air I breathe, whose
  ripples hear, lave me all over,
Bathe me, O God, in thee,
  mounting to thee,
I and my soul to range in range
  of thee.
O thou transcendent,
Nameless, the fibre and the
  breath,
Light of the light, shedding
  forth universes, thou centre
  of them.
Swiftly I shrivel at the thought
  of God,
At Nature and its wonders,
  Time and Space and Death,
But that I, turning, call to thee
  O Soul, thou actual me,
And lo, thou gently masterest
  the orbs,

Thou matest Time, smilest
content at Death,
And fillest, swellest full the
vastnesses of Space.
Greater than stars or suns,
Bounding O Soul thou
journeyest forth;
Away O Soul! hoist instantly
the anchor!
Cut the hawsers—haul out—
shake out every sail!
Reckless O Soul, exploring, I
with thee, and thou with me,

Sail forth, steer for the deep
waters only,
For we are bound where
mariner has not yet dared to
go,
And we will risk the ship,
ourselves and all.
O my brave Soul!
O farther, farther sail!
O daring joy, but safe! are they
not all the seas of God?
O farther, farther, farther sail!

MASS IN G MINOR

26 minutes

Nominally a Protestant, a member of the Church of England, Ralph Vaughan Williams did not actually practice any religion. Yet he composed his outstanding Mass in G minor for liturgical use and wrote it in a style that clearly gains from the acoustics of a church over those of a concert hall. He once commented to his wife, "There is no reason why an atheist could not write a good Mass."

Vaughan Williams worked on the Mass during 1920 and 1921 and scored it for double mixed a cappella choir, with small parts for soprano, alto, tenor, and bass soloists—though he asked that the soprano and alto parts be sung by boys, not women. Although the composer dedicated the work to Gustav Holst and his Whitsuntide Singers, the first performance was given by Joseph Lewis and the City of Birmingham Choir in December 1922.

The overall texture of the Mass is rather simple—it is often confined to either two-part polyphony or the contrasts of block-like antiphonal writing. The composer bases the tonal language on the ancient modes as well as the more familiar major and minor scales. With great skill, he blends modal melodies and harmonies (for music theorists, the two main modes are Dorian and Mixolydian) with his own twentieth-century idiom, creating a composition of great spirituality with archaic, mystical overtones.

Effectively capturing the poise and dignity of sixteenth-century vocal polyphony, Vaughan Williams constructs the *"Kyrie"* on long, strongly modal melodic lines, which he handles imitatively.

After the Priest intones the Gregorian melody, the choir launches into the *"Gloria."* The music ranges widely—now exultant and dancelike, now radiant and worshipful; sometimes with everyone singing together, sometimes divided into separate, antiphonal groups.

The *"Credo"* also starts with the Gregorian melody. To unify this extended section, Vaughan Williams uses the same melody for *"Patrem omnipotentem"* and *"Et resurrexit."* This repetition may also symbolize the concept that the same force that created the world also raised Christ from the dead.

Michael Kennedy, a friend of Vaughan Williams, compared the *"Sanctus"* to the "gentle swaying of censers."

After the comparatively spare, austere tone that predominates to this point, the *"Agnus Dei"* sounds warm and personal. By using the *"Kyrie"* melody for *"Miserere nobis"* in the *"Agnus Dei,"* Vaughan Williams brings us full circle as he ends this small-scale but glorious work.

Standard Text (see Appendix)

FLOS CAMPI

20 minutes

Vaughan Williams composed *Flos campi* ("The Flower of the Field") in 1925 for the unique combination of solo viola, small orchestra (no more than thirty-two players), and small wordless chorus (either twenty or twenty-six choristers divided into as many as eight parts). The work contains six interconnected movements, each one an "image" based on a quotation (that is not sung) from the Song of Solomon.

In writing for the choir, Vaughan Williams treats the voices instrumentally—asking the choristers to sing with such sounds as "ah," "ur," and "m," and with open, half-closed, or closed lips. On the other hand, he treats the solo viola vocally, bringing to mind the voice of the ancient singer of these songs—chanting, declaiming, beseeching.

Although the choir is wordless, Vaughan Williams quoted verses from the Song of Solomon in Latin and English at the start of each movement:

1. As the lily among thorns, so is my love among the daughters. Stay me with flagons, comfort me with apples; for I am sick of love.

The first stirrings of nature and of desire. The phrase "I am sick of love" may be misleading; a more apt translation might be "I am faint with longing." The main melodic interest in this movement is in the solo viola and the orchestra. The germinal motif—a repeated descending figure introduced at the very beginning by the oboe and solo viola—is taken to represent languishing love.

2. For lo, the winter is past, the rain is over and gone, the flowers appear on the earth, the time of the singing of birds is come, and the voice of the turtle is heard in our land.

The choir, with its varying tone colors, paints a descriptive picture of the gentle, pastoral beauties of the arriving spring.

3. I sought him whom my soul loveth, but I found him not. I charge you, O daughters of Jerusalem, if ye find my beloved, that ye tell him that I am sick of love. Whither is thy beloved gone, O thou fairest among women? Whither is thy beloved turned aside? that we may seek him with thee.

After a transition for solo viola based on the languishing love motif from the opening, the choir joins in for what can be interpreted as a love duet for choir and viola. Sadly, it ends with failure as the choir becomes silent and the lone, forsaken voice of the viola remains.

4. Behold his bed [palanquin], which is Solomon's, three score valiant men are about it. . . . They all hold swords, being expert in war.

A virile, highly rhythmic march with definite oriental overtones, this movement depicts the strength and power of the beloved. The choir only enters at the end to effect the transition to the next section.

5. Return, return, O Shulamite, return, return, that we may look upon thee. How beautiful are thy feet with shoes, O Prince's daughter.

Broad, expansive choral passages alternate with dancelike sections in this intense, impassioned movement. After a brief viola cadenza, the bassoon and French horn hint at the broad, foursquare theme that is the symbol of fulfillment and satisfaction.

6. Set me as a seal upon thine heart.

The solo viola states the complete fulfillment theme, and Vaughan Williams makes that theme the subject of an extended fugal passage for the orchestra. The choir enters with a seven-voice fugue on a different subject. After a reminder of the viola-oboe opening, the choir ends the movement and piece with a soft, distant reminder of the fulfillment theme.

Sir Henry Wood directed the premiere of *Flos campi* in London on October 10, 1925; the viola soloist was Lionel Tertis, to whom the work is dedicated.

GIUSEPPE VERDI

Born October 10, 1813, in le Roncole, Italy
Died January 27, 1901, in Milan

Giuseppe Verdi brought a few highly important skills to his music. For instance, he had amazing ability as a melodist—an uncanny ability to delineate character and mood through attractive, appealing arias. He possessed an infallible theatrical sense; he peopled his operas with characters in highly dramatic but nonetheless believable situations. He was gripped by an overwhelming fear of boring his listeners—so he filled all of his music with interest and passion. And he had a desire to compose music, not for an elite, but for the masses; opera was the "popular" music of nineteenth-century Italy, and Verdi made sure the public understood and enjoyed his works.

Born in a small village, Verdi began his musical instruction with the church organist, and by his teenage years he was already substituting for his teacher and composing on his own. A wealthy merchant offered to subsidize Verdi's further training at the Milan Conservatory, but the young man's application was rejected because he had a poor hand position when playing piano, and because his original compositions, while showing talent, displayed a lack of technical knowledge. Although both judgments were probably true, they do exhibit limited imagination and understanding on the examiners' part.

Verdi, however, did stay on in Milan, studying privately and starting a career as a conductor. The first opera he composed, *Oberto, Conte di San Bonifacio,* was presented with success at La Scala, Milan, in 1839. Over the following half century, he created a string of outstanding operas, including such popular favorites as *Rigoletto, Il trovatore, La traviata, Don Carlos,* and *Aïda.*

Verdi composed little besides his twenty-six operas; his nonoperatic oeuvre includes only eight choral works, a few songs, and a single string quartet. In each of these nonoperatic works, he adapted and modified his operatic style to the requirements of the work he was composing. Some critics complain that everything sounds as though it was composed for the opera stage. Most, though, enjoy the outpouring of beautiful melody and the intensity and accessibility of his writing, and they are delighted that he saw fit to venture outside the theater.

Most of Verdi's choral works are minor compositions that are seldom performed. *Requiem* and *Quattro pezzi sacri,* though, are major compositions that are an integral and important part of the modern choral repertoire.

REQUIEM
(Manzoni Requiem)

1 hour, 30 minutes

Verdi revered the Italian poet, novelist, and political leader Alessandro Manzoni (1785–1873) and considered him an exemplar of virtue and patriotism. After meeting Manzoni in 1868, Verdi wrote, "What can I say of Manzoni? How to describe the extraordinary, indefinable sensation the presence of that saint produced in me?"

When Manzoni died on May 22, 1873, Verdi was too grief-stricken to attend the funeral. He explained, though, that "there will have been few on that morning more sad and moved than I was, although far away. Now all is ended! And with him ends the most pure, the most holy, the most lofty of glories."

A few days later, Verdi wrote to his publisher, Giulio Ricordi, expressing his desire to compose a Requiem Mass to be performed on the first anniversary of Manzoni's death. A religious work would be a wonderful way, Verdi thought, to cap his long and highly successful career as Italy's leading opera composer and to show the world that he could do more than just compose for the theater. "I feel I have become an important person," he said. "I am no longer a barker on a platform bawling, 'Step up, Ladies and Gentlemen,' and banging on my drum." At Verdi's urging, Ricordi convinced the mayor of Milan to underwrite the expenses of the premiere, in return for which Verdi would compose the music, conduct the performance, and print the music.

Verdi started work on the *Requiem* in Paris during the summer of 1873. The first part he completed, *"Libera me,"* was apparently a reworking of something he had composed earlier. On the death of Gioacchino Rossini (November 13, 1868), Verdi had asked each of several prominent Italian composers to write one part of a Requiem Mass to honor Rossini. Although the participants completed the various sections, they bickered and squabbled so much among themselves, and those that were excluded raised such a fuss, that the project was dropped, the music was returned to the composers, and the piece was never performed.

Verdi's contribution to the Rossini *Requiem* was the *"Libera me,"* which he then used as the basis for the *"Libera me"* section of his new *Requiem*. Working very fast—and with the head start of the major *"Libera me"* section—Verdi completed the composition in less than a year, on April 16, 1874.

Assembling 4 soloists, a 100-piece orchestra, and a chorus of 120, Verdi began rehearsals at once; on May 22, 1874, he conducted the premiere of the *Requiem* at the Church of San Marco in Milan.

The church was packed, and it was obvious to all onlookers that the audience was profoundly moved by the music. Applause, however, was forbidden in the church, and there was no way the public could show its appreciation. Three days later a repeat performance was scheduled at the La Scala Opera House, where the capacity crowd received the work with a loud and enthusiastic ovation. Impresarios around Europe quickly made arrangements for Verdi to conduct performances abroad—seven in Paris and four each in London and Vienna.

To the public and most of his critics, Verdi's *Requiem* showed the composer at the height of his considerable creative power and in complete control of his musical materials. His deeply felt adoration of Manzoni, coupled with his amazing ability to create music of stunning dramatic impact, made the *Requiem* a very moving, highly emotional experience for all listeners.

Some of Verdi's adversaries, however, questioned the sincerity of the religious conviction underlying the music. Although biographers differ on the depth of his religious beliefs, most agree that he had little use for the church and its rituals. The composer often repeated the story of the trauma that occurred at age seven, when he, as an altar boy, was so transfixed by the sound of the organ that he forgot to hand the priest the wine during Mass. To rouse him, the priest gave him a powerful kick that, in one version, sent him flying down the altar steps and, in another, sent him dashing out of church, never to return.

Verdi's wife, Giuseppina, summed up his beliefs this way: "For some virtuous people a belief in God is necessary. Others, equally perfect, while observing strictly every precept of the highest moral code, are happier believing nothing."

Quite obviously, the character of Verdi's *Requiem* displeased Pope Pius X. While he did not specifically mention Verdi in his 1903 encyclical *Motu proprio,* the Pope wrote, "The theatrical style that was in the greatest vogue, especially in Italy during the last century, . . . is by its very nature diametrically opposed to Gregorian chant and classic polyphony, the most important law of all good sacred music."

Surely Verdi's *Requiem* is highly dramatic—from the hushed reverence of the *"Requiem aeternam"* to the raging fury of the *"Dies irae,"* from the overwhelming power of the *"Tuba mirum"* to the sobbing grief of the *"Lacrimosa."* Yet it is not theatrical. Verdi was very specific in the interpretation he wanted: "This Mass must not be sung the way an opera is sung, and thus colors that can be good in the theater will not satisfy me at all."

Despite the drama and passion, Verdi's *Requiem* projects great sincerity and honesty. His piety is not false, nor is it an effect achieved by a composer who is a past master in manipulating audiences' emotional response. Very personal and deeply felt, the *Requiem* rings true to Verdi's belief in a Supreme Deity

—even though he was a nonobservant Catholic—and his veneration of Manzoni.

Verdi succeeds in making real and palpable the meaning of the words of the *Requiem*—the dread of the Day of Judgment (*"Tuba mirum"*), the terror and despair of the Day of Wrath (*"Dies irae,"* which he brings back for short reprises in *"Confutatis"* and *"Libera me"*), and the touching and moving prayers in such movements as *"Recordare," "Domine Jesu Christe," "Lux aeterna,"* and *"Libera me."*

Verdi's wife, Giuseppina, a particularly perspicacious judge of his music, spoke of the *Requiem* in two letters: "A man like Verdi must write like Verdi, that is, according to his own way of feeling and interpreting the text. The religious spirit and the way in which it is given expression must bear the stamp of its period and its author's personality."

"Posterity will place it, with wings outspread, in domination of all the music of mourning ever conceived by the human brain."

Standard Text (see Appendix)

QUATTRO PEZZI SACRI
(Four Sacred Pieces)

37 minutes

Giuseppe Verdi's *Quattro pezzi sacri* began life as four separate pieces that he created from his seventy-fifth to his eighty-third year. He composed *Ave Maria* in response to a challenge posed by a Signor Crescentini in the August 3, 1888, issue of *Gazzetta Musicale di Milano,* in which he asked composers to incorporate a scale—the *"Scala enigmatica,"* which he had devised (C, D flat, E, F sharp, G sharp, A sharp, B, C)—into a musical composition.

Verdi composed *Laudi alla Vergine Maria* around the same

time as *Ave Maria*. Originally it was a setting for four solo women's voices (two sopranos, two altos) of a text from Dante's *Il Paradiso*.

Some six or seven years later, in April 1895, Verdi was asked to write a hymn on the twenty-fifth anniversary of the liberation of Rome. Verdi refused. But the idea of writing a celebratory hymn intrigued him, and he began work on the *Te Deum* at that time.

During the winter of 1896–97, Verdi wrote the *Stabat Mater,* the final composition of his life.

When someone first proposed the idea of performing these sacred pieces together, Verdi refused. In time, though, he finally agreed, and conductor Paul Taffanel led the premiere in Paris on April 7, 1898. (*Ave Maria* was performed neither at the Paris premiere nor at the subsequent Italian premiere in Turin; it was only joined with the other three at the first performance in Vienna, in November 1898.)

Verdi composed the *Ave Maria* for mixed choir a cappella. He divided the work into four sections corresponding to the four slowly ascending and descending statements of the *Scala enigmatica*. In the first three statements—by the basses, altos, and tenors, respectively—he hides the scale within the comparatively dense, polyphonic writing. Only for the last statement, by the sopranos, does he allow it to emerge as a leading voice, soaring above the others. A hushed, reverential air pervades the entire piece; the dynamic level rises above the piano or pianissimo ("soft" or "very soft") level only at the top of each scale statement.

After the quiet of the unaccompanied *Ave Maria,* the orchestral opening of *Stabat Mater* comes as a shock. The choir entrance is also striking—a unison that Verdi said should sound "sorrowful, muffled, hollow." The violins then set up a sighing, sobbing accompaniment for the succession of beautiful, moving melodies that follow, through which Verdi eloquently expresses the meaning of the text—the pain of *"O quam tristis,"* the anger and mounting fury of *"Pro peccatis,"* the buildup from the stillness of *"Fac, ut animae donetur,"* and the exuberance and exultation of *"Paradisi gloria."*

Easily overlooked in the last section of *Stabat Mater* is a rising scale sung by the sopranos and played by the first violins. The notes of this scale (A, B, C, D, E flat, F, G flat [becoming F sharp], G, A, B) are fully as "enigmatic" as the scale in *Ave Maria,* even though very different. Does this scale just appear coincidentally? Or is Verdi trying to establish some sort of linkage with *Ave Maria*?

The *Laudi alla Vergine Maria* for unaccompanied women's voices is the only one of the four pieces sung in Italian rather than Latin. In character it resembles a prayer, filled with deep religious conviction and handled with great restraint and control.

The rhythmic pattern of the word *"Ver-gi-ne"* (long/long/short) runs throughout and serves as a sort of musical signature. Although the piece starts and ends quietly, it reaches two strong, fervid climaxes.

The last and most substantial of the four pieces, *Te Deum,* is for double chorus and large orchestra. Verdi's special affection for *Te Deum* is evidenced by his request that the music be placed under his pillow when he died. The piece opens with the men of both choruses alternately intoning a chant based on a Gregorian chant. In a resplendent burst of glorious sound, both choruses and the full orchestra then enter on *"Sanctus, Sanctus."* (Verdi asked that "the choruses be divided from the orchestra and from one another.") Verdi takes us on an exciting musical journey—now whispering with quiet inner intensity, now pulsing with drama and fervor—that focuses more on the supplicating sections of the text than on those concerned with festivities and rejoicing.

In one more allusion to the scale from *Ave Maria,* Verdi sends the orchestra flutes and violins up a scale for over two octaves. The chorus (singing, *"Venerandum tuum verum, et unicum Filium")* does not follow the scale line. The entire work ends with the entry of the soprano soloist, which Verdi described as "the voice of humanity in fear of hell." (He recommended that the singer be placed far back in the choir, hidden from the audience.) Her prayer starts softly, but as she continues and the choir joins in, her prayer becomes a powerful affirmation of faith—*"In te, Domine, speravi"* ("In Thee have I trusted").

AVE MARIA

Ave, Maria, gratia plena, Dominus tecum, benedicta tu in mulieribus, et benedictus fructus ventris tui, Jesus.	Hail Mary, full of grace, the Lord is with Thee, blessed art Thou among women and blessed is Jesus the fruit of Thy womb.
Sancta Maria, Mater Dei, ora pro nobis peccatoribus nunc et in hora mortis nostrae. Amen.	Holy Mary, pray for us sinners now and at the hour of our death. Amen.

STABAT MATER
Standard Text (see Appendix)

LAUDI ALLA VERGINE MARIA

Vergine madre, figlia del tuo Figlio,	Virgin mother, daughter of thy son,
Umile ed alta più che creatura,	Humble and exalted beyond all creatures,
Termine fisso d'eterno consiglio,	Fixed goal of eternal plans,
Tu se' colei che l'umana natura	Thou art she who so ennobled
Nobilitasti, si, che'l suo Fattore	Human nature that its Creator
Non disdegnò di farsi sua fatura.	Did not disdain to make Himself its creation.
Nel ventre tuo si raccese l'amore,	Within thy womb was rekindled that love
Per lo cui caldo nell'eterna pace	By whose warmth this flower
Cosi è germinato questo fiore.	Has thus bloomed in eternal peace.
Qui se' a noi meridiana face	To us here thou art the noonday torch

Di caritate, e giuso, in tra i
  mortali,
Se' di speranza fontana vivace.
Donna, se' tanto grande, e tanto
  vali,
Che qual vuol grazia, ed a te
  non ricore,
Sua disianza vuol volar senz'
  ali.
La tua benignità non pur
  soccorre
A chi dimanda, ma molte fiate
Liberamente al dimandar
  precorre.
In te misericordia, in te pietate,
In te magnificenza, in te s'aduna

Quantunque in creatura è di
  bontate.
Ave. Ave.

Of charity, and among mortals
  below
Thou art a living fount of hope.
Lady, thou art so great and of
  such worth
That the longing of him who
  seeks grace
But turns not to thee seeks to
  fly without wings.
Thy kindness aids not only him

Who prays, but many a time
Generously anticipates his plea.

In thee is mercy, in thee is pity,
In thee magnificence, in thee the
  sum
Of all that in a creature is
  good.
Amen. Amen.

TE DEUM
Standard Text (see Appendix)

ANTONIO VIVALDI

Born March 4 (or May 6), 1678, in Venice
Died July 28, 1741, in Vienna

Despite his fame as a violinist, Vivaldi considered himself primarily an opera composer, having composed forty-six such works. Today, however, his reputation rests largely on the many instrumental works he produced—over four hundred concertos, including the oft-performed *The Four Seasons,* and nearly one hundred sonatas. Also in this vast output are some thirty-seven liturgical choral works, of which only one, the *Gloria,* holds a prominent place in the modern repertoire.

For some two hundred years after his death, Vivaldi was little known. Then, in the mid-twentieth century—with advances in musicological scholarship, the vast expansion of the recorded repertoire with the advent of long-playing records, and the tremendous popularity and appeal of his newly discovered *The Four Seasons*—Vivaldi's reputation was restored to the height it had enjoyed during his lifetime.

One unfortunate result of this long period of obscurity is a dearth of information about Vivaldi's life. We know that he entered the priesthood at age twenty-five but suffered severe chest pains (attributed to either asthma or angina) at his very first attempt to say Mass. The experience rendered him unable to continue, and he never again officiated at a Mass.

Subsequently, the Ospedale della Pietà, a charitable institution in Venice for orphaned, illegitimate, and indigent girls, engaged Vivaldi as the violin teacher. When the choirmaster left in 1713, Vivaldi took on additional duties, which included writing sacred music for various church services. Even though Vivaldi spent the next thirty-five years at Ospedale, he made numerous trips around Europe to attend productions of his various operas. The school authorities finally became annoyed at Vivaldi's long stay in Amsterdam, where he was directing a music festival, and they voted the composer out, forcing him to spend the remaining few years of his life peddling his operas and concertos around the continent.

The RV number used to identify Vivaldi's music refers to the *Ryom Verzeichnis* ("Ryom Catalog") prepared by Danish musicologist Peter Ryom in 1974.

GLORIA IN D MAJOR, RV. 589

30 minutes

The wide recognition that Vivaldi now enjoys has familiarized us with many compositions that were virtually unknown just a few generations ago. One such work is his *Gloria in D major*, RV. 589, by far the most popular of his many choral works.

No one is certain why or when Vivaldi composed the *Gloria*. Some scholars hold that Vivaldi composed the work for a function within the Ospedale della Pietà. This assumption raises a question: who sang the tenor and bass parts in the all-girl Ospedale? Perhaps the women sang the lower parts an octave higher; since their voices were doubled with bass instruments playing in the proper register, the juxtaposition could create the impression that the women were singing the lower notes.

Vivaldi surely composed a *Gloria* for the marriage of Louis XV of France in 1725. Whether he composed this particular *Gloria* for that occasion is still open to question.

Vivaldi scored the *Gloria* for two women soloists (performed today by either two sopranos, soprano and alto, or two sopranos and alto) plus choir and orchestra. An exciting piece, it is filled with all the vigor and drive of Vivaldi's instrumental music, yet it is imbued with passages of great warmth and tenderness. Vivaldi composed the soloists' sections very much in the style of the operas of his day.

Doubtless, Vivaldi conceived *Gloria* as a self-contained work; there is no evidence that it was ever performed as part of an entire Mass.

Standard Text (see Appendix)

WILLIAM WALTON

Born March 29, 1902, in Oldham, England
Died March 8, 1983, in Ischia, Italy

William Walton's music is characterized by incredible technical skill, a powerful rhythmic drive, great passion and emotion, and a spare, clean writing style. The composer embraces a broad range of forms and genres in his compositions—from intimate chamber music to monumental choral works, from symphonies to operas, along with a number of film scores.

Walton was born to a choirmaster and a music teacher, who gave him his first music instruction until age ten, when he entered Christ Church Cathedral School at Oxford. At the tender age of sixteen he entered Oxford University, and although he did extremely well in his music studies, he fared so poorly in his other courses that he flunked out at the end of his second year.

Classmate Sacheverell Sitwell invited Walton to live with him in London. There Walton met Sacheverell's older sister, poet Edith Sitwell, with whom he wrote the shocking *Façade*—an "entertainment" for speaker and small ensemble—which established Walton's reputation. With his fame came a number of wealthy sponsors who ensured the composer's future financial security.

For most of Walton's life, the English people regarded him as a sort of unofficial composer laureate. Government officials asked him to compose the ceremonial march *(Crown Imperial)* for the coronation of King George VI in 1937; similarly, he was asked to write a ceremonial march *(Orb and Sceptre)* and *Coronation Te Deum* for Queen Elizabeth II's coronation in 1953. When England's greatest actor (Laurence Olivier) filmed three plays by England's greatest playwright (William Shakespeare), Walton supplied the scores.

In spite of his great success, Walton avoided taking himself too seriously. When he and his wife were asked why he composed so little in the last twenty or thirty years of his life, she replied, "William doesn't really like music that much." He agreed, "A lot of the time, I don't. It irritates me to madness, especially my own." Often quoted is his comment "I seriously advise all sensitive composers to die at the age of thirty-seven."

Walton's choral output includes about a dozen short compositions—most of which are rarely heard—and one towering masterpiece, *Belshazzar's Feast*.

BELSHAZZAR'S FEAST

35 minutes

In 1929, despite some success as a serious composer, William Walton made his living writing jazz band arrangements. Imagine, then, his delight when the British Broadcasting Company commissioned him to write a large-scale, modern oratorio on a familiar subject to be presented at the 1931 Leeds Festival.

Ever since he had been expelled from Oxford for spending too much time on his music and not keeping up with his other courses, Walton had been living with England's renowned Sitwell family—Sacheverell, Edith, and Osbert. Walton spoke to Osbert about the commission; Osbert suggested the "handwriting on the wall" story from the Book of Daniel as a topic, and he offered to prepare the libretto.

When Walton learned that the Berlioz *Requiem,* with its huge performing forces, was being presented at the same festival, he asked conductor Sir Thomas Beecham about the advisability of including additional brass players in his work. The often dyspeptic Beecham replied, "You might as well use everything available. You'll never hear the piece again!"

At first it seemed a self-fulfilling prophecy. The festival chorus found the music extremely difficult, and the women in particular were embarrassed to sing the word "concubines." Tensions ran so high that the choir finally went on strike, refusing to perform at all. Peace was finally restored, and the performance took place as scheduled on October 10, 1931. Because of the many musical difficulties, however, the tempi were slower than those Walton had intended.

Despite these complications, the audience readily accepted *Belshazzar's Feast*. Nevertheless, there were virtually no performances for over a quarter of a century following the premiere. Then, in 1958, Walton conducted a recording of the work, including some revisions that he had made in 1948. Suddenly the whole world discovered *Belshazzar's Feast,* quickly making it a beloved and oft-performed modern choral work. Musically intense and arresting, the work is also highly dramatic, is mighty in conception, and has a powerful, barbaric drive.

Sir Osbert Sitwell drew the text for *Belshazzar's Feast* from biblical sources, using remarkable skill in compressing the material without losing any of its dramatic effect. Walton scored the work, which is in three sections, for solo baritone, mixed choir, and huge orchestra.

Opening the oratorio, the choir bleakly intones Isaiah's prophecy of the Jews' captivity in Babylon: "Thy sons that thou shalt beget/They shall be taken away/And be eunuchs." The Jews' lament, generally considered one of the most poignant and touching creations in the entire contemporary choral repertoire, follows without pause. The text is a setting of words from Psalm 137, "By the waters of Babylon."

The vigorous second part colorfully portrays the glories—as well as the debauchery—of Babylon, to the text "Babylon was a great city," which Osbert Sitwell adapted from chapter 5 of the Book of Daniel. Fluctuating rhythms conjure up the regal might of King Belshazzar and the wild abandon of the feast he commanded. Most striking in this section is the procession of the gods: God of Gold played by the full orchestra; God of Silver by glockenspiel, piccolo, and saxophone; God of Iron by blows on an anvil; God of Wood by wood block, xylophone, and strings playing with the wooden part of their bows *(col legno);* God of Stone by slapstick; and God of Brass by two brass bands placed on either side of the orchestra (courtesy of Berlioz).

There follows an absolutely terrifying moment as the solo baritone quietly intones the appearance of the hand and articulates the message it writes: *"Mene, mene, tekel upharsin."* That night, opponents slay the king and divide his kingdom. In an abrupt change of mood, the choir then sings a glorious paean of thanksgiving based on a section of Psalm 81, "Then sing aloud to God our strength." An ecstatic clamor of "Alleluias" by the different parts of the choir brings the oratorio to a brilliant conclusion.

Thus spake Isaiah:

Thy sons that thou shalt beget
They shall be taken away.
And be eunuchs
In the palace of the King of
  Babylon
    Howl ye, howl ye,
  therefore:
    For the day of the Lord is
  at hand!

By the waters of Babylon.
  By the waters of Babylon
There we sat down: yea, we
  wept
And hanged our harps upon the
  willows

For they that wasted us
Required of us mirth:
They that carried us away
  captive
Required of us a song
Sing us one of the songs of
  Zion.

How shall we sing the Lord's
  song
In a strange land?

If I forget thee, O Jerusalem,
Let my right hand forget her
  cunning.
If I do not remember thee,
Let my tongue cleave to the
  roof of my mouth.
Yea, if I prefer not Jerusalem
  above my chief joy.

By the waters of Babylon
There we sat down: yea, we
  wept.

O daughter of Babylon, who
  art to be destroyed.
Happy shall he be that taketh
  thy children
And dasheth them against
  stone.
For with violence shall that
  great city Babylon be thrown
  down
And shall be found no more at
  all.

Babylon was a great city,
Her merchandise was of gold
  and silver,
Of precious stones, of pearls, of
  fine linen,

Of purple, silk and scarlet
All manner vessels of ivory.
All manner vessels of most
   precious wood.
Of brass, iron and marble,
Cinnamon, odours and
   ointments,
Of frankincense, wine and oil,
Fine flour, wheat and beasts,
Sheep, horses, chariots, slaves
And the souls of men.

In Babylon
   Belshazzar the King
   Made a great feast,
Made a feast to a thousand of
   his lords,
And drank wine before the
   thousand.
Belshazzar, while he tasted the
   wine,
Commanded us to bring the
   gold and silver vessels:
Yea! the golden vessels, which
   his father, Nebuchadnezzar,
Had taken out of the temple
   that was in Jerusalem.

He commanded us to bring the
   golden vessels
Of the temple of the house of
   God,
That the King, his Princes, his
   wives
And his concubines might drink
   therein.

Then the King commanded us:
Bring ye the cornet, flute,
   sackbut, psaltery

And all kinds of music: they
   drank wine again.
Yea, drank from the sacred
   vessels,
And then spake the King:

   Praise ye
      The God of Gold
   Praise ye
      The God of Silver
   Praise ye
      The God of Iron
   Praise ye
      The God of Wood
   Praise ye
      The God of Stone
   Praise ye
      The God of Brass
   Praise ye the Gods!

Thus in Babylon, the mighty
   city,
Belshazzar the King made a
   great feast,
Made a feast to a thousand of
   his lords
And drank wine before the
   thousand.

Belshazzar while he tasted the
   wine
Commanded us to bring the
   gold and silver vessels
That his Princes, his wives and
   his concubines
Might rejoice and drink therein.

After they had praised their
   strange gods,
The idols and the devils,

False gods who can neither see
nor hear,
Called they for the timbrel and
the pleasant harp
To extol the glory of the King.
Then they pledged the King
before the people.
Crying, Thou, O King, art King
of Kings:
O King, live for ever . . .

And in that same hour, as they
feasted
Came forth fingers of a man's
hand
And the King saw
The part of the hand that
wrote.

And this was the writing that
was written:
'MENE, MENE, TEKEL
UPHARSIN'
'THOU ART WEIGHED IN
THE BALANCE AND
FOUND WANTING'.
In that night was Belshazzar the
King slain
And his Kingdom divided.

Then sing aloud to God our
strength:
Make a joyful noise unto the
God of Jacob.
Take a psalm, bring hither the
timbrel,

Blow up the trumpet in the new
moon.
Blow up the trumpet in Zion
For Babylon the Great is fallen,
fallen.
                         Alleluia!

Then sing aloud to God our
strength:
Make a joyful noise unto the
God of Jacob,
While the Kings of the Earth
lament
And the merchants of the Earth
Weep, wail and rend their
raiment.
Then cry, Alas, Alas, that great
city,
In one hour is her judgement
come.

The trumpeters and pipers are
silent,
And the harpers have ceased to
harp,
And the light of a candle shall
shine no more.

Then sing aloud to God our
strength.
Make a joyful noise to the God
of Jacob.
For Babylon the Great is fallen.
                         Alleluia!

APPENDIX
Standard Texts

ORDINARY OF THE MASS

Kyrie

Kyrie eleison, Christe eleison.
Kyrie eleison.

Lord, have mercy upon us.
Christ, have mercy upon us.
Lord, have mercy upon us.

Gloria

Gloria in excelsis Deo. Et in
terra pax hominibus bonae
voluntatis. Laudamus te.
Benedicimus te. Adoramus te.
Glorificamus te. Gratias agimus
tibi propter magnam gloriam
tuam. Domine Deus, Rex
coelestis, Deus Pater
omnipotens. Domine Fili
unigenite, Jesu Christe. Domine
Deus, Agnus Dei, Filius Patris.
Qui tollis peccata mundi,
miserere nobis. Qui tollis
peccata mundi, suscipe
deprecationem nostram. Qui
sedes ad dexteram Patris,
miserere nobis. Quoniam tu
solus sanctus. Tu solus

Glory be to God in the highest.
And on earth peace to men of
good will. We praise Thee. We
bless Thee. We adore Thee. We
glorify Thee. We give Thee
thanks for Thy great glory. O
Lord God, heavenly King, God
the Father almighty. O Lord
Jesus Christ, the only-begotten
Son. Lord God, Lamb of God,
Son of the Father. Who taketh
away the sins of the world,
have mercy upon us. Who
taketh away the sins of the
world, receive our prayer. Who
sitteth at the right hand of the
Father, have mercy upon us.
For Thou alone art holy. Thou

Dominus. Tu solus Altissimus,
Jesu Christe. Cum Sancto
Spiritu, in gloria Dei Patris.
Amen.

alone art Lord. Thou alone, O
Jesus Christ, art most high.
Together with the Holy Ghost,
in the glory of God the Father.
Amen.

Credo

Credo in unum Deum, Patrem
omnipotentem, factorem coeli et
terrae, visibilium omnium, et
invisibilium. Et in unum
Dominum Jesum Christum,
Filium Dei unigenitum. Et ex
Patre natum ante omnia
saecula. Deum de Deo, lumen
de lumine, Deum verum de Deo
vero. Genitum, non factum,
consubstantialem Patri: per
quem omnia facta sunt. Qui
propter nos homines, et propter
nostram salutem descendit de
coelis. Et incarnacus est de
Spiritu Sancto ex Maria Virgine;
et homo factus est. Crucifixus
etiam pro nobis; sub Pontio
Pilato passus, et sepultus est. Et
resurrexit tertia die, secundum
Scripturas. Et ascendit in
coelum: sedet ad dexteram
Patris. Et iterum venturus est
cum gloria, judicare vivos et
mortuos: cujus regni non erit
finis. Et in Spiritum Sanctum,
Dominum et vivificantem: qui
ex Patre Filioque procedit. Qui
cum Patre et Filio simul
adoratur, et conglorificatur; qui
locutus est per prophetas. Et
unam sanctam catholicam et

I believe in one God, the Father
almighty, maker of heaven and
earth, and of all things visible
and invisible. And in one Lord
Jesus Christ, the only-begotten
Son of God. Born of the Father
before all ages. God of God,
light of light, true God of true
God. Begotten, not made; of
one substance with the Father:
by whom all things were made.
Who for us men, and for our
salvation, came down from
heaven. And was made flesh by
the Holy Ghost of the Virgin
Mary: and was made man. He
was also crucified for us,
suffered under Pontius Pilate,
and was buried. And on the
third day He rose again,
according to the Scriptures. And
ascended into heaven: He sitteth
at the right hand of the Father.
And He shall come again with
glory to judge the living and the
dead; and of His Kingdom there
shall be no end. And in the
Holy Ghost, the Lord and Giver
of life, who proceedeth from the
Father and the Son. Who
together with the Father and the
Son is adored and glorified:

apostolicam Ecclesiam.
Confiteor unum baptisma in
remissionem peccatorum. Et
expecto resurrectionem
mortuorum. Et vitam venturi
saeculi. Amen.

who spoke by the prophets.
And in one holy, catholic and
apostolic Church. I confess one
baptism for the remission of
sins. And I expect the
resurrection of the dead. And
the life of the world to come.
Amen.

Sanctus

Sanctus, Sanctus, Sanctus,
Dominus Deus Sabaoth. Pleni
sunt coeli et terra gloria tua.
Osanna in excelsis.

Holy, Holy, Holy, Lord God of
hosts. Heaven and earth are
filled with Thy glory. Hosanna
in the highest.

Benedictus

Benedictus qui venit in nomine
Domini. Osanna in excelsis.

Blessed is He that cometh in the
name of the Lord. Hosanna in
the highest.

Agnus Dei

Agnus Dei, qui tollis peccata
mundi, miserere nobis. Agnus
Dei, qui tollis peccata mundi,
miserere nobis. Agnus Dei, qui
tollis peccata mundi, dona nobis
pacem.

Lamb of God, who taketh away
the sins of the world, have
mercy upon us. Lamb of God,
who taketh away the sins of the
world, have mercy upon us.
Lamb of God, who taketh away
the sins of the world, grant us
peace.

REQUIEM MASS

Introit

Requiem aeternam dona eis,
Domine: et lux perpetua luceat
eis. Te decet hymnus Deus in

Eternal rest give unto them, O
Lord: and let perpetual light
shine upon them. A hymn, O

Sion, et tibi reddetur votum in Jerusalem: exaudi orationem meam: ad te omnis caro veniet. Requiem.

God, becometh Thee in Sion; and a vow shall be paid to Thee in Jerusalem. O hear my prayer: all flesh shall come to Thee. Eternal rest.

Kyrie eleison

Kyrie eleison. Christe eleison. Kyrie eleison.

Lord, have mercy upon us. Christ, have mercy upon us. Lord, have mercy upon us.

Gradual

Requiem aeternam dona eis, Domine: et lux perpetua luceat eis. In memoria aeterna erit justus: ab auditione mala non timebit.

Eternal rest give to them, O Lord: and let perpetual light shine upon them. The just shall be in everlasting remembrance: he shall not fear the evil hearing.

Sequence

1. Dies irae, dies illa,
   Solvet saeclum in favilla:
   Teste David cum Sibylla.

   Day of wrath, O day of mourning,
   See fulfilled the prophets' warning;
   Heav'n and earth in ashes burning.

2. Quantus tremor est futurus,
   Quando judex est venturus,
   Cuncta stricte discussurus!

   Oh, what fear man's bosom rendeth
   When from heaven the Judge descendeth,
   On whose sentence all dependeth!

3. Tuba mirum spargens sonum
   Per sepulcra regionum,
   Coget omnes ante thronum.

   Wondrous sound the trumpet flingeth,
   Through earth's sepulchers it ringeth,
   All before the throne it bringeth.

4. Mors stupebit et natura,
   Cum resurget creatura,
   Judicanti responsura.

Death is struck, and nature
   quaking,
All creation is awaking,
To its Judge an answer making.

5. Liber scriptus proferetur,
   In quo totum continetur,
   Unde mundus judicetur.

Lo! the book exactly worded,
Wherein all hath been recorded:
Thence shall judgment be
   awarded.

6. Judex ergo cum sedebit,
   Quidquid latet apparebit:
   Nil inultum remanebit.

When the Judge His seat
   attaineth,
And each hidden deed
   arraigneth,
Nothing unavenged remaineth.

7. Quid sum miser tunc
   dicturus?
   Quem patronum
   rogaturus,
   Cum vix justus sit securus?

What shall I, frail man, be
   pleading?
Who for me be interceding,
When the just are mercy
   needing?

8. Rex tremendae majestatis,
   Qui salvandos salvas gratis,
   Salva me, fons pietatis.

King of majesty tremendous,
Who dost free salvation send us,
Fount of pity, then befriend us!

9. Recordare, Jesu pie,
   Quod sum causa tuae
   viae:
   Ne me perdas illa die.

Think, good Jesu, my salvation
Caused Thy wondrous
   Incarnation,
Leave me not to reprobation.

10. Quarens me, sedisti lassus:
    Redemisti crucem passus:
    Tantus labor non sit cassus.

Faint and weary Thou hast
   sought me.
On the cross of suffering bought
   me;
Shall such grace be vainly
   brought me?

11. Juste judex ultionis,
    Donum fac remissionis,
    Ante diem rationis.

Righteous Judge! for sin's
   pollution
Grant Thy gift of absolution,
Ere that day of retribution.

12. Ingemisco, tamquam reus:
    Culpa rubet vultus meus:
    Supplicanti parce, Deus.

Guilty, now I pour my moaning,
All my shame with anguish
    owning;
Spare, O God, Thy supplicant
    groaning.

13. Qui Mariam absolvisti,
    Et latronem exaudisti,
    Mihi quoque spem dedisti.

Thou the sinful woman savedst;
Thou the dying thief forgavest;
And to me a hope vouchsafest.

14. Preces meae non sunt
    dignae:
    Sed tu bonus fac benigne,
    Ne perenni cremer igne.

Worthless are my prayers and
    sighing;
Yet, good Lord, in grace
    complying,
Rescue me from fires undying.

15. Inter oves locum praesta,
    Et ab haedis me sequestra,
    Statuens in parte dextra.

With Thy favored sheep O place
    me,
Nor among the goats abase me,
But to Thy right hand upraise
    me.

16. Confutatis maledictis,
    Flammis acribus addictis,
    Voca me cum benedictis.

While the wicked are
    confounded,
Doomed to flames of woe
    unbounded,
Call me with Thy saints
    surrounded.

17. Oro supplex et acclinis,
    Cor contritum quasi cinis:
    Gere curam mei finis.

Low I kneel, with heart-
    submission,
See, like ashes, my contrition;
Help me in my last condition.

18. Lacrimosa dies illa,
    Qua resurget ex favilla

Ah, that day of tears and
    mourning!
From the dust of earth returning

19. Judicandus homo reus:
    Huic ergo parce Deus.

Man from judgment must
    prepare him.
Spare, O God, in mercy spare
    him!

20. Pie Jesu Domine, dona eis
requiem. Amen.

Lord, all pitying, Jesu blest, grant
them Thine eternal rest. Amen.

Offertory

Domine Jesu Christe, Rex
gloriae, libera animas omnium
fidelium defunctorum de poenis
inferni, et de profundo lacu:
libera eas de ore leonis, ne
absorbeat eas tartarus, ne
cadant in obscurum: sed signifer
sanctus Michael, repraesentet
eas in lucem sanctam: Quam
olim Abrahae promisisti, et
semini ejus.

O Lord, Jesus Christ, King of
Glory, deliver the souls of all
the faithful departed from the
pains of hell and from the deep
pit: deliver them from the lion's
mouth, that hell may not
swallow them up, and may they
not fall into darkness; but may
Thy holy standard-bearer,
Michael, lead them into the
holy light; which Thou didst
promise to Abraham and to his
seed.

Hostias et preces tibi,
Domine, laudis offerimus: tu
suscipe pro animabus illis,
quarum hodie memoriam
facimus: fac eas, Domine, de
morte transire ad vitam: Quam
olim Abrahae promisisti, et
semini ejus.

We offer to Thee, O Lord,
sacrifices and prayers: do Thou
receive them in behalf of those
souls whom we commemorate
this day. Grant them, O Lord,
to pass from death unto life;
which Thou didst promise to
Abraham and to his seed.

Sanctus

Sanctus, Sanctus, Sanctus,
Dominus Deus Sabaoth. Pleni
sunt coeli et terra gloria tua.
Osanna in excelsis.

Holy, Holy, Holy, Lord God of
Sabaoth. Heaven and earth are
filled with Thy glory. Hosanna
in the highest.

Benedictus

Benedictus qui venit in nomine
Domini. Osanna in excelsis.

Blessed is He who cometh in
the name of the Lord. Hosanna
in the highest.

Agnus Dei

Agnus Dei, qui tollis peccata mundi, dona eis requiem. Agnus Dei, qui tollis peccata mundi, dona eis requiem. Agnus Dei, qui tollis peccata mundi, dona eis requiem aeternam.

Lamb of God, who takest away the sins of the world, grant them rest. Lamb of God, who takest away the sins of the world, grant them rest. Lamb of God, who takest away the sins of the world, grant them eternal rest.

Communion

Lux aeterna luceat eis, Domine: cum sanctis tuis in aeternum, quia pius es. Requiem aeternam dona eis, Domine, et lux perpetua luceat eis. Cum sanctis tuis in aeternum, quia pius es.

May light eternal shine on them, O Lord. With Thy saints forever, for Thou art merciful. Eternal rest give to them, O Lord: and let perpetual light shine upon them. With Thy saints forever, for Thou art merciful.

Responsory After Absolution

Libera me, Domine, de morte aeterna, in die illa tremenda: quando coeli movendi sunt et terra: Dum veneris judicare saeculum per ignem. Tremens factus sum ego, et timeo, dum discussio venerit, atque ventura ira. Quando coeli movendi sunt et terra.

Dies illa, dies irae, calamitatis et miseriae, dies magna et amara valde. Dum veneris judicare saeculum per ignem. Requiem aeternam dona eis Domine: et lux perpetua luceat

Deliver me, O Lord, from eternal death in that awful day: when the heavens and the earth shall be moved: when Thou shalt come to judge the world by fire. Dread and trembling have laid hold on me, and I fear exceedingly because of the judgment and the wrath to come. When the heavens and the earth shall be shaken.

O that day, that day of wrath, of sore distress and of all wretchedness, that great and exceeding bitter day. When eis. (The Responsory is then repeated up to "Tremens.")

Thou shalt come to judge the world by fire. Eternal rest grant to them, O Lord, and let perpetual light shine upon them. (The Responsory is then repeated up to "Dread.")

TE DEUM

Te Deum laudamus,
te Dominum confitemur

We praise Thee, O God,
we acknowledge Thee to be the Lord,

Te aeturnum Patrem
omnis terra veneratur.

Thee, the Father everlasting,
all the earth doth worship.

Tibi omnes Angeli,
tibi Coeli et universae Potestates,
tibi Cherubim et Seraphim incessabili voce proclamant:
Sanctus, Sanctus, Sanctus Dominus
Deus Sabaoth.
Pleni sunt coeli et terra majestatis gloriae tuae.
Te gloriosus Apostolorum chorus,
te Prophetarum laudabilis numerus,
te Martyrum candidatus laudat exercitus.
Te per orbem terrarum sancta confitetur Ecclesia,

To Thee all the angels,
to Thee the heavens and the powers therein,
to Thee cherubim and seraphim cry out without ceasing:
Holy, holy, holy

God of Sabaoth.
Heaven and earth are full of the majesty of Thy glory.
The glorious company of the apostles,
the goodly fellowship of the prophets,
the noble army of martyrs praise Thee:
Throughout the world the holy Church doth acknowledge Thee,

Patrem immensae majestatis,

The Father of an infinite majesty;

venerandum tuum verum et unicum Filium,

Thine honorable,
true, and only Son,

Sanctum quoque Paraclitum
   Spiritum.

Tu Rex gloriae, Christe,

Tu Patris sempiternus et Filius.

Tu ad liberandum
suscepturus hominem,
non horruisti Virginis uterum.

Tu devicto mortis aculeo,

aperuisti credentibus
regna coelorum.
Tu ad dexteram Dei sedes,

in gloria Patris.

Judex crederis
esse venturus.
Te ergo quaesumus,
tuis famulis subveni,
quos pretioso sanguine
   redemisti.
Aeterna fac sum Sanctis tuis

in gloria numerari.
Salvum fac populum tuum,
   Domine,
et benedic hereditati tuae.
Et rege eos,
et extolle illos usque in
   aeturnum.
Per singulos dies benedicimus
   te.
Et laudamus nomen tuum in
   saeculum,
et in saeculum saeculi.

and the Holy Ghost, the
   Comforter.

Thou art the King of Glory, O
   Christ,
Thou art the everlasting Son of
   the Father.

Thou, having taken upon Thee
to deliver man,
didst not abhor the Virgin's
   womb.

Thou, having overcome the
   sting of death,
hast opened to believers
the kingdom of heaven.
Thou sittest at the right hand of
   God,
in the glory of the Father.

We believe that Thou
shalt come to be our judge.
We therefore pray Thee,
help Thy servants,
whom Thou hast redeemed with
   Thy precious blood.
Make them to be numbered
   with Thy saints
in glory everlasting.
Save Thy people, O Lord,

and bless Thine heritage.
Govern them,
and lift them up forever.

Day by day, we magnify Thee.

And we worship Thy name
   ever,
world without end.

Dignare, Domine, die isto
sine peccato nos custodire.
Miserere nostri, Domine, misere
    nostri!
Fiat misericordia tua Domine
    super nos,
quemadmodum speravimus in
    te.
In te Domine speravi:
non confundar in aeternum.

Vouchsafe, O Lord, this day
to keep us without sin.
Have mercy upon us, O Lord,
    have mercy upon us!
Let Thy mercy be upon us,

as our trust is in Thee.

In Thee, O Lord, have I trusted:
let me never be confounded.

STABAT MATER

Stabat Mater dolorosa
Juxta crucem lacrimosa

Dum pendebat Filius.

At the cross her station keeping
Stood the mournful Mother
    weeping
Close to Jesus to the last.

Cujus animam gementem

Through her heart, His sorrow
    sharing

Contristatam et dolentem
Pertransivit gladius.

All His bitter anguish bearing
Now at length the sword has
    passed.

O quam tristis et afflicta
Fuit illa benedicta
Mater Unigeniti!

Oh, how sad and sore distressed
Was that Mother highly blest
Of the sole-begotten One!

Quae maerebat et dolebat,
Pia Mater, dum videbat
Nati poenas inclyti.

Christ above in torment hangs;
She beneath beholds the pangs
Of her dying glorious Son.

Quis est homo, qui non fleret,

Is there one who would not
    weep,

Matrem Christi, si videret
In tanto supplico?

Whelmed in miseries so deep
Christ's dear Mother to behold?

Quis non posset contristari,
Christi Matrem contemplari,
Dolentem cum Filio?

Can the human heart refrain,
From partaking in her pain,
In that Mother's pain untold?

Pro peccatis suae gentis
Vidit Jesum in tormentis,
Et flagellis subditum.

Vidit suum dulcem natum
Moriendo desolatum,
Dum emisit spiritum.

Eia Mater, fons amoris,
Me sentire vim doloris
Fac, ut tecum lugeam.

Fac ut ardeat cor meum,
In amando Christum Deum,
Ut sibi complaceam.

Sancta Mater, istud agas,

Crucifixi fige plagas
Cordi meo valide.

Tui nati vulnerati,

Tam dignati pro me pati,
Poenas mecum divide.

Fac me tecum pie flere,
Crucifixo condolere,

Donec ego vixero.

Juxta crucem tecum stare,
Et me tibi sociare

In planctu desidero.

Virgo virginum praeclara,
Mihi jam non sis amara:
Fac me tecum plangere.

Fac ut portem Christi mortem,
Passionis fac consortem,

Bruis'd, derided, curs'd, defil'd,
She beheld her tender Child:
All with bloody scourges rent.

For the sins of His own nation,
Saw Him hang in desolation
Till His spirit forth He sent.

O thou Mother, fount of love!
Touch my spirit from above;
Make my heart with thine
    accord.

Make me feel as thou hast felt,
Make my soul to glow and melt
With the love of Christ our
    Lord.

Holy Mother, pierce me
    through,
In my heart each wound renew
Of my Savior crucified.

Let me share with thee His
    pain,
Who for all my sins was slain,
Who for me in torments died.

Let me mingle tears with thee,
Mourning Him who mourned
    for me,
All the days that I may live.

By the cross with thee to stay,
There with thee to weep and
    pray,
Is all I ask of thee to give.

Virgin of all virgins best,
Listen to my fond request:
Let me share thy grief divine.

Let me, to my latest breath,
In my body bear the death

Et plagas recolere.

Of that dying Son of thine.

Fac me plagis vulnerari,

Wounded with His every
    wound,

Fac me cruce inebriari,

Steep my soul till it hath
    swoon'd

Et cruore Filii.

In His very blood away.

Flammis ne urar accensus,
Per te Virgo, sim defensus

Be to me, O Virgin, nigh,
Lest in flames I burn and die

In die judicii.

In His awful Judgment day.

Christe, cum sit hinc exire,

Christ, when Thou shalt call me
    hence,

De per Matrem me venire
Ad palmam victoriae

Be Thy Mother my defense,
Be Thy cross my victory.

Quando corpus morietur,
Fac ut animae donetur

While my body here decays
May my soul Thy goodness
    praise,

Paradisi gloria

Safe in Paradise with Thee.

Amen. Alleluia.

MAGNIFICAT

1. Magnificat anima mea
   Dominum.

My soul magnifies the Lord.

2. Et exultavit spiritus meus in
   Deo salutari meo.

And my spirit rejoices in God
   my Savior.

3. Quia respexit humilitatem
   ancillae suae: ecce enim ex
   hoc beatam me dicent
   omnes generationes.

For he has regarded the low
   estate of his handmaiden: for
   behold, henceforth all
   generations will call me
   blessed.

4. Quia fecit mihi magna qui
   potens est: et sanctum
   nomen ejus.

For he who is mighty has done
   great things for me: and holy
   is his name.

5. Et misericordia ejus a progenie in progenies timentibus eum.

And his mercy is on those who fear him from generation to generation.

6. Fecit potentiam in brachio suo: dispersit superbos mente cordis sui.

He has shown strength with his arm, he has scattered the proud in the imagination of their hearts.

7. Desposuit potentes de sede, et exaltavit humiles.

He has put down the mighty from their thrones, and exalted those of low degree.

8. Esurientes implevit bonis: et divites dimisit inanes.

He has filled the hungry with good things, and the rich he has sent empty away.

9. Suscepit Israel puerum suum, recordatus misericordiae suae.

He has helped his servant Israel, in remembrance of his mercy.

10. Sicut locutus est ad patres nostros, Abraham et semini ejus in saecula.

As he spoke to our fathers, to Abraham, and to his posterity forever.

11. Gloria Patri, et Filio, et Spiritui Sancto.

Glory be to the Father, and to the Son, and to the Holy Spirit.

12. Sicut erat in principio, et nunc, et semper, et in saecula saeculorum, Amen.

As it was in the beginning is now and ever shall be; world without end, Amen.

(Luke 1:46–55)

Glossary

A cappella   In Italian, "in the chapel"; choral music performed without instrumental accompaniment.

Aria   In Italian, "air"; a composition for solo voice, usually of greater length and complexity than a song.

Canon   From the Greek word for "rule"; a polyphonic composition in which all the parts sing or play the same melody but start at different times. *"Frère Jacques"* sung as a round is an example of a canon.

Cantata   A vocal form developed in the early years of the seventeenth century, typically performed by soloists, choir, and orchestra, and usually organized into a number of arias, duets, and choruses, all based on one extended text. Although the early cantatas were largely secular, Bach, who brought the genre to its highest level, wrote sacred or religious cantatas almost exclusively.

Cantus firmus   In Latin, "fixed melody"; a borrowed melody that is used as the basis for a polyphonic composition.

Choir   Originally a group of singers in church; now any group of singers.

Choral   An adjective that means "pertaining to a choir."

Chorale   A hymn tune.

Chorister   A member of a choir.

Chorus   Music composed for a choir, or the choir itself. In this book, the word is used only with the former meaning.

Continuo   The bass part in some Baroque compositions, which is performed by a keyboard instrument (harpsichord or organ) and bass instrument (cello or viola da gamba).

Counterpoint   See *Polyphony*.

Da capo   In Italian, "from the head," an indication in music to return to the beginning and repeat either to the end or to a fixed point. A da capo aria, for example, is in three parts—the opening section (A), a contrast (B), and a repeat of the opening (A). In practice, the repeat of the opening is frequently performed with added ornamentation.

Duet   A composition for two performers.

Fugue   A composition or part of a composition in which a theme (called the subject) is stated by one voice, is then imitated by other voices in quick succession, and continues to be heard throughout the piece. The texture of a fugue is polyphonic.

Gregorian chant   The liturgical music of the Roman Catholic church, named after Pope Gregory I. Same as plainsong.

Homophony   A texture with one leading voice and accompaniment.

Hymn   A song of praise or adoration of God.

Imitation   The taking up by one voice of a melody already stated by another voice; the basic principle of the fugue and canon.

Magnificat   The song of the Virgin Mary, from St. Luke 1:46–55. Part of the Office of Vespers of the Roman Catholic church.

Mass   The central service of the Roman Catholic church. The musical portion of the Mass is divided into two parts: the Ordinary, which includes the invariable parts *(Kyrie, Gloria, Credo, Sanctus, Agnus Dei),* and the Proper, which changes with the occasion.

Oratorio   An extended composition for soloists, choir, and orchestra on either a religious or contemplative text. Although it may be dramatic in nature, it is performed without action, scenery, or costumes. The oratorio differs from a Mass in that it uses a text written for the purpose, not part of the liturgy, and it differs from a cantata in its greater length and more narrative quality.

Passion   A musical setting of the account of Christ's capture and crucifixion according to St. Matthew, St. Mark, St. Luke, or St. John. From being sung by a single priest in the fourth century, the Passion expanded until now it is usually performed by soloists, choir, and orchestra.

Plainsong   See *Gregorian chant.*

Polyphony   A musical texture that combines a number of independent, individual voices.

Recitative   A vocal style that imitates the inflections and rhythms of human speech, often used for narrative purposes to advance the story or action of an oratorio or cantata.

Requiem   The Mass for the Dead of the Roman Catholic church. The text is similar to that of the Ordinary of the Mass, with the omission of the more joyous parts *(Gloria* and *Credo)* and the addition of some parts *(Dies irae)* appropriate to the occasion.

Stabat Mater   Literally, "There stood the Mother," a poem dating from the thirteenth century that has become part of the Roman Catholic liturgy and has been set to music by any number of composers.

Te Deum   Short for *Te Deum laudamus,* "Thee, O Lord, we praise," the principal hymn of praise and rejoicing of the Christian church.

Discography

Each recording is identified by the conductor, record company, and number. All the recordings are CDs; the only exceptions are those for which no CD is available, and a recent LP is substituted. If a tape version is also available it is indicated.

Bach, Johann Sebastian

Cantata No. 4: Christ lag in Todesbanden, BWV 4. Harnoncourt. Teldec 2-35027 ZL

Cantata No. 80: Ein feste Burg ist unser Gott, BWV 80. Harnoncourt. Teldec 2-35363 ZL

Cantata No. 106: Gottes Zeit ist die allerbeste Zeit, BWV 106, "Actus Tragicus." Leonhardt. Teldec 2-42602-2 ZK

Jesu, meine Freude, BWV 227. Harnoncourt. Teldec 2-42663 ZK

Mass in B minor, BWV 232. Solti. London 2-430-353-2

Magnificat in D major, BWV 243. Shaw. Telarc CD-80194

Passion According to St. Matthew, BWV 244. Gardiner. Deutsche Grammophon 3-427648-2 AH3

Passion According to St. John, BWV 245. Newman. Newport Classic NCD 60015

Christmas Oratorio, BWV 248. Gardiner. Deutsche Grammophon 2-423232-2 AH2 (tape)

Beethoven, Ludwig van

Fantasia for Piano, Chorus, and Orchestra, Op. 80. Ax (piano), Mehta. RCA 61213-2 (tape)

Christ on the Mount of Olives, Op. 85. Baudo. Harmonia Mundi HMC-90.5181

Mass in C major, Op. 86. Shaw. Telarc CD-80248
Missa solemnis, Op. 123. Shaw. Telarc 2-CD-80150
Symphony No. 9, Op. 125, "Choral Symphony." Mehta. RCA
    60477-2-RV

Berlioz, Hector
Requiem, Op. 5. Inbal. Denon 81757-3205/6
Te Deum, Op. 22. Abbado. Deutsche Grammophon 410696-2
    GH
La Damnation de Faust, Op. 24. Munch. RCA 7940-2-RG
L'Enfance du Christ, Op. 25. Inbal. Denon 2-81757-6863-2

Bernstein, Leonard
Chichester Psalms. Litton. MusicMasters 7049-2-C
Mass. Bernstein. CBS 2-M2K-44593

Bloch, Ernest
Sacred Service (Avodath hakodesh). Bernstein. Sony Classical
    SMK 47533

Brahms, Johannes
Ein deutsches Requiem, Op. 45. Shaw. Telarc CD-80092
Alto Rhapsody, Op. 53. Horne, Shaw. Telarc CD-80176
Schicksalslied, Op. 54 Shaw. Telarc CD-80176

Britten, Benjamin
A Ceremony of Carols, Op. 28. Willcocks. Angel CDC-47709
War Requiem, Op. 66. Britten. London 2-414383-2 LH2

Bruckner, Anton
Mass No. 2 in E minor. Jochum. Deutsche Grammophon
    4-423-127-2 GX4
Te Deum. Barenboim. Seraphim 4XG-60427
Psalm 150. Jochum. Deutsche Grammophon 4-423-127-2 GX4

Delius, Frederick
A Mass of Life. Del Mar. Intaglio 2-INCD 702-2

Duruflé, Maurice
Requiem, Op. 9. Marlow. Conifer CDCF 176

Dvořák, Antonin
Stabat Mater, Op. 58. Sawallisch. Supraphon 2-103561-2
Requiem, Op. 89. Sawallisch. Supraphon 2-10-4241

Elgar, Edward
The Dream of Gerontius, Op. 38. Britten. London 2-421381-2
   LM2

Fauré, Gabriel
Requiem, Op. 48. Rutter. Collegium COLCD-109

Gounod, Charles
St. Cecilia Mass. Prêtre. Angel CDC-47094

Handel, George Frideric
Israel in Egypt. Mackerras. Deutsche Grammophon 2-429530-2
   AGA2
Messiah. Shaw. Telarc 2-CD-80093-2 (Note: The Shaw record-
   ing, which is "patterned" on the May 15, 1754, performance,
   although with some exceptions, is one of the best of the many
   Messiah recordings. For those interested in hearing various
   different versions, the McGegan recording [Harmonia Mundi
   3-HMU 907050.52] includes alternate sections that enable
   the listener to re-create nine different performances from the
   time of Handel.)
Samson. Leppard. Erato STU-71240 (LP)
Judas Maccabaeus. Abravanel. MCA Classics 3-MCAD3-10515
Solomon. Gardiner. Philips 2-412612-2 PH2 (tape)
Jephtha. Gardiner. Philips 3-422351-2 PH33

Haydn, Franz Joseph
The Seven Last Words of Christ, Hob. XX:2. Bernius. Intercord
860.950
The Creation, Hob. XXI:2. Marriner. Philips 2-416449-2 PH2
The Seasons, Hob. XXI:3. Dorati. London 2-425708-2 LM2
Six Last Masses, Hob. XXII:9–14
No. 9. Missa in tempore belli ("Paukenmesse"). Bernstein.
Philips 412734-2 PH
No. 10. Missa Sancti Bernardi von Offida ("Heiligmesse").
Willcocks. London 421146-2 LM
No. 11. Missa in angustiis ("Nelson Mass"). Marriner. Lon-
don 421146-2 LM
No. 12. Missa ("Theresienmesse"). Guest. London 430159-2
LM
No. 13. Missa solemnis ("Schöpfungmesse"). Hinreiner.
Charlin AMS 35 (LP)
No. 14. Missa ("Harmoniemesse"). Guest. London 430162-2
LM

Honegger, Arthur
Le roi David. Abravanel. Vanguard Classics OVC 4038
Jeanne d'Arc au bûcher. Baudo. Supraphon 2-11 0557-2
Une cantate de Noël. Baudo. Supraphon 2-11 0557-2

Janáček, Leoš
Glagolitic Mass. Tilson Thomas. Sony Classical 47182

Josquin des Prez
Missa Pange Lingua. Pérès. Harmonia Mundi 901239

Kodály, Zoltán
Psalmus hungaricus, Op. 13. Dorati. Hungaroton HCD-11392
(tape)
Budavári Te Deum. Ferencsik. Hungaroton MK-11397
Missa brevis. Ferencsik. Hungaroton MK-11397

Mahler, Gustav
Symphony No. 8 in E flat major, "Symphony of a Thousand."
Bernstein. CBS 3-M3K-42199

Mendelssohn, Felix
St. Paul, Op. 36. Masur. Philips 2-420212-2 PH2
The First Walpurgis Night, Op. 60. Dohnányi. Telarc CD-80184
Elijah, Op. 70. Sawallisch. Philips 2-420106-2 PH2

Monteverdi, Claudio
Vespro della Beata Vergine. Herreweghe. Harmonia Mundi
2-HMC-90.1247/8

Mozart, Wolfgang Amadeus
Mass in C major, "Coronation," K. 317. Flor. RCA 60812-2
Vesperae solennes de confessore, K. 339. Pearlman. Harmonia
Mundi HMU 907021 (tape)
Mass in C minor, "The Great," K. 427 (K. 417a). Shaw. Telarc
2-CD-80150
Ave verum corpus, K. 618. Guest. London 430159-2 LM
Requiem, K. 626. Shaw. Telarc CD-80128

Orff, Carl
Carmina burana. Ozawa. RCA 6533-2-RG (tape)

Palestrina, Giovanni Pierluigi da
Pope Marcellus Mass. Christophers. Collins Classics 50092

Poulenc, Francis
Gloria. Bernstein. CBS MK-44710

Prokofiev, Sergey
Alexander Nevsky, Op. 78. Slatkin. Vox Box 2-CDX 5021

Purcell, Henry
Ode to St. Cecilia. Tippett. Vanguard OVC 8020

Te Deum and Jubilate. Deller. Harmonia Mundi HMA-190.207

Rachmaninoff, Sergey
The Bells, Op. 35. Slatkin. Vox Box 3-CD3X-3002

Rossini, Gioacchino
Stabat Mater. Hickox. Chandos CHAN-8780 (tape)
Petite messe solennelle. Scimone. Philips 2-412548-2 PH2

Schoenberg, Arnold
Gurre-Lieder. Ozawa. Philips 2-412511-2 PH2

Schubert, Franz
Mass No. 2 in G major, D. 167. Shaw. Telarc CD-80212
Mass No. 5 in A flat major, D. 678. Sawallisch. Angel CDM-69222
Mass No. 6 in E flat major, D. 950. Sawallisch. Angel CDM-69223

Stravinsky, Igor
Les Noces. Eotvos. Hungaroton HCD-12989
Symphony of Psalms. Shaw. Telarc CD-80254
Mass. O'Donnell. Hyperion CDA 66437 (tape)
Canticum sacrum. O'Donnell. Hyperion CDA 66437 (tape)
Threni. Stravinsky. Arkadia 2-CDGI 766.2

Thompson, Randall
Americana. Hilbish. New World 219 (LP)
The Peaceable Kingdom. Lyrichord 7124 (LP)
Alleluia. Ross. Arkay AR6110
The Testament of Freedom. Hanson. Pfeiffer 8777 (LP)

Tippett, Michael
A Child of Our Time. Davis. Philips 420075-2

Vaughan Williams, Ralph
Symphony No. 1, "A Sea Symphony." Rozhdestvensky. Melodiya SUCD 10-00234

Mass in G minor. Best. Hyperion CDA-66076
Flos campi. Imai (viola), Best. Hyperion CDA-66420

Verdi, Giuseppe
Requiem. Karajan. Verona 2-27060/1
Quattro pezzi sacri. Shaw. Telarc CD-80254

Vivaldi, Antonio
Gloria in D major, RV. 589. Shaw. Telarc CD-80194

Walton, William
Belshazzar's Feast. Slatkin. RCA 60813-2

MELVIN BERGER is the author of a number of books on musical subjects and is program annotator for several symphonic and chamber music organizations. He has a B.M. from the Eastman School of Music, holds an M.A. from Teacher's College, Columbia University, and is an Associate of London University. He has written liner notes for RCA Records, contributed articles to *World Book,* directed music programs at Ball State University and Silvermine Guild, and taught at the City University of New York. At present, he is writing, performing, and lecturing in the New York City area.